THE
CARLOW
WAR DEAD

THE
CARLOW
WAR DEAD

A HISTORY OF THE CASUALTIES OF THE GREAT WAR

TOM BURNELL

The
History
Press
Ireland

Many thanks to Carmel Flahavan, Local Studies, Carlow County Library.

First published 2011

The History Press Ireland
119 Lower Baggot Street
Dublin 2, Ireland
www.thehistorypress.ie

© Tom Burnell, 2011

British Library Cataloguing in Publication Data.
A catalogue record for this book is available from the British Library.

ISBN 978 1 84588 691 2

Typesetting and origination by The History Press
Printed in Great Britain
Manufacturing managed by Jellyfish Print Solutions Ltd

Contents

Foreword

This book is a record of the 556 Carlow men and women who died in the military and associated services during and just after the Great War. This list includes personnel buried in Carlow from other locations. They died in the service of the British Army, the Australian Army, the New Zealand Army, the American Army, the Indian Army, the Canadian Army, the South African Army, the Royal Navy and the British Mercantile Marine and various war worker and nursing services. In the words of Kevin Myers, 'the only axe being ground in these pages which follow is that of the steel of truth, tempered as it has been by decades of falsehood and neglect about the Irish involvement in the Great War.'

Sources

Blackrock College Roll of Honour, Bond of Sacrifice, British Medical Journal, Carloviana, Carlow County Library, *Carlow Nationalist*, *Carlow Sentinel*, Commonwealth War Graves Commission registers for the Irish Free State, De Ruvignys Roll of Honour, Death in the Irish Sea, by Roy Stokes, Great War Memorial, Milford Street, Leighlinbridge, County Carlow, and 'Irelands Memorial Records', *Kilkenny Journal*, *Kilkenny People*, *King's County Chronicle*, *Leinster Express*, *London Gazette*, *Munster Express*, *Nationalist and Leinster Times*, New Zealand Roll of Honour, Nominal Rolls of the New Zealand Expeditionary Force.

Officers died in the Great War, *Our Heroes*, *Scarborough Evening News*, Soldiers Died in the Great War, Soldiers of the Great War, The Commonwealth War Graves Commission, The National Archives of Australia, The New Library and Archives Canada, The Offaly War Dead, *The People*, *The Tipperary War Dead*, The War Graves of the British Empire, *The Waterford News*, *The Wexford War Dead*, *The Wicklow War Dead*.

Abbreviations & Terminology

CWGC: Commonwealth War Graves Commission.

ODGW: Officers Died in the Great War.

SDGW: Soldiers Died in the Great War.

IMR: Ireland's Memorial Records.

Killed in action: The soldier was killed during engagement with the enemy.

Died of wounds: The soldier was not killed outright and may have made it back to the Regiments Aid Post or Casualty Clearing Station before he eventually died of his wounds.

Died at home: Death by drowning, suicide, accident or illness in the UK. Home in these cases means back in England and not necessarily where he lived. Many times I have come across this and it turned out to be that the soldier died in a UK hospital.

Died of wounds at home: The soldier was not killed outright and may have made it back to the Regiments Aid post or Casualty Clearing Station before he eventually died of his wounds back in the UK or Ireland.

Died: Death by drowning, suicide, accident or illness.

A

ABEL, GEORGE: Rank: Private. Regiment or service: Royal Munster Fusiliers. Unit: 2nd Battalion. Date of death: 22 March 1918 (SDGW, CWGC, IMR), 22 March 1916 (Great War Memorial, Milford Street). Age at death: 19. Service No.: 18135. Formerly he was with the Royal Army Service Corps where his number was 66615. Born in Carlow. Enlisted in Shirehampton, Bristol while living in Celbridge, County Kildare. Killed in action.

Supplementary information: Son of Mary Abel, of Main Street, Celbridge, County Kildare, and the late William Abel.

Grave or memorial reference: Panel 78 and 79. Memorial: Pozieres Memorial in France. Also listed under Carlow/Graigue on the Great War Memorial, Milford Street, Leighlinbridge, County Carlow.

ALBOROUGH, GEORGE: Rank: Sergeant. Regiment or service: King's Royal Rifle Corps. Unit: 3rd Battalion. Date of death: 3 February 1915. Age at death: 31. Service No.: 1774. Born in Carlow. Enlisted in Carlow while living in Winchester, Hants. Killed in action.

Supplementary information: Son of George James and Annie Alborough, of 3 Greyfriars Terrace. Winchester.

Grave or memorial reference: Panel 51 and 53. Memorial: Ypres (Menin Gate) Memorial in Belgium. Also listed under Carlow/Graigue on the Great War Memorial, Milford Street, Leighlinbridge, County Carlow.

ALEXANDER, DAVID: Rank: Private. Regiment or service: Australian Infantry, AIF. Unit: 13th Battalion. Date of death: 15 August 1915. Service No.: 1509. Died of wounds. Born, St Mullins, later changed to Clonygoose, and again to Ballytiglea, Borris, County Carlow. Occupation on enlistment: Barman, and Farmer. Age on enlistment: 24 years, 10 months.

Supplementary infortmation: Son of Mrs Annie Sophia Alexander, Ballytiglea (mentioned in his will as Balytighe and in a letter by his mother as Ballytiglea), Borris, County Carlow. Educated at the National School, Borris and the Christian Brothers School, Bagenalstown. Age on entering Australia: 22. He was very fond of sports and excelled in boxing, handball and cycling, and won many prizes and competitions and could speak Latin and French fluently and won two scholarships, also medals. Place and date of enlistment: 24 December 1914 at Liverpool, N. S. W. Weight, 9st 12lbs. Height, 5 feet, 5 inches. Complexion, dark. Eyes, blue. Hair, brown. Wounded in at Suvla Bay, Gallipoli on 15 August 1915 by a shrapnel wound to the side. Evacuated to the hospital ship 'REWA'. Died and was buried at sea the next day by Reverend V. L. Keelan. A pension of £2 per fortnight was awarded to his mother from

Pte David Alexander, letter from records.

19 September 1915. The missing articles in the image above were never found.

Grave or memorial reference: 36. He has no known grave but is listed on the Lone Pine Memorial in Turkey. Also listed under Borris/Ballyellin on the Great War Memorial, Milford Street, Leighlinbridge, County Carlow.

ALEXANDER, WALTER LORENZO: Rank: Lieutenant Colonel. Regiment or service: Yorkshire Regiment. Unit: Cdg. 2nd Battalion. Date of death: 14 May 1915. Age at death: 42. Killed in action.

Supplementary information: Son of George and Susan Alexander, of Erindale, County Carlow; husband of Mrs A. M. Alexander, of The Thatched Cottage, Northiam, Sussex. From *Bond of Sacrifice*:

Lieutenant-Colonel Walter Lorenzo Alexander, Commanding 2nd Battalion, Alexandra, Princess of Wales's Own (Yorkshire Regiment). Born at Rathvindon, County Carlow, on the 8th September, 1872, was the youngest son of George Alexander, of Rathvindon, and a cousin of Major John Alexander, of Milford, County Carlow. He was educated at Densotone College, and the R. M. C., Sandhurst, from which he was gazetted to the Yorkshire Regiment in May, 1892, becoming Lieutenant in July, 1896, and Captain in 1900. In the Tirah Camapign of 1897-8 he was present with his battalion at the capture of Sampagha and Arhanga Passes, and took part in the reconnaissance of the Saran Sar and the attack of the 9th November, 1897, in the operations against Khani Kel Chamkunis; and in the Bazar Valley, also at the affair of Shinkamar, on the 28th January, 1898. For his services in the campaign he

Lt Col. Alexander, from *Bond of Sacrifice*.

received the medal with two clasps.

Becoming Major in February, 1898, he succeeded to the command of the 2nd Battalion of his Regiment in September, 1914, and proceeded to France. Lieutenant-Colonel Alexander was wounded at Ypres in October, but returned to the front towards the end of December, and led his Battalion during the hard fighting at Neuve Chapelle in March. He was killed on the 14th may, 1915, during the fighting south of the River Lys. For his services in the field Lieutenant-Colonel Alexander was mentioned in Sir John French's Despatches of the 31st May, and the 30th November, 1915. Lieutenant-Colonel Alexander, who was a member of the Army and Navy Club, married Mabel, daughter of Colonel Maurice Tweedle, late Indian Army, and left one son.

From *Carlow Sentinel*, May 1915:

Lieutenant-Colonel Alexander. Carlow is contributing a heavy toll to the "Roll of Honor", both amongst Officers and Rank and File. To-day we regret having to add to the list Lieutenant-Colonel W. L. Alexander, Yorks Regiment, who was killed in action in France on 14th inst, was the youngest son of the late Mr George Alexander, Rathvindon, Carlow, and cousin of Major Alexander, Milford House. He was 43 years of age and had seen much service in India, winning the medal with two clasps for gallantry.

Grave or memorial reference: II. D. 11. Cemetery; Le Touret Military Cemetery, Richebourg-L'Avoue in France. Also listed under Carlow/Graigue on the Great War Memorial, Milford Street, Leighlinbridge, County Carlow.

APPLEBY, PATRICK: Rank: Unknown. Regiment or service: Rifle Brigade. Date of death: 6 November 1922. Recorded in an article by John Kenna in Carlowviana 2003. Born: 4 August 1888 in Carlow.

Supplementary information: Son of Edward and Alice Appleby (listed in the 1911 census in Kilcarrig Street, Bagenalstown and brother of Mary Alice, Nellie and Maggie Appleby). Suffered from the effects of poison gas. Died after discharge on 6 November 1922 and buried in Dunleckney Cemetery, Bagenalstown, County Carlow.

ASHMORE, LUKE: Rank: Private. Regiment or service: Irish Guards. Unit: 3rd Reserve Battalion. Date of death: 3 September 1915. Age at death: 26. Service No.: 8815. Born in Palatine, Carlow. Enlisted in Naas, County Kildare. Died at home.

Supplementary information: Son of Mrs Florence Loftus, of Knockbane House, Palatine, Carlow. Alternative Commemoration – buried in Joyce Green Cemetery.

Grave or memorial reference: Screen Wall. Cemetery: Gravesend Cemetery in Kent. Also listed under Palatine/ Urglin on the Great War Memorial, Milford Street, Leighlinbridge, County Carlow.

ASPLE, MICHAEL: Rank: Private. Regiment or service: Royal Inniskilling Fusiliers. Unit: 8th Battalion. Date of death: 15 March 1917 Service No.: 80321(CWGC) and 40321(SDGW). Age at death: 21. Born in Borris, County Carlow. Enlisted in Kilkenny while living in Borris, County Carlow. Died. Formerly he was with the Royal Dublin Fusiliers where his number was 19460.

Supplementary information: Son of Patrick and Margaret Asple, of Borris, County Carlow.

Grave or memorial reference: Panel 22. Memorial: Ypres (Menin Gate) Memorial in Belgium. Also listed under Borris/Ballyellin on the Great War Memorial, Milford Street, Leighlinbridge, County Carlow.

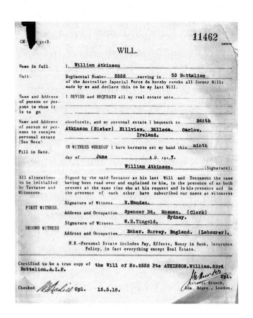

Pte Atkinson's Will.

ATKINSON, WILLIAM: Rank: Private. Regiment or service: Australian Infantry, A. I. F. Unit: 53rd Battalion. Date of death: 27 April 1918. Age at death: 23, also listed as 24. Service No.: 2552.

Supplementary information: Son of Samuel and Jeanie Atkinson, of Hillview, Bilboa, Carlow, Ireland. Born, listed as Hillview, Bilboa and Cloydah, Carlow, Queen's County(sic), Ireland. Educated at the nationals school at Bilboa. Age on entering Australia: 21. No previous military experience. Before leaving for Australia he was a crack shot with a shotgun, was fond of riding horses and was a fairly good photographer. Occupation on enlistment: Tram guard, conductor on tramway in Sydney, N. S. W. Age on enlistment: 23 years. Among other debilities he suffered from pulmonary T. B. S., tonsilitis and bronchitis during his service. Next of kin details; Samuel Atkinson, of Hillview, Bilboa, Carlow, Ireland. Effects sent to Edith Atkinson at the same address. Place and date of enlistment: 14 June 1916 in Liverpool, N. S. W. Weight, 138lbs. Height, 5 feet, 5¾ inches. Complexion, fresh. Eyes, brown. Hair, brown. Killed in action and initially (the same day) buried in an isolated grave 1 mile west of Hamel, 1¾ miles east south east of Corbie and transferred to Villers-Brettonneux Military Cemetery in October 1923. An application for a pension by his mother was rejected in September 1918 as she was not dependent on him.

Grave or memorial reference: II. A. 3. Cemetery: Villers-Bretonneux Military Cemetery in France. Also listed under Leighlinbridge/Old Leighlin on the Great War Memorial, Milford Street, Leighlinbridge, County Carlow.

AYLWARD, EDWARD: Rank: Private. Regiment or service: Irish Guards. Unit: 2nd Battalion. Date of death: 28 October 1918. Service No.: 2255. Born in Carlow. Enlisted in Dublin. Died at home. Grave or memorial reference: In the North East part. Cemetery: Coon Catholic Churchyard in Kilkenny. Also listed under Carlow/ Graigue on the Great War Memorial, Milford Street, Leighlinbridge, County Carlow.

B

BAILEY, ALEXANDER: Rank: lance Corporal. Regiment or service: Princess Patricia's Canadian Light Infantry (Eastern Ontario Regiment). Unit: No 4 Company. Date of death: 7 May 1915. Age at death: 27. Service No.: 1570.

Supplementary information: Son of the Reverend Robert Taylor Bailey, MA and Alice Magil, his wife. Ex-member of R. N. W. M. P. and Legion of Frontiersmen. Sub-manager of Royal Trust Company, Winnipeg. Enlisted in 1914. Born in Strangford in 1887, County Down. Enlisted in Ottowa, 21 August 1914. Height, 5 feet 7 inches. Complexion, fair. Hair, dark brown. Eyes, grey. Next of kin listed as Reverend R. J. Bailey, MA, The Manse, Carlow. Occupation on enlistment, Clerk with the Royal Trust Company. Spent two years serving with the Royal North West Mounted Police. From *Carlow Sentinel*, May, 1915:

> Lance Corporal Alex Bailey.
> The recent casualties also include Alexander Bailey, Princess Patricia's Canadian Light Infantry. He was elder son of the late Rev. R. T. Bailey, M. A., Carlow, and grandson of Rev. George Magill, D. D., senior minister of Cliftonville Presbyterian Chirch, Belfast. When war was proclaimed Mr Bailey was in a responsible and lucrative situation in Winnipeg, Canada. As is well-known a wave of local enthusiasm swept over the Dominion, and Mr Bailey, with many personal friends, volunteered as a private in the Princess Patricia's Canadian Light Infantry. Though he might have had a commission in another regiment he preferred to serve in the now famous corps. He was sent to the front before Christmas. After being some time in the trenches, enduring the hardships of trench life, he caught enteric, and was sent to hospital. On recovery he was granted a short leave to see his friends in Ireland. He left his grandfather's house about four weeks ago, and returned to duty full of health and hope.
> News just arrived that he was killed last week by a shell. Mr bailey was a young man of great promise, who has left no enemies or bitter memories behind him. To Dr Magil—the highly-respected "father" of the Presbytery of Belfast—and the other relatives deep sympathy will be extended in their bereavement.

Grave or memorial reference: Panel 10. Memorial: Ypres (Menin Gate) Memorial in Belgium.

BAILEY, PATRICK: Rank: Lance Corporal. Regiment or service: Royal Dublin Fusiliers. Unit: 2nd Battalion. Date of death: 22 May 1915. Age at death: 19. Service No.: 11641. Born in Clonmore, County Wicklow. Enlisted in Carlow. Killed in action.

Supplementary information: Son of Christopher and Margaret Bailey, of Arnold, Coolkenno, Tullow, County Carlow. Effects and property received by: (Mother) Mrs Bailey, Aghold, Coolkenno, Tullow, County Carlow.

Grave or memorial reference: He has no known grave but is listed on Panel 44 and 46 on the Ypres (Menin Gate) Memorial in Belgium. Also listed under Clonmore on the Great War Memorial, Milford Street, Leighlinbridge, County Carlow.

BAIRD, DAVID EUGENE: Rank: Company Sergeant Major. Regiment or service: Border Regiment. Unit: 1st Battalion. Date of death: 6 July 1916. Age at death: 34. Service No.: 7516. Born; Aldershot, Hants. Enlisted in Woolwich in Kent while he was living in Borris County Carlow. Died of wounds.

Supplementary information: Son of Captain David Baird, of Ullard House, Borris, County Carlow; husband of Elizabeth M. F. Baird, of Ash Brook, Roscrea, County Tipperary.

Grave or memorial reference: F. 7. Cemetery; Beauval Communal Cemetery in France.

BARNES, JOHN: Rank: Sapper. Regiment or service: Royal Engineers. Unit: 264th Railway Construction Company. Date of death: 16 August 1917. Age at death: 42. Service No.: 267176(CWGC), 267167. Enlisted in Newtownbarry, County Wexford while living in Clonegal, County Carlow. Killed in action. Formerly he was with the Royal Irish Rifles where his number was 6079.

Supplementary information: Son of James Barnes and Ellen Barnes (*née* Smyth); husband of Margaret Barnes, of Johnstown, Clonegal, County Carlow.

Grave or memorial reference: IV. B. 36. Cemetery: Bard Cottage Cemetery in Belgium. Also listed under Clonegal/Kildavin on the Great War Memorial, Milford Street, Leighlinbridge, County Carlow.

BARRON, WILLIAM W.: Rank: Gunner. Regiment or service: Royal Garrison Artillery. Unit: 38th Siege Battery. Date of death: 17 July 1917. Age at death: 24. Service No.: 38573. Born in Ballyellen, County Carlow. Enlisted in Carlow. Died of wounds.

Supplementary information: Son of Mrs James Barron, of Ballyellin, Goresbridge.

Grave or memorial reference: In north-west corner. Cemetery: Ballyellin Cemetery, County Carlow. Also listed under Borris/Ballyellin on the Great War Memorial, Milford Street, Leighlinbridge, County Carlow.

BECKER, JOHN: Rank: Lance Corporal. Regiment or service: Royal Irish Regiment. Unit: 3rd Battalion. Date of death: 1 June 1917. Age at death: 36. Service No.: 7739 Born in Carlow. Enlisted in Carlow. Died at home. From *Nationalist* and *Leinster Times*, June 1917:

BECKER--In loving memory of Lance-Corporal John Becker, 18th Royal irish Regiment, of Pollerton Road, Carlow, who died of Dysentery in Tipperary Hospital on the 1st June, 1917. Interred in

St Mary's Cemetery, Carlow. On whose soul, Sweet Jesus, have mercy.

I stood beside your dying bed,
To take a last farewell,
With tearful eyes I watched you,
And say you pass away.
Although I dearly loved you.
I could not make you stay
Dearest husband, thou hast left us,
And thy loss we deeply feel,
But the God that hath bereft us,
He can all our sorrows heal.
May his spirit now repose,
In thy great protecting arms.
Free from care and earthly woes.

Inserted by his sorrowing wife and children.

Grave or memorial reference: 5. 3. 14. Cemetery: Carlow (St Mary's) Cemetery, County Carlow. Also listed under Carlow/Graigue on the Great War Memorial, Milford Street, Leighlinbridge, County Carlow.

BELL, RICHARD: Rank: Corporal. Regiment or service: Royal Horse Artillery and Royal Field Artillery. Unit: 5th Divisonal Ammunition Column. Date of death: 17 March 1915. Age at death: 34. Service No.: 10622. Born in Dublin. Enlisted in Dublin. Died at home.

Supplementary information: Husband of Agnes M. Power (formerly Bell), of 20 Coral Street, Chorlton-on-Medlock, Manchester.

Grave or memorial reference: R.C. 445. Cemetery: Grangegorman Military Cemetery, Dublin. Also listed under Carlow/Graigue on the Great War Memorial, Milford Street, Leighlinbridge, County Carlow.

BENSON, MICHAEL VINCENT FRANCIS: Rank: Private. Regiment or service: Cheshire Regiment. Unit: 15th Battalion. Date of death: 19 July 1916. Age at death: 25. Service No.: 19043. Born in Carlow, County Kildare (sic). Enlisted in Birkenhead. Killed in action.

Supplementary information: Son of Mrs C. Benson, of Staplestown Road, Carlow.

Grave or memorial reference: Pier and Face 3 C and 4 A. Memorial: Thiepval Memorial in France. Also listed under Carlow/Graigue on the Great War Memorial, Milford Street, Leighlinbridge, County Carlow.

BERNARD, ROBERT: Rank: Lieutenant. Regiment or service: Royal Dublin Fusiliers. Unit: 1st Battalion. Date of death: 25 April 1915. Age at death: 23. Killed in action.

Supplementary information: Son of the Most Reverend and Right Honourable J. H. Bernard, DD, and Maud, his wife, of Provost's House, Trinity College, Dublin. Educated at Marlborough College and Sandhurst. From *Carlow Sentinel,* May 1915:

Lieutenant Robert Bernard.
The casualties announced on Monday include the name of Lieutenant Robert Bernard, younger son of the Bishop of Ossory, Ferns and Leighlin, and Mrs

Bernard, the Palace, Kilkenny, who was killed in action on Sunday, 25th April. He was born 21st, December, 1891, and was gazetted from Sandhurst Second Lieutenant, Royal Dublin Fusiliers in March, 1912, and promoted Lieutenant November, 1913.

On Sunday last, previous to the 11. 30 o'clock Service in St Canice's Cathedral, a muffled peal was rung by the members of the Change Ringers Society as a mark of respect to the memory of the deceased.

From *Kilkenny People*, May 1915:

The Late Lieutenant Robert Bernard.

At a meeting of the County Kilkenny Relief Committee held in the Assembly Room, City Hall, on Monday last, the Mayor, Mt John Magennis, P. L. G., who resided, proposed the following resolution; -- "That we, the members of the County Kilkenny Relief Committee, respectfully tender to His Lordship the Right Rev Dr. Bernarg, Bishop of Ossory, and esteemed member of this committee, and expression of our sincere condolence and sympathy in the great loss he has sustained by the death of his gallant son, Lieutenant Robert Bernard, who nobly fell in action in the Dardanelles, and that this meeting be adjourned as a mark of respect. "

Very Rev. Dean Barry, D. D. P. P., V. F., Ballyragget, seconded the resolution which was passed in silence.

Grave or memorial reference: Special Memorial A. 6. Cemetery: V. Beach Cemetery in Turkey. He is also commemorated on the Great War Memorial in St Canice's Cathedral, Kilkenny... 'To the Glory of God and in loving memory of the following members of the Diocese of Ossory who gave their lives for their country in the Great War 1914-1918'.

BERRY, THOMAS: Rank: Private. Regiment or service: Royal Irish Regiment. Unit: 2nd Battalion. Date of death: 19 October 1914. Age at death: 38. Service No.: 7253. Born in St Marys, Wexford. Enlisted in Enniscorthy while living in Tullow, County Carlow. Killed in action.

Supplementary information: Husband of Margaret Jordan (formerly Berry) of 18 Married Quarters, 8th Hussars, Cavalry Barracks, York. Date of will: 9 August 1918. Effects and property received by: (Wife) Mrs Margaret Barry, Bridge Street, Tullow, County Carlow. From an article in a Wexford newspaper:

Private Thomas Berry, Royal Irish Regiment is a native of Newtownbarry district. He had eleven years' service with the colours and had been stationed in India. At the outbreak of the war his regiment was drafted out to Flanders, and in the terrible combats in the earlier stages of the war Private Berry took part. After the second Battle of Mons Private Berry was reported missing. His brother, Patrick, who has had twelve years service with the 11th Hussars, is also in the firing line, where on two occasions he was wounded. [See Patrick Berry in the *Wexford War Dead*.]

Grave or memorial reference: Has no known grave but is commemorated on Panel 11 and 12. Memorial: Le Touret Memorial in France. Also listed under Tullow on the Great War Memorial, Milford Street, Leighlinbridge, County Carlow.

BLACKETT, WILLIAM STEWART BURDETT: Rank: Lieutenant. Regiment or service: Household Cavalry and Cavalry of the line including the Yeomanry and Imperial Camel Corps. Unit: Leicestershire Yeomanry. Date of death: 25 November 1914. Age at death: 41.

Supplementary information: Son of Captain Blackett (RN); husband of Mrs Blackett Swiny, of Arbigland, Dumfries. Served in the South African Campaign with Grenadier Guards. From De Ruvignys Roll of Honour:

...of Arbigland, co, Dubfries, and Manton Grange, Oakham, co. Rutland, Captain, Leicestershire Yeomanry, late Grenadier Guards, eldest son of the late Captain Archibald Campbell Stewart Blackett, R. N., by his wife, Clara Blanche Harriet, eldest daughter of Lieutenant Colonel Charles Sedley Burdett, Coldstream Guards, and nephew and heir of Christopher Edward Blackett of Arbigland, J. P., Lieutenant Colonel, 26th and 93rd Regiments, and Coldstream Guards (a cadet of the family of Blackett,

of Wylam, co. Northumberland. Born in London, 24 October 1873. Educated at Wellington and Sandhurst. Joined the 3rd Grenadier Guards, 8th May, 1895, becoming Lieutenant, 12 February, 1898, and Captain, 1901. He served through the South African War, 1899-1902, in the 8th Division under General Rundle. Was present at the Battle of Biddulphsberg, and received the King's medal with two clasps. He retired in 1903, but on the outbreak of war joined the Leicestershire Yeomanry, and was gazetted, 15th August, 1914. He went to France with the Expeditionary Force, was wounded in action near Ypres on 20 November 1914, and died in a French hospital at Poperinghe, 24 November following, and was buried there. He married at Staplestown Church, Carlow, 6th April, 1907, Kathleen Prudence Eiene (Arbigland, Dumfries), daughter of Beauchamp Frederick Bagenal, of Benekerry House, County Carlow, D. L., and had a son, Christopher William Stewart Blackett, now of Arbigland, born 27 April 1908.

He is also listed (with a different photograph) in *Our Heroes* with no further information. Kathlene Prudence Eirene Bagenal is listed in the 1901 census under Prudence Bagenal, born in Carlow. From the *Carlow Sentinel*, and the *Nationalist* and *Leinster Times*, December 1914:

Roll of Honour.
We regret to find in the list of casualties issued this week, the name of

Captain William Stewart Burdett Blackett [late Grenadier Guards], of Arbigland, Dunfries, and Matnon[?] Grange, Oakham. While serving with the Leicestershire Yeomanry he was wounded about November 21st, 1914, died in Hospital de Notre Dame, in Poperinghe, on November 24th, and buried there on Noveber 26th, aged 41 years. He was married in 1907 to the youngest daughter of Mr Beauchamp F. Bagenal, D. L., Bennekerry House, Carlow.

From *Bond of Sacrifice, Volume 1*:

...born in 1873, and was the only son of Commander A. S. Blackett, R. N. Captain Blackett was the nephew and heir of his uncle, Colonel Blackett, of Arbigland, Dumfries. He was educated at Wellington College, and at the R. M. C., Sandhurst, and joined the Grenadier Guards in May, 1895, being promoted Lieutenant in February, 1898, and Captain in May, 1900. With the 3rd Battalion, he served during the whole of the South African War, for which he received the Queen's medal with three clasps, and the King's medal with two clasps. In the Great War he was attached for service to the Leicestershire Yeomanry, a died on the 24th November.

Captain Blackett was a keen fisherman and cricketer, and fond of hunting and shooting. He was a member of the Guards', Bachelors', and Army and Navy Clubs.

He married Kathleen Prudence Eirene, youngest daughter of B. F. Bagenal, D. L., of Benekerry, Carlow,

Lt Blackett, from De Ruvinys Roll of Honour, Volume 1.

and left one son, C. W. S. Blackett, born 1908.

Grave or memorial reference: I. B. 1. Cemetery: Poperinghe Communal Cemetery in Belgium.

BOLGER, JAMES: Rank: Private. Regiment or service: Durham Light Infantry. Unit: 15th Battalion. Date of death: 12 September 1918. Age at death: 20. Service No.: G/385(CWGC), 91358 (SDGW). Born in Tullow, County Carlow. Enlisted in Naas while living in Tullow, County Carlow. Died of wounds. Formerly he was with the Royal Dublin Fusiliers where his number was 43095.

Supplementary information: Foster son of Bridget Bolger, of Paulville, Tullow, County Carlow.

Grave or memorial reference: III. L. 10. Cemetery: Varennes Military Cemetery in France. Also listed under Tullow on the Great War Memorial, Milford Street, Leighlinbridge, County Carlow.

BOLGER, KATIE: Rank: Staff Nurse. Regiment or service: Queen Alexandra's Imperial Military Nursing Service. Date of death: 5 March 1916. Age at death: 30. Service No.: 2/Res/B/1257.

Supplementary information: Died of pneumonia. Daughter of Edward and Margret Bolger, of Tullow, County Carlow. From the *Nationalist* and *Leinster Times*, 1916:

The Late Nurse Bolger. Interred with Full Honours.
Mr T Bolger, Downings, Tullow, has received the following from Father Corcoran;
London Irish Rifles, No 6 Camp. Suttonveny, Warminster, Wilts.

6th March, 1916.

Dear Mr Bolger—As Senior Catholic Chaplain who attended your sister in her last illness, I write to tell you how highly Sister Bolger was appreciated by all with whom she came in contact—a fact which was clearly evidenced at her funeral. At the same time a short account of what happened may help to comfort you in your great loss. Katie Bolger came to Suttonveny Military Hospital about four months ago, to take up the duties of Staff Sister, with the military rank of Lieutenant. Her bright and happy disposition son made her a favourite, not only with the Matron and staff, but particularly with the patients, and her loss is greatly felt by all. She contracted pneumonia only a week ago, and although she received every care and attention, she passed away on Sunday evening last, fortified with all the rites of the Holy Church. As she had expressed a wish to be buried in the local Churchyard, her desire was acceded to. The funeral procession fell in at 10 o'clock, March 7th, in the hospital grounds, to proceed to Suttonveny Church.

As she had the military status of officer, an officer of the 15th London Regiment was in command of the firing party, which headed to procession with reversed arms. Next came the coffin, covered with the Union Jack and Flag of the R. A. M. C., hidden with wreaths, and carried on a gun carriage, drawn by black horses of the 12th London F. A. Immediately behind were Mr Bolger, brother of the deceased, and Father R. Corcoran, S. C. F., London Irish Rifles. The bearer party furnished by the sergeant of the R. A. M. C., walked on either side of the gun carriage. Then followed the Matron, Staff Sisters and Nurses of the Hospital, and the War Office was represented by Miss Tours, Principal Matron. The Band of the R. A. M. C., kindly lent by the Colonel Segbie, Salisbury Training Centre, played the Dead March on the way to the Churchyard, and the procession was completed by 250 men of the R. A. M. C., under the command of Lieutenant J. D. Ryan, R. A. M. C., the colonel and other officers of the Corps being also present. When the funeral party arrived at the Church, the body was met and blessed by Father Corcoran, and carried to the graveside. Here the hospital staff—firing party—buglers and men were formed up and listened attentively to the solemn words of the funeral service. When the priest had concluded his duties, the firing party discharged three volleys, and the buglers sounded the Last Post, a sad and mournful note—heard by the soldiers every evening—and sounded finally over his grave. Thus was laid to rest, with full military honours, the body of Sister Bolger.

At a time, when every man and woman is needed to combat an inhuman foe, she bravely came forward to do her share, and sacrificed her life in the service of her fellows. Example will lend others to do likewise. May we hope that her "greater love hath no man than this." In return her country honoured her, she died as a soldier, she was buried as a soldier; all along the line of march were officers and men of all Nationalities standing at attention as she passed on her last journey. May God rest her soul. The many beautiful wreaths which covered the coffin and gun carriage were sent by the following; --The Matron and Sisters, the Colonel and Officers, R. A. M. C., R. A. M. C. Regimental Crest, Sergeants Mess, Wreath, Corporals and Lance Corporals; White Lillies and Shamrock Wreath, Orderlies and G. D. O. s; Wreath, from Servants of

Sisters Quarters, etc. The arrangements were most efficiently carried out by Dr and Lieutenant J. D. Ryan, of Rathdrum, County Wicklow, himself almost a neighbour of Sister Bolger, at home. From beginning of the war he has also afforded an example of the duty incumbent on all Irishmen at the present crisis, and whose services have been particularly at the disposal of his countrymen and countrywomen in the British Army. Yours very sincerely.
Richard Corcoran, S. C. F.
London Irish Rifles.

Grave or memorial reference: 411. Cemetery: Sutton Veny (St John) Churchyard, Wiltshire, UK.

BOLGER, PATRICK: Rank: Private. Regiment or service: Royal Dublin Fusiliers. Unit: 2nd Battalion. Date of death: 24 May 1915. Age at death: 22. Service No.: 11479. Born in Borris, County Carlow. Enlisted in Naas while living in Borris, County Carlow. Killed in action.

Supplementary information: Son of James and Mary Dowling Bolger, of Inch, Ballymurphy, Borris, County Carlow.

Grave or memorial reference: Panel 44 and 46. Memorial: Ypres (Menin Gate) Memorial in Belgium. Also listed under Borris/Ballyellin on the Great War Memorial, Milford Street, Leighlinbridge, County Carlow.

BOLGER, PIERCE: Rank: Private. Regiment or service: Machine Gun

Corps (Infantry). Unit: 89th Company. Date of death: 12 October 1916 (CWGC, SDGW, IMR) 12 December 1916 (Great War Memorial, Milford Street, Leighlinbridge). Service No.: 36402. Born in Graiguenaugh, County Kilkenny. Enlisted in Dublin while living in Graiguenanaugh, County Kilkenny. Killed in action. Formerly he was with the Royal Irish Regiment where his number was 9802.

Supplementary information: Brother of William Bolger, of Tinnahinch East, Graiguenamanagh, County Kilkenny.

Grave or memorial reference: Pier and Face 5 C and 12 C. Memorial: Thiepval Memorial in France. Also listed under Tinnehinch on the Great War Memorial, Milford Street, Leighlinbridge, County Carlow.

BOLGER, THOMAS: Rank: Private. Regiment or service: Leinster Regiment. Unit: A Company. 1st Battalion. Date of death: 19 May 1915 (SDGW, CWGC), 18 May 1915 (IMR, Great War Memorial, Milford Street). Age at death: 18. Service No.: 3407. Born in Tullow, County Carlow. Enlisted in Maryborough. Died of wounds.

Supplementary information: Son of Sarah Bolger, of Barrack Street, Tullow, County Carlow, and the late Edward Bolger. From the *Nationalist* and *Leinster Times,* May 1915:

Tullow Soldier's Death.
Mr P Bolger, Barrack Street, Tullow, has received the following letter; --
Dear Mrs Bolger—I regret to announce the death of your son, No

3407, Private Thomas Bolger, who was killed in action on the 19th inst. We were holding a osition a short distance behind the firing line. He was struck by a stray bullet, and expired shortly afterwards. His death is much regretted by the officers and men of his regiment; he is laid to rest in the wood where he fell, an a cross has been erected to his memory. I am forwarding you photographs which were found upon him. I may point out that on the previous night he took part with his company in a fierce attack on a German position, and proved himself a brave soldier and a man. On behalf of officers and men of "A" Company, we tender you, in this your great trouble, our deepest sympathy. —I remain, yours sincerely,
J. Matthews
Company Sergeant Major,
1st Leinster Regiment.

Grave or memorial reference: Panel 44. Memorial: Ypres (Menin Gate) Memorial in Belgium. Also listed under Tullow on the Great War Memorial, Milford Street, Leighlinbridge, County Carlow.

BOLTON, HENRY: Rank: Private. Regiment or service: Royal Irish Regiment. Unit: 2nd Battalion. Date of death: 13 November 1918 (two days after the war ended). Service No.: 12336. Formerly he was with the Royal Dublin Fusiliers where his number was 29096. Born in Bagenalstown, County Carlow. Enlisted in Carlow while living in Bagenalstown, County Carlow. Died of wounds. After his death his effects and property were received by: (Wife) Mrs H Bolton, Clowater, Gores Bridge, County Kilkenny, Ireland. Grave or memorial reference: I. C. 33. Cemetery: Cemetery: Valenciennes (St Roch) Communal Cemetery in France. Also listed under Bagenalstown/Fenagh on the Great War Memorial, Milford Street, Leighlinbridge, County Carlow.

BOURKE, BERTRAM WALTER: Rank: Captain. Regiment or service: Royal Dublin Fusiliers. Unit: 5th Battalion, attached to the 2nd Battalion. Date of death: 9 May 1915. Age at death: 33. Born in Mayo. Killed in action.

Supplementary information: Son of Major William H. Bourke (Connaught Rangers), of Heathfield, Ballina, County Mayo; husband of Eileen N. Newsam (formerly Bourke, née Ussher). From De Ruvignys Roll of Honour:

...only surviving son of the late Major William Henry Bourke, of Heathfield, Ballina, County Mayo, Connaught Rangers, by his wife, Sarah Louisa, daughter of James John Young. Born 09-December-1882. Educated in Saint Servant, France. Served with the Royal Engineers (Militia) from which he exchanged into the 5th Battalion, Royal Dublin Fusiliers in 1904. Passed the school of instruction for employment with the Regular Forces, and obtained the rank of Captain, 24-February-1912. He left for the front on 2-May-1915, was attached to the 2nd Battalion, Royal Dublin Fusiliers, and was killed in action while gallantly lead-

ing his men near Ypres, just a week later, 09-May-1915. Captain Bourke married at Staplestown, Carlow, 19-April-1913, Eileen, daughter of George Neville Usher, of Carlow, and had two sons; Vivienne Neville, born 29-January-1911; and Patricia Berttram, born 04-November-1915.

Grave or memorial reference: He has no known grave but is listed on Panel 44 and 46 on the Ypres (Menin Gate) Memorial in Belgium.

BOWLER, EDWARD (Eddie) ST KENTIGERN: Rank: Private. Regiment or service: Machine Gun Corps. Unit: Infantry, 72nd Company. Date of death: 12 August 1916. Age at death: 22/23. Service No.: 27747. Formerly he was with the Royal Irish Rifles where his number was 10728. Born in Keswick (Soldiers died in the Great War), Irelands Memorial Records state he was born in Kings County. Enlisted in Cork. Died of wounds at the Casualty Clearing Station based in Corbie, France.

Supplementary information: Son of Staff QMS Bowler (Royal Army Service Corps) and Mrs W. J. Bowler, of Bough, Rathvilly, County Carlow.

Grave or memorial reference: Plot 2 Row A Grave 90. Cemetery: Corbie Communal Cemetery Extension in France.

BRADY, JOHN: Rank: Rifleman. Regiment or service: London Regiment. Unit: 18th (County of London) Battalion (London Irish Rifles). Date of death: 7 November

1917. Service No.: 502946(SDGW), 592946(CWGC). Formerly he was with the Royal Army Medical Corps where his number was 44209. Born in Dublin. Enlisted in Dublin while living in Carlow. Killed in action in Egypt. Grave or memorial reference: 51. Cemetery: Jerusalem War Cemetery, Israel. Also listed under Carlow/Graigue on the Great War Memorial, Milford Street, Leighlinbridge, County Carlow.

BRAY, EDWARD: Rank: Private. Regiment or service: Royal Irish Regiment. Unit: 6th Battalion. Date of death: 9 September 1916. Age at death: 34. Service No.: 2751. Born in Ballincarrig, County Carlow. Enlisted in Carlow while living in Ballincarrig. Killed in action. Grave or memorial reference: Pier and Face 3 A and 4 A. Memorial: Thiepval Memorial in France. Also listed under Tinryland on the Great War Memorial, Milford Street, Leighlinbridge, County Carlow.

BREEN, JOSEPH: Rank: Private. Regiment or service: Royal Irish Regiment. Unit: 1st Battalion. Date of death: 24 April 1915 (IMR, CWGC, SDGW) 24 May 1915 (Great War Memorial, Milford Street, Leighlinbridge, County Carlow). Age at death: 18. Service No.: 4660. Born in Bride Street Wexford. Enlisted in Wexford while living in Tullow, County Carlow. Killed in action.
Supplementary information: Son of Moses and Annie Breen of 7 Ruskin Avenue, Rock Ferry, Birkenhead. From a newspaper article:

Mr Moses Breen of King Street, has been notified by the War Office that his son Joseph, a Private in the Royal Irish Regiment, was killed in action.

Only a short time previously another son of Mr Breen's, John who was also with the Royal Irish- was killed on active service. Both young men were exceedingly popular in Wexford and the greatest sympathy is felt with Mr Breen on his double berevement.

Grave or memorial reference: Has no known grave but is commemorated on Panel 33. Memorial: Ypres (Menin Gate) Memorial in Belgium. Also listed under Tullow on the Great War Memorial, Milford Street, Leighlinbridge, County Carlow.

BRENNAN, JAMES: Rank: Shoeing Smith. Regiment or service: Royal Army Service Corps. Unit: No. 1 Company, 12th Div. Train. Date of death: 10 November 1918 (the day before the war ended). Age at death: 26. Service No.: TS/5925. Born in Donnane, Queen's County. Enlisted in Carlow while living in Ballickmoyler. Died.
Supplementary information: Son of James and Elizabeth Brennan, of Aughaterry, Ballickmoyler, County Carlow.
Grave or memorial reference: D. 1. Cemetery: Brebieres British Cemetery, Pas-de-Calais, France.

BRENNAN, JAMES: Rank: Private. Regiment or service: Machine Gun Corps. Unit: 11th Company, Infantry.

Date of death: 9 April 1917. Service No.: 36397. Formerly he was with the Leinster Regiment where his number was 5076. Born in Leighlinbridge, County Carlow. Enlisted in Carlow while living in Leighlinbridge. Killed in action. Grave or memorial reference: Bay 10. Memorial: Arras Memorial in France. Also listed under Leighlinbridge/Old Leighlin on the Great War Memorial, Milford Street, Leighlinbridge, County Carlow.

BRENNAN, JAMES: Rank: Gunner. Regiment or service: Royal Garrison Artillery. Unit: 24th Siege Battery. Date of death: 12 September 1916. Service No.: 34541. Born in Mayo, Queen's County. Enlisted in Carlow while living in Chelland, Lanark. Killed in action. James was brother of Mrs Mulhall, of Ravenshall Cottage, Cleland, with whom he lived. He worked in Howmuir Colliery, Cleland, Lanarkshire, Scotland. Grave or memorial reference: I. G. I. Cemetery: Peronne Road Cemetery, Maricourt in France. Also listed under Carlow/Graigue on the Great War Memorial, Milford Street, Leighlinbridge, County Carlow.

BRENNAN, JOSEPH: Rank: Private. Regiment or service: Connaught Rangers. Unit: 1st Battalion. Age at death: 37. Date of death: 19 August 1917. Service No.: 415814(CWGC), 5814(SDGW) 4/5814 (last will and testament). Born in Carlow. Enlisted in Carlow while living in Carlow. Died in Mesopotamia.
Supplementary information: Son of Mrs Ann Brennan, of Barrack Street, Carlow. Date of will: 27 June 1915. Effects and property received by: (Sister) Lizzie Leonard, Pollton Road, Carlow, County Carlow. From the *Nationalist* and *Leinster Times,* May 1916:

A Carlow Soldier in the Balkans Corporal Christy Brennan, 6th Leinster Regiment, Balkan Ex, Force, writes us to thank the Carlow ladies for parcels received. Corporal Brennan, who has served in France, where he received wounds, is a native of Barrack Street, Carlow. [Christopher Brennan in the above snippet survived the war. He was a younger brother of Joseph.]

Grave or memorial reference: XI. K. 6. Cemetery: Baghdad (North Gate) War Cemetery, Iraq.

BRENNAN, PATRICK: Rank: Private. Regiment or service: King's Liverpool Regiment. Unit: 19th Battalion. Date of death: 29 April 1918. Age at death: 40. Service No.: 48259. Born in Carlow, Leinster. Enlisted in Liverpool while living in Liverpool. Killed in action.
Supplementary information: Husband of Margaret Brennan, of 3 Ivor Street, Kirkdale, Liverpool.
Grave or memorial reference: XIV. F. 8. Cemetery: Voormezeele Enclosures No. 3 in Belgium. Also listed under Carlow/Graigue on the Great War Memorial, Milford Street, Leighlinbridge, County Carlow.

BRENNAN, PATRICK: Rank: Private. Regiment or service:

Northumberland Fusiliers. Unit: 9th Battalion. Date of death: 16 May 1917. Service No.: 48467. Formerly he was with the T. RES, where his number was TR/5/52621. Born in Ballyalln(sic), County Carlow. Enlisted in Dublin. Killed in action.

Supplementary information: Son of Mrs A. Brennan, of Bevllafallen, Goresbridge, County Kilkenny.

Grave or memorial reference: I. B. 43. Cemetery: Highland Cemetery, Roclincourt, Pas-de-Calas, France.

BRESLIN, THOMAS: Rank: Private. Regiment or service: Australian Infantry, A. I. F. Unit: 59th Battalion. Date of death: 19 July 1916. Service No.: 1914.

Supplementary information: Son of Thomas and Mary Breslin; husband of Mary Breslin, of North Clermiston Farm, Davidson's Mains, Edinburgh, Scotland. Native of County Clare, Ireland. His records, however, state he was born in Carlow. Died on the Somme. Born, Clonmore, Carlow. Occupation on enlistment: Labourer. Age on enlistment: 25 years 6 months. Next of kin details: (Mother) Mary Breslin. Clonmore, County Carlow. His mother re-married and recoded in the records as Mrs Robert Rutchinson (sic), North Clermirston Farm, Davidsons Mains, Edinburgh, Scotland. Place and date of enlistment, 14 January 1915, Melbourne, Victoria. Weight, 14st 7lbs. Height, 6 feet ¾ inches. Complexion, ruddy. Eyes, blue. Hair, dark brown. Fought in Gallipoli, the Dardanelles and France. Also served in Egypt and Marseilles. Reported 'wounded in action' on 28 July 1916. Later changed to 'wounded and missing in action' on 15 September 1916. Changed again to 'Missing' on 24 October 1916. Changed

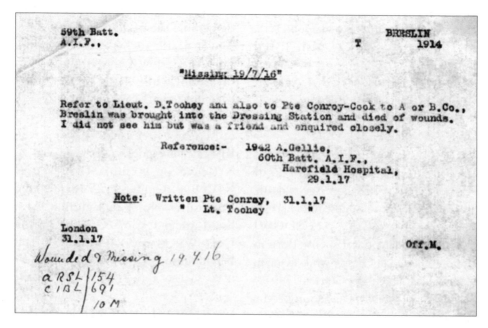

Pte Breslin, from his records.

to 'Killed in action' on 29 August 1917 after a court of enquiry held 'in the field'. 'Presumed buried in no-man's-land at approx 5 JGO 43 to 5 K 0. Q. 51. 'Another report; – Graves Regristratuon units, Breslin, 19-7-16 (buried) Ration Farm Military, 1½ miles south of Armentieres.

Grave or memorial reference: VI. D. 46. Cemetery: Ration Farm Military Cemetery, La Chapelle-Darmentieres, Nord in France.

BRESTLAUN, OWEN: Rank: Private. Regiment or service: Royal Dublin Fusiliers. Unit: 1st Battalion. Date of death: 29 June 1915. Age at death: 28. Service No.: 10053. Born in Carnew, Wexford. Enlisted in Carlow while living in Taney, County Wexford. Killed in action in Gallipoli.

Supplementary information: Son of the late Daniel Brestlaun of Ballyellis, Gorey, County Wexford and of Bessie McGuinness (formerly Brestlaun) of Ardoyne, Tullow, County Carlow.

Grave or memorial reference: Panel 190 to 196. Memorial: Helles Memorial in Turkey. Also listed under Tullow on the Great War Memorial, Milford Street, Leighlinbridge, County Carlow.

BRIEN, CHARLES: Rank: Lance Sergeant. Regiment or service: Irish Guards. Unit: 1st Battalion. Date of death: 10 May 1917. Age at death: 24. Service No.: 3790. Born in Killeshin, County Carlow. Enlisted in Carlow. Died of wounds.

Supplementary information: Son of Mrs Sarah Brien, of 5 Sleaty Street, Graigue-

Cullen, Carlow. Date of will: 4 August 1917. Effects and property received by: (Mother) Sarah O'Brien, Sleaty Street, Carlow. Witnesses: M. Bruce, Wellington Barracks, H. Richardson, Wellington Barracks. Mother also an executor.

Grave or memorial reference: Near the north boundary. Cemetery: Sleaty Old Burial Ground in County Laoise. Also listed under Carlow/Graigue on the Great War Memorial, Milford Street, Leighlinbridge, County Carlow.

BROOKS, JOHN: Rank: Private. Regiment or service: Royal Dublin Fusiliers. Unit: 1st Battalion. Date of death: 4 September 1918. Service No.: 5008. He won the Military Medal and is listed in the *London Gazette*. Born in Carlow. Enlisted in Carlow. Killed in action. Date of will: 1 July 1916. Effects and property received by: (Mother) Mrs M. Brookes, Lowery's Lane, Carlow. Grave or memorial reference: II. M. 20. Cemetery: Trois Arbres Cemetery, Steenerck in France. Also listed under Carlow/Graigue on the Great War Memorial, Milford Street, Leighlinbridge, County Carlow.

BROPHY, DANIEL: Rank: Private. Regiment or service: Machine Gun Corps. Unit: 62nd Battalion, Infantry. Date of death: 4 November 1918. Service No.: 130656. Formerly he was with the Royal Dublin Fusiliers where his number was 30946. Born in St Catherines, Dublin. Enlisted in Carlow while living in Leighlinbridge, County Carlow. Killed in action. Grave or memorial reference: I. D. 1.

Cemetery: Ruesnes Communal Cemetery, Nord, France. Also listed under Leighlinbridge/Old Leighlin on the Great War Memorial, Milford Street, Leighlinbridge, County Carlow.

BROPHY, JAMES: Rank: Private. Regiment or service: Royal Dublin Fusiliers. Unit: 1st Battalion. Date of death: 30 July 1915. Age at death: 22. Service No.: 19737. Born in Borris, County Carlow. Enlisted in Carlow. Killed in action in Gallipoli.

Supplementary information: Son of Thomas and Elizabeth Brophy, of Borris, County Carlow.

Grave or memorial reference: VII. E. 4. Cemetery: Twelve Tree Copse Cemetery in Turkey. Also listed under Borris/Ballyellin on the Great War Memorial, Milford Street, Leighlinbridge, County Carlow.

BROPHY, MICHAEL: Rank: Private. Regiment or service: Royal Irish Regiment. Unit: Depot. Date of death: 19 September 1914. Age at death: 39. Service No.: 8113. Born in Rathue, Gibberstown, County Carlow. Enlisted in Carlow while living in Ballon, County Carlow. Died at home.

Supplementary information: Son of the late John and Brigid Brophy; husband of Brigid Lawless (formerly Brophy). From the *Nationalist* and *Leinster Times,* September 1914:

A man named Brophy, a soldier reservist, and a native of Rathrush, County Carlow, was accidentally killed at Newbridge on Saturday

last. It appears that the deceased was about to go to Tullow for a few days vacation when the accident occurred at the railway station. An inquest was held on Monday. On Tuesday the remains were conveyed to Tullow by the morning train, and the internment took place at Rathoe immediately afterwards. The deceased leaves a wife and two children to mourn his loss. For them sincere sympathy is felt.

Grave or memorial reference: South-East of Church. Cemetery: Rathtoe Catholic Cemetery, County Carlow. Also listed under Ballon/Rathoe/Aghade on the Great War Memorial, Milford Street, Leighlinbridge, County Carlow.

BROPHY, MICHAEL: Rank: Gunner. Regiment or service: Royal Horse Artillery and Royal Field Artillery. Unit: 2nd Trench Mortar Battery. Date of death: 27 September 1916. Service No.: 46212. Born in Baynalstowe(sic), County Carlow. Enlisted in Milston. Died of wounds. Grave or memorial reference: II. C. 13. Cemetery: Gezaincourt Communal Cemetery Extension in France. Also listed under Bagenalstown/Fenagh on the Great War Memorial, Milford Street, Leighlinbridge, County Carlow.

BROWN, BRIAN STEWART: Rank: Rifleman. Regiment or service: Rifle Brigade Unit: 1/28th Regiment. Date of death: 5 April 1918. Age at death: 21. Service No.: B/201487. Born in County Carlow. Enlisted in Dublin while living in Bagenalstown, County Carlow. Killed in action. Formerly he was with the Royal Army Service Corps where his number was M/2/264388.

Supplementary information: Son of Frank B. and Jane Brown, of Bagenalstown, County Carlow, Ireland.

Grave or memorial reference: II. F. 33/37. Cemetery: Hamel Military Cemetery, Beaumont-Hamel, France. Also listed under Bagenalstown/ Fenagh on the Great War Memorial, Milford Street, Leighlinbridge, County Carlow.

BUCHANAN, GEORGE: Rank: Rifleman/Lance Corporal. Regiment or service: King's Royal Rifle Corps. Unit: 2nd Battalion. Date of death: 14 September 1914. Age at death: 23. Service No.: 7211. Born in Carlow. Enlisted in Carlow. Killed in action. Was a member of the Carlow Company of the Boy's Brigade.

Supplementary information: Son of Thomas and Mary Buchanan, of 15, Little Barrack Street, Carlow. From *Carlow Sentinel*, December 1914:

Six Carlow Sons in the Army.
Mr Thomas Buchannan, Little Barrack Street, Carlow (late Sergeant Major, Carlow Rifles), has received the following letter, with reference to which, on the part of Carlow Loyalists, we heartily congratulate him.

Privy Council Office.
Bucking Palace
26 November, 1914.

Sir—I have the honour to inform you that the King has heard with much interest that you have at the present moment, six sons in the Army.

I am commended to express to you the King's congratulations, and to ensure you that His Majesty much appreciates the spirit of patriotism which prompted this example in one family of loyalty and devotion to their Soverign and Empire—I have the honour to be, Sir,
Your Obedient Servant,
F. M. Ponsonby,
Keeper of the Privy Purse.

Rifleman Buchanan is also listed in De Ruvigny's Roll of Honour with no new information. Memorial: La Ferte-Sous-Jouarre Memorial in France. Also listed under Carlow/Graigue on the Great War Memorial, Milford Street, Leighlinbridge, County Carlow.

BURGESS, RUPERT WILLIAM: Rank: Private. Regiment or service: Australian Infantry, A. I. F. Unit: 47th Battalion. Date of death: 7 June 1917. Age at death; 21 years 10 ½ months. Service No.: 1635. Reported 'missing in action' 16 June 1917. Proceedings of Court of Enquiry (24 November 1917) 'in the field' findings: Killed in action in Messines on the night of 6/7 June 1917.

Supplementary informaion: Born, Tobinstown House, Tullow, Carlow, Ireland. Occupation on enlistment: Labourer. Age on enlistment: 20 years 5 months. Educated at D'Israeli School, Rathvilly, County Carlow. Age entering Australia: 16½ years. Next of kin details:

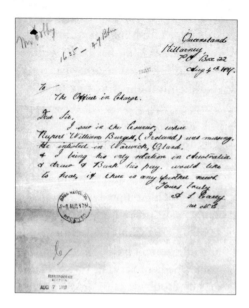

Pte Burgess, letter from records.

(Mother) Mrs Lucy Williams Burgess, Tobinstown House, Tullow, County Carlow. Place and date of enlistment: Warwick, Queensland, 10 January 1916. Weight, 130¾lbs. Height, 5 feet, 5½ inches. Complexion, dark. Eyes, brown. Hair, dark brown.

Grave or memorial reference: Panel 7 – 17 – 23 – 25 – 27 – 29 – 31. Memorial: Ypres (Menin Gate) Memorial in Belgium. Also listed under Rathvilly on the Great War Memorial, Milford Street, Leighlinbridge, County Carlow.

BURKE,   FRANCIS COLLINGWOOD: Rank: Private. Regiment or service: Leinster Regiment. Unit: 2nd Battalion. Date of death: 4 May 1918. Age at death: 20. Service No.: 3704. Born in County Carlow. Died of gas wounds.

Supplementary information: Son of Francis R. Burke (late QMS King's Royal Rifle Corps) and Janet Burke, of Dean Cottage, Browne's Hill, Carlow. Enlisted in Maryborough, Queen's County. Date of will: 5 January 1917. Effects and property received by; (Father) Mr F. R. Burke From the *Nationalist* and *Leinster Times*, May 1918:

BURKE—May 4th, 1918, died of gas wounds, Private Francis C Burke, Leinster Regiment, the dearly beloved son of Francis R Burke, Barrack Warden, Carlow, aged 20 years. -R. I. P.

Grave or memorial reference: I. E. 18. Cemetery: Ebblinghem Military Cemetery, Nord in France. Also listed under Carlow/Graigue on the Great War Memorial, Milford Street, Leighlinbridge, County Carlow.

BURKE, JOHN: Rank: Private. Regiment or service: Irish Guards. Unit: 2nd Battalion. Date of death: 30 September 1915. Age at death: 21. Service No.: 6039. Born in Carlow. Enlisted in Belfast, County Antrim while living in Cornakinega, County Armagh. Killed in action.

Supplementary information: Son of Michael and Nora Burke, of 81 North Street, Lurgan, County Armagh.

Grave or memorial reference: Panel 9 and 10. Memorial: Loos Memorial in France. Also listed under Carlow/Graigue on the Great War Memorial, Milford Street, Leighlinbridge, County Carlow.

BURKE, RUSSELL JAMES: Rank: Bugler. Regiment or service: King's Royal Rifle Corps. Unit: A Company, 2nd Battalion. Date of death: 31 October 1914. Age at death: 31. Service No.: 8856. Born in Gibralter. Enlisted in Colhenry while living in Carlow. Died of wounds.

Supplementary information: Son of Francis R. Burke (late QMSKRRC), of 'Dean Cottage', Browne's Hill, Carlow.

Grave or memorial reference: Has no known grave but is commemorated on Panel 51 and 53. Memorial: Ypres (Menin Gate) Memorial in Belgium. Also listed under Carlow/Graigue on the Great War Memorial, Milford Street, Leighlinbridge, County Carlow.

BURNS, THOMAS: Rank: Private. Regiment or service: Royal Army Service Corps. Unit: 866th H. T. Company. Date of death: 12 April 1918. Service No.: T/370041(SDGW), T3/70041(CWGC). Born in Hacketts Town, Carlow. Enlisted in Perth while living in Dunfermline. Died at home. Grave or memorial reference: In the south east part. Cemetery: Rathmore Church of Ireland Churchyard, Kildare. Also listed under Hacketstown on the Great War Memorial, Milford Street, Leighlinbridge, County Carlow.

BURTON, ALFRED HENRY WELLESLEY: Rank: Captain. Regiment or service: Lincolnshire Regiment. Unit: 7th Battalion attached to 2nd Battalion. Date of death: 23 October 1916. Killed in action. From the *Carlow Sentinel*, January 1917:

Captain A. H. W. Burton, Lincolns, previously reported wounded and missing, and since then killed, was the third son of Mr W. Fitzwilliam Burton, of Burton Hall, Carlow.

From the *Nationalist* and *Leinster Times*.

Roll of Honour.
Captain A. H. W. Burton, 3rd suriving son of W. F. Burton, Esq, of Burton Hall, Carlow, is reported wounded and missing on October 23rd. He was commanding one of the two leading Companies of the 2nd Batt, Lincolns in an assault on the trenches west of Lesoup, and was the first officer to fall up to the present time. He has not been traced since he was seen badly wounded, early in March this year, near Ypres, but, had returned to the front last July. His next brother, now Captain Gerald Burton, K. R. R. C., has made a good recovery from severe burns received at the front. He belongs to the Yeoman Battalion, raised and commanded by the late Lord Feversham.

From *Carlow Sentinel*, November 1916:

Roll of Honour.
…The youngest brother, E. T. Burton, is a Lieutenant in the R. F. A., at the front. An older brother, Captain B. W. Burton, is commanding a Company in the Cadet Battalion at the Curragh.

Grave or memorial reference: I. F. 7. Cemetery: Thiepval Anglo-French Cemetery, Authuille, Somme, France.

BUTLER, JAMES: Rank: Private. Regiment or service: Royal Dublin Fusiliers. Date of death: 25 February 1916. Age at death: 38. Service No.: 13367.

Supplementary information: Husband of Mary Anne Butler, of 4 Pollerton Road, Carlow. This man is not in any other database.

Grave or memorial reference: 5. 4. 1. Cemetery: Carlow (St Mary's) Cemetery, County Carlow. Also listed under Carlow/Graigue on the Great War Memorial, Milford Street, Leighlinbridge, County Carlow.

BUTLER, JOHN: Rank: Gunner. Regiment or service: Royal Garrison Artillery. Unit: 34th Siege Battery. Date of death: 11 November 1917. Service No.: 32321. Born in Grange Tullow, County Carlow. Enlisted in Glasgow while living in Kildare. Died of wounds. Grave or memorial reference: III. F. 34. Cemetery: Hazebrouck Communal Cemetery, Nord, in France.

BUTLER, WILLIAM: Rank: Gunner. Regiment or service: Royal Garrison Artillery. Unit: 185th Siege Battery. Date of death: 25 June 1917. Service No.: 30302. Born in Carlow. Enlisted in Maryborough while living in Carlow. Killed in action. From the *Nationalist and Leinster Times,* June 1918:

> Butler—1st Anniversary—In loving memory of my beloved son, 30302, Gunner William Butler, Royal Garrison Artillery, of Bridge Street, Carlow, who was killed in action in France, June 26th, 1917, on whose soul,

> Sweet Jesus, have mercy. Immaculate heart of Mary pray for him.
> One sad long year has passed away
> since my great sorrow fell.
> Yet in my heart I mourn the loss of
> him I loved so well.
> When last I saw your smiling face
> you seemed so strong and brave.
> I little thought you soon would be
> laid in a soldier's grave.
> The one I loved is now laid low, his
> fond true heart is still.
> Wherever I may roam, dear William,
> forget you I never will.
> I often sit and think of you; your
> name I often call.
> And there is nothing left to answer
> me but your photo on the wall.

> Inserted by his sorrowing mother and brothers and sister.

Grave or memorial reference: II. D. 5. Cemetery: Cemetery: Vlamertinghe New Military Cemetery in Belgium. Also listed under Carlow/Graigue on the Great War Memorial, Milford Street, Leighlinbridge, County Carlow.

BYRNE, BERNARD: Rank: Corporal. Regiment or service: Army Cyclist Corps. Unit: 6th Battalion. Date of death: 19 February 1917. Service No.: 5040. Formerly he was with the Connaught Rangers where his number was 442. Born in Carlow. Enlisted in Dublin while living in Carlow. Killed in action. Grave or memorial reference: O. V. K. 2. Cemetery: St Sever Cemetery Extension, Rouen in France. Also listed under Carlow/Graigue on the

Great War Memorial, Milford Street, Leighlinbridge, County Carlow.

BYRNE, CORNELIUS: Rank: Private. Regiment or service: Royal Dublin Fusiliers. Unit: 2nd Battalion. Date of death: 17 October 1918. Service No.: 24662. Born in Hackettstown, Carlow. Enlisted in Naas while living in Hackettstown. Killed in action. Date of will: 1 November 1916. Effects and property received by: Mrs Mary Byrne, Hacketstown, County Carlow. Grave or memorial reference: IV. A. 5. Cemetery: Highland Cemetery, Roclincourt, Pas-De-Calais, France. Also listed under Hacketstown on the Great War Memorial, Milford Street, Leighlinbridge, County Carlow.

BYRNE, EDWARD: Rank: Lance Corporal. Regiment or service: Royal Dublin Fusiliers. Unit: 1st Battalion. Date of death: 28 August 1918. Age at death: 19. Service No.: 27194. Born in Tullow, County Carlow. Enlisted in Carlow while living in Tullow. Killed in action. S

Supplementary information: Son of the late Mr and Mrs P. Byrne, of Tullow, County Carlow.

Grave or memorial reference: II. D. 13. Cemetery: Outtersteene Communal Cemetery Extension, Bailleul in France. Also listed under Tullow on the Great War Memorial, Milford Street, Leighlinbridge, County Carlow.

BYRNE, EDWARD: Rank: Private. Regiment or service: East Lancashire

Regiment. Unit: 2nd Battalion. Date of death: 1 July 1916. Service No.: 8364. Born in Bagenalstown, County Carlow. Enlisted in Portadown, Armagh while living in London, Middlesex. Killed in action. Grave or memorial reference: Pier and Face 6 C. Memorial: Thiepval Memorial in France. Also listed under Bagenalstown/Fenagh on the Great War Memorial, Milford Street, Leighlinbridge, County Carlow.

BYRNE, JAMES: Rank: Private. Regiment or service: Australian Infantry, A. I. F. Unit: 15th Battalion. Date of death: 27 April 1915. Service No.: 116. Killed in action on the Gallipoli Peninsula.

Supplementary infortmation: Son of Michael Byrne, Pollerton, Carlow. His father died soon after he enlisted and the next of kin details were changed to (sister) Mrs Mary Drury, 140 Minet Avenue, Harlesden, London, N. W. England. However, his personal effects were sent to Rose Byrne, formerly of Pollerton. Born, Carlow, Ireland. Occupation on enlistment: Labourer. Age on enlistment: 32 years – months. Previous military experience: Completed 8 years in the Royal Garrison Artillery and 4 years in the reserve. Place and date of enlistment: Townsville, Queensland, 26 September 1914. Weight, 140lbs. Height, 5 feet, 8 inches. Complexion, dark. Eyes, blue. Hair, black.

Grave or memorial reference: 14. He has no known grave but is listed on the Lone Pine Memorial, Gallipoli. Also listed under Palatine/Urglin on the Great War Memorial, Milford Street, Leighlinbridge, County Carlow.

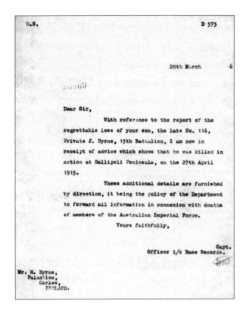

Pte Byrne, letter from records.

BYRNE, JAMES: Rank: Private. Regiment or service: Royal Munster Fusiliers. Unit: 2nd Battalion. Date of death: 6 November 1914. Age at death: 33. Service No.: 8474. Born in St John's, Kildare. Enlisted in Carlow while living in Craigue, County Carlow. Died of wounds.

Supplementary information: Son of Peter and Kate Byrne, of Derrymoyle, Ballickmoyler Road, Carlow.

Grave or memorial reference: IV. A. 8. Cemetery: White House Cemetery, St Jean-Les-Ypres in Belgium. Also listed under Carlow/Graigue on the Great War Memorial, Milford Street, Leighlinbridge, County Carlow.

BYRNE, JAMES: Rank: Private. Regiment or service: Royal Irish Fusiliers. Unit: 5/6th Battalion(SDGW), 7th Battalion(CWGC). Date of death: 26 April 1916. Age at death: 37. Service

No.: 21390. Born in Tullow, County Carlow. Enlisted in Marybororugh while living in Tullow. Killed in action.

Supplementary information: Son of William and Elizabeth Byrne, of Tullow, County Carlow.

Grave or memorial reference: II. H. 39. Cemetery: Vermelles British Cemetery in France. Also listed under Tullow on the Great War Memorial, Milford Street, Leighlinbridge, County Carlow.

BYRNE, JAMES: Rank: Private. Regiment or service: Royal Munster Fusiliers. Unit: 8th Battalion. Date of death: 9 September 1916. Service No.: 870. Born in Clonmore, County Carlow. Enlisted in Carlow while living in Clonmore, County Carlow. Killed in action.

Supplementary information: Brother of Miss Elizabeth Byrne, of Belmount, Clonmore, Hacketstown, County Carlow.

Grave or memorial reference: Pier and Face 16C. Memorial: Thiepval Memorial in France. Also listed under Clonmore on the Great War Memorial, Milford Street, Leighlinbridge, County Carlow.

BYRNE, JOHN JOSEPH: Rank: Private. Regiment or service: Royal Munster Fusiliers. Unit: 2nd Battalion. Date of death: 4 October 1916. Age at death: 22. Service No.: 4772. Born in Carlow. Enlisted in Glasgow while living in Anderston, Lanarkshire. Died of wounds.

Supplementary information: Son of Mr and Mrs Peter Byrne, of 1 Hope Street, Anderston, Glasgow.

Grave or memorial reference: B 20. 12. Cemetery: St Sever Cemetery, Rouen in France. Also listed under Carlow/ Graigue on the Great War Memorial, Milford Street, Leighlinbridge, County Carlow.

BYRNE, MICHAEL: Rank: Private. Regiment or service: Royal Dublin Fusiliers. Unit: 2nd Battalion. Date of death: 24 February 1917. Service No.: 10945. Born in Carlow. Enlisted in Naas while living in Carlow. Died of wounds. Grave or memorial reference: N. 50. Cemetery: Kemmel Chateau Military Cemetery in Belgium.

BYRNE, MICHAEL: Rank: Private. Regiment or service: Royal Dublin Fusiliers. Unit: 2nd Battalion. Date of death: 23 October 1916(CWGC, SDGW) 24 October 1916, (IMR) Age at death: 30. Service No.: 16392. Born in Myshall, County Carlow. Enlisted in Kilkenny while living in Myshall, County Carlow. Killed in action.

Supplementary information: Son of Andrew Byrne; husband of Margaret Byrne, of Johnstown, Clonegal: Ferns, County Carlow. Grave or memorial reference: Pier and Face 16C. Memorial: Thiepval Memorial in France. Also listed under Carlow/Graigue and Myshall on the Great War Memorial, Milford Street, Leighlinbridge, County Carlow.

BYRNE, MICHAEL: Rank: Private. Regiment or service: Royal Dublin Fusiliers. Unit: Depot. Date of death: 16 January 1915(CWGC, IMR, SDGW) 16 April 1915 (Great War Memorial, Milford Street). Age at death: 47. Service No.: 17369. Born in Carlow. Enlisted in Naas while living in Kildare. Died at home.

Supplementary information: Husband of Mary Byrne, of New Row, Naas.

Grave or memorial reference: E. 13. 39. Cemetery: Naas (St Corban's) Catholic Cemetery, County Kildare. Also listed under Carlow/Graigue on the Great War Memorial, Milford Street, Leighlinbridge, County Carlow.

BYRNE, PATRICK: Rank: Sapper. Regiment or service: Corps of Royal Engineers. Unit: 175th Tunnelling Company, R. E. Date of death: 6 March 1917. Age at death: 41. Service No.: 157759. Born in Rathvilla, County Wicklow. Enlisted in Hamilton, Lanarkshire while living in Glenboig, Lanarkshire. Killed in action.

Supplementary information: Son of Patrick and Bridget Byrne, of Kiltegan, County Wicklow; husband of Anna Maria Byrne, of 242, Annathill, Glenboig, Lanarkshire.

Grave or memorial reference: M. 17. Cemetery; Aveluy Communal Cemetry Extension in France. Also listed under Rathvilly on the Great War Memorial, Milford Street, Leighlinbridge, County Carlow.

BYRNE, PATRICK: Rank: Corporal. Regiment or service: Royal Irish Regiment. Unit: 2nd Battalion. Date of death: 21 March 1918. Age at death: 36. Service No.: 18212. Formerly he was with the Yorks and Lancs Regiment where his number was 38205. Born in Carlow. Enlisted in Hull while living in Carlow. Killed in action.

Supplementary information: Son of Mrs Elizabeth Byrne, of Castle Hill, Carlow.

Grave or memorial reference: Panel 30 and 31. Memorial: Pozieres Memorial in France. Also listed under Carlow/Graigue on the Great War Memorial, Milford Street, Leighlinbridge, County Carlow.

BYRNE, PATRICK: Rank: Private. Regiment or service: Royal Dublin Fusiliers. Unit: 1st Battalion. Date of death: 1 July 16, first day of the Battle of the Somme. Age at death: 39. Service No.: 24591. Born in Ballyconnell, County Wicklow. Enlisted in Wicklow while living in Garryhoe, County Wicklow. Killed in action.

Supplementary information: Son of Patrick Byrne. Enlisted in 1915.

Grave or memorial reference: He has no known grave but is listed on Pier and Face 16 C on the Theipval Memorial in France. Also listed under Carlow/Graigue on the Great War Memorial, Milford Street, Leighlinbridge, County Carlow.

BYRNE, PATRICK: Rank: Private. Regiment or service: Royal Dublin Fusiliers. Unit: 2nd Battalion. Date of death: 26 April 1915. Age at death: 31. Service No.: 5227. Born in Tullow, County Carlow. Enlisted in Naas while living in Carlow. Killed in action.

Supplementary information: Son of John and Jane Byrne, of Barrack Street, Tullow, County Carlow. From the *Nationalist* and *Leinster Times*, April 1915:

> Private Pat Byrne, 2nd R. D. F., writes to thank the Carlow ladies for the parcel received. He states the Government is doing all possible for them, but the Carlow ladies have gone one better, as these parcels were most necessary, and the weather has been very inclement.

Grave or memorial reference: Has no known grave but is commemorated on Panel 44 and 46. Memorial: Ypres (Menin Gate) Memorial in Belgium. Also listed under Carlow/Graigue on the Great War Memorial, Milford Street, Leighlinbridge, County Carlow.

BYRNE, PATRICK: Rank: Private. Regiment or service: Royal Dublin Fusiliers. Unit: 1st Battalion. Date of death: 1 March 1917. Service No.: 27193. Born in Tullow, County Carlow. Enlisted in Carlow while living in Tullow. Killed in action. Grave or memorial reference: Pier and Face 16 C. Memorial: Thiepval Memorial in France. Also listed under Tullow on the Great War Memorial, Milford Street, Leighlinbridge, County Carlow.

BYRNE, RICHARD: Rank: Private. Regiment or service: Royal Dublin Fusiliers. Unit: 2nd Battalion. Date of death: 24 April 1915 (SDGW, CWGC) 25 April 1915, (IMR). Service No.: 4599. Born in Carlow. Enlisted in Carlow. Killed in action. Grave or memorial reference: Panel 44 and 46. Memorial: Ypres

(Menin Gate) Memorial in Belgium. Also listed under Carlow/Graigue on the Great War Memorial, Milford Street, Leighlinbridge, County Carlow.

BYRNE, SIMON: Rank: Private. Regiment or service: Royal Irish Fusiliers. Unit: 2nd Garrison Battalion. Date of death: 30 October 1917. Age at death: 45. Service No.: 1052 and G-1052. Previously he was with the Royal Dublin Fusiliers where his number was 20350. Born in Hacketstown, County Carlow. Enlisted in Wicklow while living in Rathdrum, County Wicklow. Died in Salonika.

Supplementary information: Son of Cornelius and Kate Byrne; husband of Annie Byrne, of Shroughmore, Avoca, County Wicklow.

Grave or memorial reference: 139. Cemetery: Mikra British Cemetery, Kalamaria in Greece. Also listed under Hacketstown on the Great War Memorial, Milford Street, Leighlinbridge, County Carlow.

BYRNE, THOMAS: Rank: Private. Regiment or service: Royal Dublin Fusiliers. Unit: 9th Battalion. Date of death: 13 March 1916. Service No.: 23174. Enlisted in Ballyvonan, County Carlow while living in Bagnaltown, County Carlow. Died of wounds. Grave or memorial reference: V. B. 15. Cemetery: Bethune Town Cemetery in France. Also listed under Bagenalstown/Fenagh on the Great War Memorial, Milford Street, Leighlinbridge, County Carlow.

BYRNE, THOMAS: Rank: Private. Regiment or service: Royal Dublin Fusiliers. Unit: 10th Battalion. Date of death: 30 November 1917. Service No.: 25007. Born in Tullow, County Carlow. Enlisted in Carlow while living in Tullow. Killed in action. Two graves up from him in this row lies Private Wiliam Howard, another Carlowman who died with the same unit on the same day. Grave or memorial reference: II. F. 17. Cemetery: Croiselles British Cemetery in France. Also listed under Tullow on the Great War Memorial, Milford Street, Leighlinbridge, County Carlow.

BYRNE, THOMAS: Rank: Private. Regiment or service: Royal Dublin Fusiliers. Unit: 2nd Battalion. Date of death: 13 January 1915. Service No.: 5334. Born in Carlow. Enlisted in Carlow. Killed in action.

Supplementary information: Son of Mrs A. Byrne, of Barnhill. Castledermot, County Kildare. From De Rivigny's Roll of Honour. Byrne 5334:

…son of the late Thomas Byrne, Royal Irish Rifles, by his wife, Anne (Castledermot, co. Kildare), daughter of James Grace. Born Carlow 14-August-1895. Educated at Castledermot. Joined the Army in August-1911, and was killed in action at Ypres on 13-January-1915.

Grave or memorial reference: I. E. 9. Cemetery: Prowse Point Military Cemetery in Belgium. Also listed under Carlow/Graigue on the Great War Memorial, Milford Street, Leighlinbridge, County Carlow.

BYRNE, THOMAS: Rank: Private. Regiment or service: Royal Dublin Fusiliers. Unit: 1st Battalion. Date of death: 1 July 1916. Age at death: 29. Service No.: 8941 Born in Carlow. Enlisted in Carlow. Killed in action.

Supplementary information: Son of Patrick and Alice Byrne, of 4, Charlotte Street, Carlow.

Grave or memorial reference: Pier and Face 16 C. Memorial: Thiepval Memorial in France. Also listed under Carlow/Graigue on the Great War Memorial, Milford Street, Leighlinbridge, County Carlow.

BYRNE, WILLIAM: Rank: Private. Regiment or service: Royal Irish Regiment. Unit: 2nd Garrison Battalion. Secondary Regiment: Labour Corps Secondary. Unit: transf. (275868) Age at death: 53. Date of death: 1 April 1919. Service No.: 1743. This man is not in any other database.

Supplementary information: Son of William and Eliza Byrne; husband of Mary Anne Byrne, of Tullowbeg Street, Tullow.

Grave or memorial reference: Adjoining East wall. Tullow (The Abbey) Cemetery, County Carlow.

BYRNE, WALTER: Rank: Lance Corporal. Regiment or service: Royal Dublin Fusiliers. Unit: 1st Battalion. Date of death: 30 April 1915. Service No.: 11265. Born in Carlow. Enlisted in Carlow while living in Regents Park, London. Killed in action in Gallipoli.

Supplementary information: Brother of Mary Byrne, of 5 Princes Terrace, Queen's Road, Westgate-on-Sea. From the *Nationalist* and *Leinster Times*, May 1915:

Byrne—May 11th, (sic) killed in action at the Dardanelles Lance Corporal Walter Byrne, 1st Battalion, Royal Dublin Fusiliers; aged 19 years 6 months, Carlow. Deeply regretted by his brother and sisters. Sweet Jesus, have mercy on him.

His name is dear to memory
'Tis graven on our hearts
His kindly smile is with us,
Still lingering, loath to part
'Tis sweet to know we'll meet again,
Where parting is no more;
And that the one we loved so well,
Is but one day, gone before.

Grave or memorial reference: A. 17. V Beach Cemetery in Turkey. Also listed under Carlow/Graigue on the Great War Memorial, Milford Street, Leighlinbridge, County Carlow.

C

CAHILL, JOHN NUGENT: Rank: Captain. Regiment or service: Royal Irish Rifles. Unit: 13th Battalion. Date of death: 16 August 1917. Killed in action. From *Leinster Express* and *Carlow Sentinel*, August 1917:

Captain J. N. Cahill.

Captain J. N. Cahill, Royal Irish Regiment (attached Royal Irish Rifles), was killed in action on the 16th August. He was the eldest son of Molonel J. N. Cahill, Ballyconra, County Kilkenny. Captain Cahill's colonel writes of him; - "He was hit leading his company like the gallant soldier he was. We were all so fond of him, and I always considered him as good a company commander as there was in----, and he had trained and led one of the best companies going. We buried him that night at dark, and I will get a proper cross put up as soon as possible." He was a great favourite with everyone who knew him. A good, all-round sportsman, he was a fine rider across a country, and was well known with the Kilkenny Hounds and other packs in the South of Ireland.

From *Kilkenny People*, January 1918:

Death of Colonel J. N. Cahill
We regret to announce the death of Colonel John Nugent Cahill, J. P., Ballyconra House, Ballyragget, which occurred on Wednesday. He was the fourth son of Mr Michael Cahill, D. L., and joined the Royal Irish Regiment early in life. His eldest son, Captain J. N. Cahill, joined his father's regiment and was killed on active service on August 16-1917. Colonel Cahill was a fine sportsman and was exceedingly popular with all classes in the County Kilkenny. He was an extensive land agent in the old days, and always maintained friendly relations with the tenantry. His daughter is the wife of Mr E. J. McElligott, K. C., one of the leaders of the Munster Bar.

From the *Carlow Sentinel*, January 1918:

Death of Colonel John Nugent Cahill.
The announcement of the death of Colonel J. N. Cahill, which occurred on Wednesday last will be received with very genuine regret in Kilkenny and the adjoining counties, where, for many years he was a prominent figure in the public life of the country. He wad the fourth son of the late Michael Cahill, D. L., of Ballyclera House, ballyragget, County Kilkenny, and was educated at Stoneyhurst College. Early in life he joined the 4th Royal Irish Regiment at, which he subsequently commanded for many years. He married in 1889, Emily, daughter of the late Mr Henry Hodges, of Beaufort, Rathfarnham, and is survived by three sons and four daugh-

ters. His eldest son, the late Captain J. N. Nugent Cahill, joined his fathers regiment eight years ago and was killed on active service on the 16th August, 1917. Colonel Cahill was a very fine sportsman, and was exceedingly popular with all classes.

Grave or memorial reference: Panel 138 to 140 and 162 to 162A and 163A. Memorial: Tyne Cot Memorial in Belgium.

CALLINAN, MATTHEW: Rank: Sergeant. Regiment or service: Leinster Regiment. Unit: 1st Battalion. Date of death: 6 September 1915. Service No.: 3011. Born in Carlow. Enlisted in Carlow. Killed in action. From the *Nationalist* and *Leinster Times*, September 1915:

CALLINAN—6th September, 1915, killed in action in France, Matthew Callinan, 4th Leinster Regiment, late of Carlow-Graigue. Sacred Heart of Jesus have mercy on him. —R. I. P.

The voice is now silent, the heart is now cold.
The smile and the welcome, that met us of old.
We miss him, and mourn him, in sorrow unseen.
And dwell on the memory of days that have been.

Inserted by his sorrowing wife and child.

From the *Nationalist* and *Leinster Times*, September 1918:

CALLINAN—3rd Anniversary—in sad and loving memory of Sergeant Matthew Callinan, Church Street, Graiguecullen, Carlow, killed in action, in France, September 6th, 1915. Sacred Heart of Jesus have mercy on him. Immaculate Heart of Mary pray for him. —R. I. P.

Grave or memorial reference: I. C. 28. Cemetery: Houplines Communal Cemetery Extension in France. Also listed under Carlow/Graigue on the Great War Memorial, Milford Street, Leighlinbridge, County Carlow.

CALLINAN, PETER: Rank: Private. Regiment or service: Royal Dublin Fusiliers. Unit: 1st Battalion. Date of death: 12 July 1915. Age at death: 19. Service No.: 5685. Born in Carlow Graigue, Carlow. Enlisted in Carlow. Killed in action in Gallipoli.

Supplementary information: Son of Matthew and Julia Callinan, of Church Street, Graigue Cullen, Carlow.

Grave or memorial reference: Panel 190 to 196. Memorial: Helles Memorial in Turkey. Also listed under Carlow/ Graigue on the Great War Memorial, Milford Street, Leighlinbridge, County Carlow.

CANAVAN, HUGH: Rank: Lance Corporal. Regiment or service: Connaught Rangers. Unit: 1st Battalion. Date of death: 20 October 1918. Service No.: 9707. Born in Carlow. Enlisted in Dublin while living in Kinsale. Died in Egypt. Grave or memorial reference: B. 17. Cemetery: Haifa War Cemetery in Israel. Also listed under Carlow/ Graigue on the Great War Memorial, Milford Street, Leighlinbridge, County Carlow.

CANAVAN, MATHEW/ MATTHEW: Rank: Private. Regiment or service: Royal Irish Regiment. Unit: 2nd Battalion. Date of death: 19 October 1914. Service No.: 7667. Born in Clonegal, County Wexford. Enlisted in Carlow while living in Ballon, County Carlow. Killed in action. Grave or memorial reference: He has no known grave but is listed on Panels 11 and 12 on the Le Touret Memorial in France. Also listed under Clonegal/Kildavin on the Great War Memorial, Milford Street, Leighlinbridge, County Carlow.

CANAVAN, WILLIAM: Rank: Private. Regiment or service: Royal Dublin Fusiliers. Unit: 2nd Battalion. Date of death: 28 August 1914. Age at death: 26. Service No.: 9223. Born in Tullow, County Carlow. Enlisted in Carlow. Died.

Supplementary information: Son of Hugh and Mary Canavan; husband of Bridgid Canavan, of The Green, Tullow, County Carlow.

Grave or memorial reference: C. 95. Cemetery: Shorncliffe Military Cemetery, UK. Also listed under Tullow on the Great War Memorial, Milford Street, Leighlinbridge, County Carlow.

CANTAN, HENRY THOMAS: Rank: Lieutenant Colonel. Regiment or service: Duke of Cornwall's Light Infantry. Unit: 1st Battalion. Date of death: 16 April 1916. Age at death: 47. Killed in action.

Supplementary information: Won the CMG. Husband of Mabel Margaret Cantan (formerly Kidd), of Tullow Lodge, Tullow, County Carlow. Served in the Boer War as a Captain in the Duke of Cornwall's Light Infantry. From *Carlow Sentinel*, April 1916:

> Lieutenant Colonel Cantan Killed in action.
> We regret to learn that the "Roll of Honor" just issued, includes the name pf Lieutenant Colonel Cantan, Duke of Cornwall's Light Infantry, who was killed in action on the 16th inst. This gallant officer was son-in-law of Dr Kidd, Tullow, and was well known in Carlow hunting and other sporting circles, by whom his death will be deeply deplored. We heartily join with his many mourning friends in tendering sincere sympathy to his bereaved widow and other relatives.

Grave or memorial reference: II. A. 49. Cemetery: Faubourg D'Amiens Cemetery, Arras in France.

CANTLON, WILLIAM ROBERT: Rank: Gunner. Regiment or service: Royal Garrison Artillery. Unit: 231st Siege Battery. Date of death: 23 December 1917. Age at death: 33. Service No.: 157977. Enlisted in Liverpool while living in Kilkenny. Died of wounds. Formerly he was with the Lancs and Ches, R. G. A., where his number was 1417.

Supplementary information: Son of the late Philip and A. Cantlon, of Ballyellen, Goresbridge, County Kilkenny.

Grave or memorial reference: II. B. 43. Cemetery: Bleuet Farm Cemetery in Belgium. Also listed under Borris/ Ballyellin on the Great War Memorial, Milford Street, Leighlinbridge, County Carlow.

CAREY, MICHAEL (Listed as **CAREY, MATTHEW** in Irelands Memorial Records, and on the Great War Memorial, Milford Street): Rank: Private. Regiment or service: Royal Inniskilling Fusiliers. Unit: 1st Battalion. Date of death: 9 August 1916. Service No.: 24030. Born in Carlow. Enlisted in Carlow. Died of wounds. From the *Nationalist and Leinster Times*, August 1917:

CAREY—In sad and loving memory of Matthew Carey, Hanover, Carlow, aged 21 years, who died from wounds received in action, on the 9th August, 1916, at the Canadian Clearing Hospital, Remy Station, Belgium. On whose soul Sweet Jesus have mercy. Queen of Peace pray for him.

In far off Belgium the stars are shin-
ing.
Shining on a hero's grave.
Where the one we loved is sleeping,
He was a soldier brave.
In the prime of manhood days,
None knew him but to love him,
None mentioned his name but with
praise.
He bade us not a last farewell,
He said good-bye to none,

His spirit flew before we knew
That from us he had gone.
He sleeps beside his comrades,
In hallowed grave unknown
But "memory is the only friend that
grief can call its own. "

Inserted by his sorrowing parents, sisters and brothers.

Grave or memorial reference: XXVIII. E. 19. Cemetery: Lijssenthoek Military Cemetery in Belgium. Also listed under Carlow/Graigue on the Great War Memorial, Milford Street, Leighlinbridge, County Carlow.

CARROLL, PATRICK: Rank: Lance Corporal. Regiment or service: Royal Dublin Fusiliers. Unit: 6th Battalion. Date of death: 9 October 1918. Age at death: 19. Service No.: 5593. Born in Leighlinbridge, County Carlow. Enlisted in Carlow. Died of wounds.

Supplementary information: Son of William and Ann Carroll, of Rathellin, Bagenalstown, County Carlow. Native of Leighlinbridge. Date of will: 22 October 1917. Effects and property received by: (Father) Mrs William Carroll, Bagenalstown, County Carlow. Witnesses: P Curry, Sergeant, E Company, 3 Royal Dublin Fusiliers, R. Stokes, CQMS, E Company, 3.

Grave or memorial reference: I. F. 2. Cemetery: Doingt Communal Cemetery Extension, Somme, France. Also listed under Leighlinbridge/Old Leighlin on the Great War Memorial, Milford Street, Leighlinbridge, County Carlow.

CARSON, GEORGE ALFRED:
Rank: Sergeant. Regiment or service: Princess Patricia's Canadian Light Infantry (Eastern Ontario Regiment). Unit: 2nd Company. Date of death: 18 May 1915. Age at death: 30. Service No.: 811.

Supplementary information: Son of Edward and Annie Carson, of 74, Sandy Lane, Chorlton-cum-Hardy, Manchester, England. Born, Manchester, England. Occupation on enlistment: Letter carrier for the GPO Canada. Previous military experience: Pivate, 16th Queen's Lancers. Age on enlistment: 29 years - months. Date of birth: 13 March 1885. Next of kin details: (Wife) Frances Emily Carson, Regina College, Sask. Place and date of enlistment: Ottowa, 27 August 1914. Height, 5 feet, 7½ inches. Complexion, fair. Eyes, brown. Hair, brown. From De Ruvigny's Roll of Honour:

Sgt Carson, from De Ruviny's Roll of Honour, Volume 1.

Carson, George Alfred, Sergeant, No 811, Princess Patricia's Canadian Light Infantry. Youngest son of the late Edward Carson, of Manchester, Draper, by his wife, Annie (74, Sandy Lane, Chorlton-cum-Hardy, Manchester). Daughter of Thomas Wallworth, of Manchester. Born Bradford, 13 March 1885. Educated Manchester Higher Grades School, and the Science and Art School. Enlisted in the 16th (Queen's) Lancers in 1902, and served two years in South Africa. Obtained his discharge by purchase on the death of his father in 1905. Went to Canada in 1909 to take up farming, but afterwards went into the Post Office in Regina. Volunteered for Imperial service on the outbreak of war and joined the Regina Legion of Frontiersmen, 09 August 1914, subsequently transferring to Princess Patricia's Canadian Light Infantry; came over in October, 1914, went to France in December. Was in action on the 25th, and was promoted Sergeant on the field; was wounded by a stray shell while going to Headquarters at Ypres, Boulogne, on the 18th. Buried in the Military Cemetery at Boulogne. He greatly distinguished himself after the repulse of the German attack on 8 May by bringing in the wounded, and a comrade wrote; "He returned (from support trenches to the open) and carried a wounded man back to our trenches. To do this he had to cross an open space 300ft wide swept by shrapnel and machine guns, he returned four times and brought back a wounded man each time—how he escaped unhurt I cannot imagine. Our company sergeant, shook him by the hand and said 'You are the bravest man I ever met. '" Captain Adamson also wrote speaking highly of his conduct, and added "No braver man ever gave his life for his country." He married at Regina, Saskatchewan, Canada, 22 August 1914, Frances Emily, youngest daughter of Thomas (and Marcell) Bolton, of Carlow.

[This entry is included as his wife was born in Carlow and is listed in the 1901 census in Ballinnabranagh, Clongrennane].

Grave or memorial reference: VIII. D. 19. Cemetery: Boulogne Eastern Cemetery in France.

CARTHY, MARTIN: Rank: Private. Regiment or service: leinster Regiment. Unit: 1st Battalion. Date of death: 12 May 1915. Service No.: 3821. Born in Carlow. Enlisted in Maryborough, Queen's County. Killed in action. Grave or memorial reference: Panel 44. Memorial: Ypres (Menin Gate) Memorial in Belgium. Also listed under Carlow/Graigue on the Great War Memorial, Milford Street, Leighlinbridge, County Carlow.

CASEY, JOHN: Rank: Private. Regiment or service: Labour Corps. Unit: 200th Company. Date of death: 6 November 1918. Service No.: 553809. Born in Carlow. Enlisted in Dublin while living in Carlow. Died. Grave or memorial reference: VII. D. 2. Cemetery:

Terlincthun British Cemetery, Wimille, France. Also listed under Carlow/Graigue on the Great War Memorial, Milford Street, Leighlinbridge, County Carlow.

CLARKE, ROBERT WILLIAM: Rank: Gunner. Regiment or service: Royal Horse Artillery and Royal Field Artillery. Unit: 277th Brigade, B Battery. Date of death: 5 April 1918 (SDGW, CWGC, IMR) 6 April 1918 (Great War Memorial, Milford Street, Leighlinbridge). Service No.: L/27536. Born in Bagnals Town, County Carlow. Enlisted in Sheffield in Yorkshire. Killed in action. Grave or memorial reference: Panel 7 to 10. Memorial: Pozieres Memorial in France. Also listed under Bagenalstown/Fenagh on the Great War Memorial, Milford Street, Leighlinbridge, County Carlow.

CLARKE, THOMAS: Rank: Private. Regiment or service: Royal Dublin Fusiliers Unit: 2nd Battalion. Date of death: 15 January 1915. Age at death: 28. Service No.: 5579. Born in Bagnalstown, County Carlow. Enlisted in Carlow. Killed in action.

Supplementary information: Son of Patrick Clarke, of Leighlinbridge, County Carlow.

Grave or memorial reference: I. E. 9. Cemetery: Prowse Point Military Cemetery in Belgium. Also listed under Leighlinbridge/Old Leighlin on the Great War Memorial, Milford Street, Leighlinbridge, County Carlow.

CLARKE, THOMAS: Rank: Private. Regiment or service: Scottish Rifles. Unit: 9th Battalion. Date of death: 25 September 1915. Service No.: 11526. Born in Williamstown, County Carlow. Enlisted in Glenboig while living in Rathvilly. Killed in action. Grave or memorial reference: Panel 57 to 59. Memorial: Loos Memorial in France. Also listed under Rathvilly on the Great War Memorial, Milford Street, Leighlinbridge, County Carlow.

CLARKE, THOMAS: Rank: Private. Regiment or service: Labour Corps. Unit: 2nd Battalion. Date of death: 14 March 1918. Age at death: 52. Service No.: 492901. Formerly he was with the Royal Dublin Fusiliers where his number was 15720. Born in Leighlin Bridge, Bagnalstown County Carlow. Enlisted in Carlow while living in Leighlin Bridge, County Carlow. Died at sea.

Supplementary information: Son of Mr and Mrs Clarke, of Leighlinbridge; husband of Margaret Clarke, of Poes Hill, Leighlinbridge, Muine Bheag, County Carlow.

Grave or memorial reference: Hollybrook Memorial, Southampton, Hampshire, UK. Also listed under Leighlinbridge/Old Leighlin on the Great War Memorial, Milford Street, Leighlinbridge, County Carlow.

CLARKE, WILLIAM JOHN: Rank: Private. Regiment or service: Royal Dublin Fusiliers. Unit: A Company, 2nd Battalion. Date of death: 25 April 1915 (SDGW, CWGC, IMR) 25 May 1915 (Great War Memorial, Milford Street, Leighlinbridge) Age at death: 23. Service No.: 11803. Born in Galway. Enlisted in Carlow while living in Inglestone, Essex. Killed in action.

Supplementary information: Son of Mary Warrin (formerly Clarke), of 32, Killeen Road, Rathmines, County Dublin, and the late Matthew Todd Burne Clarke (Royal Welch Fusiliers). Educated at the Royal Hibernian Military School, Pheoonix Park, Dublin.

Grave or memorial reference: Panel 44 and 46. Memorial: Ypres (Menin Gate) Memorial in Belgium. Also listed under Clonegal/Kildavin on the Great War Memorial, Milford Street, Leighlinbridge, County Carlow.

COADY, JAMES: Rank: A/C. S. M. Regiment or service: South Staffordshire Regiment. Unit: 8th Service Battalion. Date of death: 20 May 1917. Service No.: 20652. Born in Southwark, Surrey. Enlisted in Southwark while living in Glynn, County Carlow. Killed in action. Grave or memorial reference: A. 45. Cemetery: Fampoux Military Cemetery, Pas-De-Calais, France.

COBURN, NOTLEY: Rank: Sergeant. Regiment or service: Leinster Regiment. Unit: 2nd Battalion. Date of death: 11 November 1916. Service No.: 3590. Born in Clonegale, County Carlow. Enlisted in Edenderry, King's County. Died of wounds. Grave or memorial reference: I. L. 8. Cemetery: Maroc British Cemetery, Grenay in France. Also listed under Clonegal/Kildavin on the Great War Memorial,

Milford Street, Leighlinbridge, County Carlow.

COE, THOMAS: Rank: Private. Regiment or service: Canadian Infantry (Alberta Regiment). Unit: 50th Battalion. Date of death: 23 June 1917 Age at death: 32. Service No.: 435071.

Supplementary information: Son of Mary Louisa Coe, of Rathrush, Tullow, County Carlow, Ireland, and the late John Coe. From the *Nationalist* and *Leinster Times,* June 1917:

> COE—June 23rd, 1917, killed in action. Thomas Coe, Canadians, fourth son of John and Mary Louisa Coe, Rathrush, Tullow, County Carlow, aged 32 years.
> Those that die in Christ shall first arise at the last triumphant sound.

Memorial: Vimy Memorial, Pas-de-Calais, France.

COLEMAN, SAMUEL: Rank: Private. Regiment or service: Royal Dublin Fusiliers. Unit: 1st Battalion. Formerly he was with the Royal Irish Regiment where his number was 10019. Date of death: 28 October 1916. Service No.: 43104. Born in Carlow. Enlisted in Carlow. Died of wounds.

Supplementary information: Husband of Mary Coleman, of Spratstown, Colbinstown, County Wicklow. Grave or memorial reference: VIII. E. 7. Cemetery: Etaples Military Cemetery in France. Also listed under Carlow/Graigue on the Great War Memorial, Milford Street, Leighlinbridge, County Carlow.

CONDON, JOHN: Rank: Private. Regiment or service: Irish Guards. Unit: 1st Battalion. Date of death: 13 September 1917. Service No.: 5222. Born in Tullow, County Carlow. Enlisted in Carlow. Died of wounds. Date of his informal will: 2 February 1915. Effects and property received by: (Brother) James Condron, Ballyrale, Ballon, County Carlow. Grave or memorial reference: Cemetery: IV. D. 12. Mendingham Military Cemetery in Belgium. Also listed under Tullow on the Great War Memorial, Milford Street, Leighlinbridge, County Carlow.

CONDRON, J.: See **CONDRON, THOMAS.**

CONDRON, PATRICK: Rank: Private. Regiment or service: Scottish Rifles. Unit: 1st Battalion. Age at death: 21. Service No.: A/7579. Formerly he was with the Leinster Regiment where his number was 3157. Born in Doonane, County Carlow, Ireland. Enlisted in Maryborough while living in Longriggend, Glasgow. Killed in action.

Supplementary information: Son of the late Michael and Catherine Condron, East Longrigg, Longriggend, Lanarkshire; brother of Catherine Condron of East Longrigg.

Grave or memorial reference: 6. G. 24. Cemetery: London Cemetery and Extension, Longueval in France.

CONDRON, THOMAS (SDGW, IMR)**, J.** (CWGC): Rank: Private.

Regiment or service: Royal Irish Fusiliers. Unit: 1st Battalion. Date of death: 11 April 1917 (SDGW) 16 April 1917 (CWGC). Service No.: 24941. Born in Dublin. Enlisted in Glasgow. Killed in action. Grave or memorial reference: III. D. 47. Cemetery: Brown's Copse Cemetery, Roeux, Pas-de-Calais, France.

CONNOR, WILLIAM JOSEPH SANDERSON:

Rank: Lieutenant. Regiment or service: Canadian Field Artillery. Unit: 4th Battery. 1st Brigade. Age at death: 31. Date of death: 5 July 1916.

Supplementary information: Son of Abner and Mary Anne Connor, of Barrow House, Carlow, Ireland; late of 620, Ontario Street, Toronto. Place and date of birth: Carlow, 21 February 1885. Occupation on enlistment: Mounted police constable. Previous military experience, 10 years with the Canadian Field Artillery. Place and date of enlistment: 16 September 1914, Valcartier. Height, 6ft ½inch. Complexion, dark. Eyes, brown. Hair, dark. From the *Carlow Sentinel*, October 1914:

Another Carlow Volunteer from Canada.
…We take the following for the Toronto "Sentinel" of September 3, which gives a portrait of the young volunteer; -
Sergeant Major, W. J. S. Connor a volunteer for active service in defence of his country and the old Union Jack, was paid a surprise visit in the form of a corn roast at his home, 620 Ontario Street by a host of his old comrades and well wishers on Thursday night, 27th ult, on the eve of his departure from Toronto, with the 6th Battery, Canadian Field Artillery.

Many were the expressions of regret and sorrow indulged in by those present, at losing the presence of one who had endeared himself to all, by his social and amiable disposition. Anyone coming in contact with Bill Connor found him a true friend. Before separating an expression of good luck and God speed in his arduous undertaking, with a triumphant return home, was tendered to this gallnt young volunteer. A suitable reply was drowned in an outburst of applause, and with the singing of "Rule Brittania", and the National Anthem, the party took their departure, with many handshakes, and expressions of good will.

Sergeant Major Connor joined the Battery when he only a lad out from the County Carlow, Ireland. Promotion was his ambition. With close attention to discipline, and ever mindful of his several duties, his promotion was rapid. Taking a course of instruction at Kingstown, he qualified for a Sergeant Major's rank, which position he held during the remainder of his time with the battery. On expiration of his time he joined the police force. On the declaration of war he offered his services with his old associate officers in the battery, which was accepted, and left on Friday for camp.

Sergeant Major Connor is a member of the Masonic Order, Scarlet and Black knights of Ireland. Many and varied gifts were bestowed on the young soldier as he shipped out to do his duty, to uphold the honor of England and the Flag of our Country. Sergeant Major Connor represented the battery in London in the Coronation ceremony of our present King.

From the *Carlow Sentinel*, July 1916:

Roll of Honour.
Lieutenant W. J. S. Connor.
We regret to have to add to the long list of the Roll of Honour, another young Carlow Officer, Lieutenant Connor, Canadian F. A., who died of wounds sustained while gallantly taking his part in the great advance of the Allies. A few weeks since we recorded the death of his brother, Mr James Connor, Carlow, who was fired on by Sinn Feiners while motoring at Stephen's Green on Easter Monday, and died in hospital on the 15th inst. Much sympathy is felt for the family in their double bereavement.

Grave or memorial reference: II. A. 15. Cemetery: Vlamertinghe Military Cemetery in Belgium. Also listed under Carlow/Graigue on the Great War Memorial, Milford Street, Leighlinbridge, County Carlow.

CONNORS, JAMES: Rank: Private. Regiment or service: Royal Irish Regiment. Unit: 2nd Battalion. Date of death: 19 July 1916. Service No.: 4891. Born in Tryerland(sic), County Carlow. Enlisted in Carlow while living in Ballycarney, County Carlow. Died of wounds. After his death his effects and property were received by his mother, Mrs Mary Connors, Bally Carney, County Carlow. Grave or memorial reference: II. D. 26. Cemetery: Heilly Station Cemetery, Mericourt-L'Abbe in France. Also listed under Tinryland on the Great War Memorial, Milford Street, Leighlinbridge, County Carlow.

CONORAN, WILLIAM: Rank: Private. Regiment or service: Royal Dublin Fusiliers. Unit: 1st Battalion. Age at death: 32. Date of death: 10 October 1918. Service No.: 43637. Formerly he was with the Leincester(sic) Regiment where his number was 3408. Born in Leighlinbridge, County Carlow. Enlisted in Maryborough, Queen's County while living in Leighlinbridge. Killed in action.

Supplementary information: Youngest son of John and Anastatia Conoran, of Chapel Street, Leighlinbridge, County Carlow. After his death his effects and property were received by his mother, Mrs A. Conoran, Leighlin Bridge, County Carlow. His Nuncupative (or missing) will was witnessed by Mary Kenna (daughter of A. Conoran) and Arthur McLintock, JP Carlow.

Grave or memorial reference: Panel 144 to 145. Memorial: Tyne Cot Memorial in Belgium. Also listed under Leighlinbridge/Old Leighlin on the Great War Memorial, Milford Street, Leighlinbridge, County Carlow.

CONROY, DANIEL: Rank: Private. Regiment or service: Royal Dublin Fusiliers. Unit: 8th Battalion. Date of death: 29 April 1916. Age at death: 34. Service No.: 5726. Born in Carlow. Enlisted in Naas while living in Carlow. Killed in action.

Supplementary information: Son of Nicholas and Ellen Conroy, of Pollerton Road, Carlow.

Grave or memorial reference: Panel 127 to 129. Memorial: Loos Memorial in France. Also listed under Carlow/Graigue on the Great War Memorial, Milford Street, Leighlinbridge, County Carlow.

CONROY/CONRON, JAMES: Rank: Private. Regiment or service: Royal Dublin Fusiliers. Unit: 2nd Battalion. Date of death: 16 October 1916. Service No.: 4660. Born in Tullow, County Carlow. Enlisted in Carlow while living in Dublin. Killed in action. Grave or memorial reference: Pier and Face 16 C. Memorial: Thiepval Memorial in France. Also listed under Tullow on the Great War Memorial, Milford Street, Leighlinbridge, County Carlow.

CONROY, PATRICK: Rank: Private. Regiment or service: Royal Dublin Fusiliers. Unit: 1st Battalion. Date of death: 21 July 1916. Age at death: 37. Service No.: 5442. Born in County Carlow. Enlisted in Garlow (sic). Killed in action.

Supplementary information: Son of Nicholas and Ellen Conroy, of Carlow; husband of Ellen Conroy, of Pollerton Road, Carlow. Date of will: 12 July 1916. Effects and property received by: (Mother) Mrs Ellen Conroy, Pollerton Road. Carlow.

Grave or memorial reference: Pier and Face 16 C. Memorial: Thiepval Memorial in France. Also listed under Carlow/Graigue on the Great War Memorial, Milford Street, Leighlinbridge, County Carlow.

COOGAN, HUGH: Rank: Private. Regiment or service: Royal Dublin Fusiliers. Unit: 8th Battalion. Date of death: 6 July 1916. Age at death: 18. Service No.: 20073. Born in Bagnalstown County Carlow. Enlisted in County Carlow. Killed in action.

Supplementary information: Son of Thomas and Kate Coogan, of Kilcarrig, Bagnalstown, County Carlow.

Grave or memorial reference: I. C. 3. Cemetery: Philosophe British Cemetery, Mazingarbe in France. Also listed under Bagenalstown/Fenagh on the Great War Memorial, Milford Street, Leighlinbridge, County Carlow.

COOGAN, THOMAS: Rank: Private. Regiment or service: Royal Inniskilling Fusiliers. Unit: 1st Battalion. Date of death: 23 April 1917. Age at death: 21. Service No.: 16971. Born in Bagnalstown County Carlow. Enlisted in County Carlow. Killed in action.

Supplementary information: Son of Thomas and Kate Coogan, of Kilcarrig, Bagnalstown, County Carlow. Also served at Gallipoli.

Grave or memorial reference: Bay 6. Memorial: Arras Memorial in France. Also listed under Bagenalstown/Fenagh on the Great War Memorial, Milford Street, Leighlinbridge, County Carlow.

CORCORAN, THOMAS: Rank: Private. Regiment or service: Royal Dublin Fusiliers. Unit: 2nd Battalion. Date of death: 14 March 1919. Service No.: 5578. This man is not in any other database.

Supplementary information: Son of Mr T. Corcoran, of Kill, Tullow.

Grave or memorial reference: south-west of entrance. Cemetery: Mullawn (St Bridget's) Cemetery, Carlow. Also listed under Tullow on the Great War Memorial, Milford Street, Leighlinbridge, County Carlow.

CORRIGAN, ALBERT VICTOR ERNEST: Rank: Lance Corporal. Regiment or service: Canadian Infantry (British Columbia Regiment). Unit: 7th Battalion. Date of death: 27 March 1917. Age at death: 25. Service No.: 442038.

Supplementary information: Son of Thomas and Adelaide Corrigan, of 118, East 59th Street, Chicago, USA. Born at Killerig, Carlow, Ireland. Next of kin listed as (mother), Mrs Adelaide Corrigan, PO Box 426, Winnipeg. Place of birth, Carlow, Ireland. Date of birth: 21 August 1891. Occupation on enlistment: Clerk. Place and date of enlistment: Chernon, 31 May 1915. Height, 5 feet, 11 inches. Complexion, dark. Eyes, blue. Hair, dark brown. From the *Nationalist* and *Leinster Times*, April 1917:

> CORRIGAN—March 27th, 1917, at Horton war Hospital, Epsom, of "endocarditis", contracted on active service, Lance Corporal Albert V. E. Corrigan, Canadians, aged 25 years, dearly loved youngest son of the late

Thomas Corrigan, Killerig, Carlow. Funeral took place Monday, April 2nd, at Epsom.

Grave or memorial reference: Screen Wall. K. 737. Cemetery: Epsom Cemetery, UK. Also listed under Tullow on the Great War Memorial, Milford Street, Leighlinbridge, County Carlow.

CORRIGAN, ALFRED: Rank: Private. Regiment or service: South Irish Horse Date of death: 19 June 1917. Age at death: 22. Service No.: 1532. Born in Rathfilly. Enlisted in Riverstown while living in Rathfilly. Killed in action.

Supplementary information: Son of William and Susan Corrigan, of Garrettstown, Rathvilly, County Carlow.

Grave or memorial reference: XIX. A. 21. Cemetery: Loos British Cemetery in France. Also listed under Rathvilly on the Great War Memorial, Milford Street, Leighlinbridge, County Carlow.

CORRIGAN, GEORGE HENRY SYKES: Rank: Private. Regiment or service: South Irish Horse. Date of death: 21 March 1917. Age at death: 21. Service No.: 1540. Born in Rathfilly. Enlisted in Dublin while living in Rathfilly. Died at home.

Supplementary information: Son of Thomas and Sarah Corrigan, of Maplestown, Rathvilly, County Carlow.

Grave or memorial reference: Q. 387 (Screen Wall). Cemetery: Manchester Southern Cemetery, UK. Also listed under Rathvilly on the

Great War Memorial, Milford Street, Leighlinbridge, County Carlow.

COSGROVE (IMR, SDGW, CWGC), **COSGRAVE** (Great War Memorial, Milford Street, Leighlinbridge, County Carlow), **JOHN:** Rank: Corporal. Regiment or service: Royal Dublin Fusiliers. Unit: 9th Battalion. Date of death: 7 November 1914. Age at death: 49. Service No.: 15553 Born in Tullow, County Carlow. Enlisted in Naas while living in Tullow, County Carlow. Died at home. Grave or memorial reference: In North-East corner. Tullow (The Abbey) Cemetery, County Carlow. Also listed under Tullow on the Great War Memorial, Milford Street, Leighlinbridge, County Carlow.

COSTIGAN, WILLIAM: Rank: Private. Regiment or service: Royal Irish Regiment. Unit: 2nd Battalion. Date of death: 3 September 1916. Age at death: 23. Service No.: 9700. Born in Muckalee, County Kilkenny. Enlisted in Kilkenny while living in Coolcullen, County Kilkenny. Killed in action.

Supplementary information: Son of Michael and Ellen Costigan, of Coolcullen, Bagnalstown, County Kilkenny. From the *Kilkenny People*, September 1916:

"Killed in action."
Private William Costigan, son of Mr Michael Costigan, Coolcullen, who was in the Royal Irish Regiment, having enlisted as a voluntary recruit about two years ago, was "killed in action", on the 3rd September. He

was a young man, fired with a young Irishman's love of his own country, and under the belief that his own country would be served best by his action.

Grave or memorial reference: Pier and Face 3 A. Memorial: Thiepval Memorial in France. Also listed under Leighlinbridge/Old Leighlin on the Great War Memorial, Milford Street, Leighlinbridge, County Carlow.

CRAMPTON, THOMAS: Rank: Private. Regiment or service: Royal Irish Fusiliers. Unit: 9th Battalion. Date of death: 16 August 1917. Age at death: 21. Service No.: 24927. Born in Kilkenny. Enlisted in Enniskillen while living in Mountcharles, County Donegal. Killed in action.

Supplementary information: Son of William and Elizabeth Crampton, of the Club House Hotel, Carlow.

Grave or memorial reference: Panel 140 to 141. Memorial: Tyne Cot Memorial in Belgium. Also listed under Carlow/Graigue on the Great War Memorial, Milford Street, Leighlinbridge, County Carlow.

CRIMMIN (CWGC, SDGW, IMR) **CREMIN** (Great War Memorial, Milford Street, Leighlinbridge), **DENIS:** Rank: Private. Regiment or service: Royal Dublin Fusiliers. Unit: 1st Battalion. Date of death: 26 April 1915. Service No.: 9819. Born in Rathvilly, County Carlow. Enlisted in Naas while living in Ferrybank, County Wicklow. Joined the Army in 1907. Killed in action in Gallipoli. He had two brothers who also served, Thomas in the Royal Navy and William in the Royal Field Artillery.

Grave or memorial reference: D. 13. V Beach Cemetery in Turkey. Also listed under Rathvilly on the Great War Memorial, Milford Street, Leighlinbridge, County Carlow.

CROMBIE, WILLIAM: Rank: Regimental Quartermaster Sergeant. Regiment or service: King's Own Scottish Borderers. Unit: 1st Battalion. Date of death: 4 October 1917. Age at death: 29. Service No.: 8214 Died of wounds.

Supplementary information: Son of Sergeant William Crombie (King's Royal Rifle Corps) and Sarah Crombie, of Garden House, Hanover, Carlow, County Carlow. Awards: DCM. Born in Gosport, Hants. Enlisted in Dublin while living in Carlow. From the *Nationalist* and *Leinster Times*, October 1917:

CROMBIE—October 4th, 1917, died of wounds received in action, William Crombie, Regimental Quartermaster Sergeant, King's Own Scottish Borderers, eldest son of the late Sergeant W. Crombie, Per. Staff—K. R. R, Corps, and Mrs B. H. Hopkins, Hanover, Carlow. —R. I. P.

From De Ruvigny's Roll of Honour:

... eldest son of the late William Crombie, Sergeant, King's Royal Rifle Corps, by his wife, Sarah)now wife of Benjamin Herbert Hopkins,

of Hanover, Carlow), daughter of Denis Cahill, of Limerick. Born at Parkhurst, Isle of Wight, 20-February-1889. Educated at the Royal Hibernian Military School, Dublin. Enlisted 06-February-1903. Served in Egypt and with the Mediterranean Expeditionary Force at Gallipoli from April, 1915. Took part in the landing there on the 25th, and on the evacuation in January, 1916. Landed in France 20-March-1916, and died at No 47 Casualty Clearing Station 04-October-1917, from wounds received in action. Buried in Dozingham Cemetery, eight and a half miles north-west of Ypres. His Commanding Officer in recommending him for the D. C. M., wrote; "Regimental Quartermaster-Sergeant Crombie has done very good work throughout the whole campaign. In Gallipoli he superintended the bringing up of rations under very difficult circumstances and in many instances under very heavy fire. By his zeal and devotion to duty he has shown a very fine example to all ranks." He was awarded the Distinguished Conduct Medal, also a Parchment Conduct Certificate (posthumously), "for gallantry and devotion to duty."

Grave or memorial reference: VI. G. 18. Cemetery: Dozinghem Military Cemetery in Belgium.

CULLEN, JOHN: Rank: Private/ Lance Corporal. Regiment or service: Royal Irish Regiment. Unit: 1st Battalion. Date of death: 3 May 1915.

Age at death: 25. Service No.: 4078. Born in Bagenalstown, County Carlow. Enlisted in Kilkenny while living in Graiguenamanagh, County Kilkenny. Killed in action.

Supplementary information: Son of John and Julia Cullen, of High Street, Graiguenamanagh; husband of Mary Cullen, of High Street, Graiguenamanagh, County Kilkenny.

Grave or memorial reference: Panel 33. Memorial: Ypres (Menin Gate) Memorial in Belgium. Also listed under Bagenalstown/Fenagh on the Great War Memorial, Milford Street, Leighlinbridge, County Carlow.

CULLEN, JOHN: Rank: Private. Regiment or service: Irish Guards. Unit: 2nd Battalion. Date of death: 27 November 1917. Service No.: 2670. Born in Tullow, County Carlow. Enlisted in Dublin while living in King's Cross, Middlesex. Killed in action. Michael Hawe is on the same panels and died the same day with the same unit. Both are killed in action and neither of them have graves. Grave or memorial reference: Panel 2 and 3. Memorial: Cambrai Memorial in Louveral in France. Also listed under Tullow on the Great War Memorial, Milford Street, Leighlinbridge, County Carlow.

CULLETON, THOMAS: Rank: Private/Lance Corporal. Regiment or service: Royal Irish Regiment. Unit: 1st Battalion. Date of death: 30 December 1917. Service No.: 8675. Born in Bagenalstown, County Carlow. Enlisted in Carlow while living in Bagenalstown, County Kilkenny (sic). From the *Nationalist* and *Leinster Times*, June 1916:

Soldiers Furlough.
Thomas Culleton, Bagnalstown, is home on eight days furlough, having been twice wounded at the front by a bullet and a piece of shrapnel. He stated that there were times when they have been as near as 50 yards from the German trenches. Died at Sea.

Grave or memorial reference: Chatby Memorial Cemetery in Egypt. Also listed under Bagenalstown/Fenagh on the Great War Memorial, Milford Street, Leighlinbridge, County Carlow.

CULLETON(CWGC and the Great War Memorial, Milford Street, Leighlinbridge, County Carlow), **CULLERTON**(SDGW, IMR), **THOMAS:** Rank: Private. Regiment or service: Leinster Regiment. Unit: 2nd Battalion. Date of death: 15 March 1916. Age at death: 23. Service No.: 3491. Born in Gores Bridge, County Kilkenny. Enlisted in Maryborough, Queen's County. Killed in action.

Supplementary information: Son of William and Ellen Culleton, of Near Grange, Goresbridge, County Kilkenny. Grave or memorial reference: I. K. 5. Cemetery: Menin Road South Military Cemetery in Belgium.

D

DALTON, JAMES: Rank: Private. Regiment or service: Leinster Regiment. Unit: 1st Battalion. Date of death: 16 March 1918. Service No.: 4125. Born in Clanmore, County Carlow. Enlisted in Glasgow, Lanarkshire. Killed in action in Egypt.

Supplementary information: Son of Peter and Mary Tompkins.

Grave or memorial reference: U. 63. Cemetery: Ramleh War Cemetery in Israel.

DALTON, MICHAEL: Rank: Private. Regiment or service: Royal Dublin Fusiliers. Unit: 2nd Battalion. Date of death: 27 August 1914. Age at death: 35. Service No.: 8950. Born in Hackettstown, County Carlow. Enlisted in Carlow. Killed in action.

Supplementary information: Son of John and Jean Dalton, of Hacketstown, County Carlow.

Memorial: La Ferte-Sous-Jouarre Memorial in France. Also listed under Hacketstown on the Great War Memorial, Milford Street, Leighlinbridge, County Carlow.

DALTON, PETER: Rank: Private. Regiment or service: Irish Guards. Unit: 1st Battalion. Date of death: 15 November 1914. Age at death: 21. Service No.: 4564. Born in Hackettstown, County Carlow. Enlisted in Boyle, County Roscommon. Died of wounds.

Supplementary information: Son of James and Jane Dalton, brother of Michael, Winifred K., Margaret H. and Kate Dalton. Listed in the 1911 census in Cloonyquin, Roscommon. In his will, written on 5 August 1914 he leaves his property and estate was received by his mother, Jane Dalton, Cloonymun, Castlerea, County Roscommon, and his will was also executed by her.

Grave or memorial reference: III. C. 32. Cemetery: Boulogne Eastern Cemetery in France. Also listed under Hacketstown on the Great War Memorial, Milford Street, Leighlinbridge, County Carlow.

DALY, JOHN: Rank: Private. Regiment or service: Royal Dublin Fusiliers. Unit: 8th Battalion. Date of death: 6 September 1916. Age at death: 40. Service No.: 23010. Born in Bagnalstown County Carlow. Enlisted in Carlow while living in Bagenalstown County Carlow. Killed in action.

Supplementary information: Son of Patrick and Nora Daly; husband of Brigid Daly, of Pump Street, Leighlinbridge, County Carlow.

Grave or memorial reference: XXV. J. 6. Cemetery: Serre Road Cemetery No. 2 in France. Also listed under Leighlinbridge/Old Leighlin on the Great War Memorial, Milford Street, Leighlinbridge, County Carlow.

DALY, RICHARD: Rank: Private. Regiment or service: Irish Guards. Unit: 1ˢᵗ Battalion, Machine Gun Section. Date of death: 15 September 1916. Service No.: 4916. Born in Carlow. Enlisted in Dublin. On the second anniversary of his death a newspaper records that his parents resided at Barrack Street. Killed in action. Grave or memorial reference: Pier and face 7 D. He has no known grave but is listed on the Thiepval Memorial in France. Also listed under Carlow/Graigue on the Great War Memorial, Milford Street, Leighlinbridge, County Carlow.

DAVIS, MICHAEL: Rank: Private. Regiment or service: Leinster Regiment. Unit: A Company, 1ˢᵗ Battalion. Date of death: 14 March 1915. Age at death: 29. Service No.: 3350. Born in Bagnalstown, County Carlow. Enlisted in Carlow. Killed in action.

Supplementary information: Son of the late Mr and Mrs Michael Davis.

Grave or memorial reference: Panel 44. Memorial: Ypres (Menin Gate) Memorial in Belgium. Also listed under Bagenalstown/Fenagh on the Great War Memorial, Milford Street, Leighlinbridge, County Carlow.

DELANEY, JAMES: Rank: Private. Regiment or service: Highland Light Infantry. Unit: 2ⁿᵈ Battalion. Date of death: 28 April 1917. Service No.: 1541. Born in Carlow, Queen's County. Enlisted in Wishaw, Lanarkshire while living in Cleland, Lanarkshire. Killed in action during the Battle of the Lys. Grave or memorial reference: He has

no known grave but is listed in Bay 8 on the Arras Memorial in France. Also listed under Carlow/Graigue on the Great War Memorial, Milford Street, Leighlinbridge, County Carlow.

DELANEY, JOHN: Rank: Private. Regiment or service: Royal Dublin Fusiliers. Date of death: 1914. Age at death: 41. I have no additional information on this man. Data above is listed under Leighlinbridge/Old Leighlin on the Great War Memorial, Milford Street, Leighlinbridge, County Carlow.

DELANEY, MICHAEL: Rank: Sergeant. Regiment or service: Highland Light Infantry. Unit: 10/11ᵗʰ Battalion. Date of death: 15 September 1917. Service No.: 9395. Born in, Carlow, Queen's County (sic). Enlisted in Wishaw, Lanarkshire while living in Cleland, Lanarkshire. Killed in action. This man may be related to James Delaney, No. 1541 above. Also listed De Ruvigny's Roll of Honour with no new information. Grave or memorial reference: Pier and face 15 C. He has no known grave but is listed on the Thiepval Memorial in France. Also listed under Carlow/Graigue on the Great War Memorial, Milford Street, Leighlinbridge, County Carlow.

DELANEY, MICHAEL: Rank: Sergeant. Regiment or service: Royal Sussex Regiment. Unit: 2ⁿᵈ Battalion. Date of death: 30 October 1914. Age at death: 25. Service No.: L/9490. Killed in action.

Supplementary information: Son of William and Mary Delaney, of Dublin Road, Carlow. Born in Carlow. Enlisted in Carlow. Date of will: 19 August 1914. His name on the will is Delany L (sic) Effects and property received by: (Mother) Mrs Delaney, Dublin Road, Carlow.

Grave or memorial reference: Panel 20. Memorial: Ypres (Menin Gate) Memorial in Belgium. Also listed under Carlow/Graigue on the Great War Memorial, Milford Street, Leighlinbridge, County Carlow.

DELANEY, THOMAS: Rank: Private. Regiment or service: Royal Dublin Fusiliers. Date of death: 16 November 1925. Age at death: 25. I have no additional information on this man. Data above is listed under Leighlinbridge/Old Leighlin on the Great War Memorial, Milford Street, Leighlinbridge, County Carlow.

DELANEY, WILLIAM: Rank: Private. Regiment or service: Connaught Rangers. Unit: 2nd Battalion. Date of death: 29 November 1920. Age at death: 44. Service No.: 7144866. This man is not in any other database. Grave or memorial reference: East of Church. Cemetery: Ballinabrannagh Catholic Churchyard, County Carlow. Also listed under Leighlinbridge/Old Leighlin on the Great War Memorial, Milford Street, Leighlinbridge, County Carlow.

DEMPSEY, JAMES: Rank: Rifleman. Regiment or service: London Regiment. Unit: 8th (City of London) Battalion (Post Office Rifles). Date of death: 30 October 1917. Service No.: 371324. Born in Carlow. Enlisted in Carlow while living in Carlow. Killed in action. Grave or memorial reference: Panel 150 to 151. Memorial: Tyne Cot Memorial in Belgium. Also listed under Carlow/Graigue on the Great War Memorial, Milford Street, Leighlinbridge, County Carlow.

DENNIS, CECIL: Rank: Private. Regiment or service: Army Cyclist Corps. Unit: 19th Corps Cyclist Battalion. Date of death: 21 April 1918. Service No.: 2716. Formerly he was with the Somerset Light Infantry where his number was 11942. Born in Dunleckney, Baymalstown(sic), County Carlow. Enlisted in Taunton in Somerset. Killed in action. Grave or memorial reference: IV. B. 15. Cemetery: Premont British Cemetery, Aisne, France. Also listed under Bagenalstown/Fenagh on the Great War Memorial, Milford Street, Leighlinbridge, County Carlow.

DERMODY, THOMAS: Rank: Lance Corporal. Regiment or service: Royal Dublin Fusiliers. Unit: 2nd Battalion. Date of death: 24 May 1915. Age at death: 21. Service No.: 5313. Born in Leighlinbridge, County Carlow. Enlisted in Carlow. Killed in action.

Supplementary information: Son of Patrick and Julia Dermody, of Harrow Goss, Bagenalstown, County Carlow.

Grave or memorial reference: Panel 44 and 46. Memorial: Ypres (Menin Gate) Memorial in Belgium. Also listed under Leighlinbridge/Old Leighlin on

the Great War Memorial, Milford Street, Leighlinbridge, County Carlow.

DIGGES LA TOUCHE, AVERELL: See **LA TOUCHE, AVERELL DIGGES.**

DIGNAM, GEORGE: Rank: Private. Regiment or service: Royal Munster Fusiliers. Unit: 1st Battalion. Date of death: 31 July 1917. Service No.: 15038. Formerly he was with the South Lancashire Regiment where his number was 24383.

Supplementary information: Born in Castleknock, County Dublin. Enlisted in Naas, County Kildare while living in Tullow, County Carlow. Killed in action. After his death his effects and property were received by: (A dear friend) Mrs Pat Curran, Aghade, County Carlow.

Grave or memorial reference: II. A. 13. Cemetery: Potijze Chateau Lawn Cemetery in Belgium. Also listed under Tullow on the Great War Memorial, Milford Street, Leighlinbridge, County Carlow.

DILLON, PATRICK: Rank: Lance Corporal. Regiment or service: Royal Munster Fusiliers. Unit: 2nd Battalion. Date of death: 8 September 1916. Age at death: 23. Service No.: 5116. Born in Tynerland, County Carlow. Enlisted in Carlow while living in Palatine, County Carlow. Killed in action.

Supplementary information: Son of Patrick and Mary Dillon (*née* Byrne), of Palatine, Carlow, County Carlow.

Grave or memorial reference: Pier and Face 16 C. Memorial: Thiepval Memorial in France. Also listed under Tinryland on the Great War Memorial, Milford Street, Leighlinbridge, County Carlow.

DILLON, THOMAS: (Alias, correct name is *FRASER, THOMAS*) Rank: Gunner. Regiment or service: Royal Garrison Artillery. Unit: 70th Siege Battery. Date of death: 1 May 1918 Service No.: 140251. Born in

Pte Dillon's (Fraser) headstone.

Bagnalstown County Carlow. Enlisted in Kilkenny while living in Bagnalstown County Carlow. Killed in action.

Supplementary information: Son of Peter Fraser, of 74, Kilcarrig Street, Bagenalstown, County Carlow.

Grave or memorial reference: XXVIII. E. 19. Cemetery: Lijssenthoek Military Cemetery in Belgium. Also listed under Bagenalstown/Fenagh on the Great War Memorial, Milford Street, Leighlinbridge, County Carlow.

DONOHOE, JAMES: Rank: Private. Regiment or service: Royal Dublin Fusiliers. Unit: 2nd Battalion. Date of death: 26 April 1915. Age at death: 29. Service No.: 4997. Born in Leighlinbridge, County Carlow. Enlisted in Carlow while living in Leighlinbridge, County Carlow. Killed in action.

Supplementary information: Son of James Donohoe, of Pump Street, Leighlinbridge, County Carlow.

Grave or memorial reference: Panel 44 and 46. Memorial: Ypres (Menin Gate) Memorial in Belgium. Also listed under Leighlinbridge/Old Leighlin on the Great War Memorial, Milford Street, Leighlinbridge, County Carlow.

DONOHUE, JOHN: Rank: Private. Regiment or service: Royal Irish Regiment. Unit: 2nd Battalion. Date of death: 14 July 1916. Service No.: 11243. Born in Killeshin, County Carlow. Enlisted in Athy, County Kildare while living in Carlow. Killed in action. Grave or memorial reference: Pier and face 3A. He has no known grave but is listed

on the Thiepval Memorial in France. Also listed under Carlow/Graigue on the Great War Memorial, Milford Street, Leighlinbridge, County Carlow.

DONOHUE, PATRICK: Rank: Sergeant. Regiment or service: Connaught Rangers. Unit: 1st Battalion. Date of death: 10 October 1918. Age at death: 38. Service No.: 7023. Born in Carlow. Enlisted in Naas while living in Gorey. Died in Egypt.

Supplementary information: Son of Patrick and Sarah Donohue; husband of Sarah Williams (formerly Donohue) of 7 Newtown, Cwmbran, Monmouthshire. Served in the Boer War. Born at Carlow.

Grave or memorial reference: A. 87. Cemetery: Haifa War Cemetery in Israel. Also listed under Carlow/Graigue on the Great War Memorial, Milford Street, Leighlinbridge, County Carlow.

DONOHUE, PATRICK: Rank: Gunner. Regiment or service: Royal Garrison Artillery. Unit: 20th Heavy Battery. Date of death: 20 September 1915. Service No.: 31939. Born in Carlow. Enlisted in Carlow. Killed in action. Grave or memorial reference: 8. Cemetery: Pommer Communal Cemetery, Pas-De-Calais, France. Also listed under Carlow/Graigue on the Great War Memorial, Milford Street, Leighlinbridge, County Carlow.

DOODY, JOHN: Rank: Sergeant. Regiment or service: Royal Iniskilling Fusiliers. Unit: 3rd Battalion. Date of death: 29 August 1918. Age at death: 40. Service No.: 5157. Born in Castledermott, County Kidlare (IMR), Carlow(SDGW). Enlisted in Carlow while living in Castledermott. Died at home.

Supplementary information: Husband of Sarah Doody, of Railway Terrace, Omagh.

Grave or memorial reference: Screen Wall. EE. 26. Cemetery: Belfast (Milltown) Roman Catholic Cemetery, County Antrim.

DOOLEY, JAMES: Rank: Corporal. Regiment or service: Corps of Royal Engineers. Unit: RETC, Deganwy. Date of death: 8 May 1916. Service No.: 985. Born in Hackettstown, County Carlow. Enlisted in Dublin. Died at home. Grave or memorial reference: St Patrick's. UL. 156. Cemetery: Glasnevin Cemetery, Dublin. Also listed under Hacketstown on the Great War Memorial, Milford Street, Leighlinbridge, County Carlow.

DORAN, MICHAEL: Rank: Private. Regiment or service: Royal Dublin Fusiliers. Unit: A Company. 9th Battalion. Date of death: 10 January 1916. Age at death: 22. Service No.: 16077. Born in Newtown, County Carlow. Enlisted in Carlow while living in Fenagh, County Carlow. Killed in action.

Supplementary information: Son of Steven and Margaret Doran, of Killane, Ballon, County Carlow; husband of Bridget Doran, of Rathrush, Tullow, County Carlow.

Grave or memorial reference: Panel 127 to 129. Memorial: Loos Memorial in France. Also listed under Ballon/Rathoe/Aghade on the Great War Memorial, Milford Street, Leighlinbridge, County Carlow.

DOWLEY, PATRICK: Rank: Private. Regiment or service: King's Liverpool Regiment. Unit: 1/8th and 8th Battalion. Date of death: 20 November 1917. Service No.: 325106. Formerly he was with the London Regiment where his number was 4802. Born in Carlow, Ireland. Enlisted in London while living in Newbridge, Ireland. Died of wounds. Grave or memorial reference: Pier and Face 1 D 8 B and 8 C. Memorial: Thiepval Memorial in France. Also listed under Carlow/Graigue on the Great War Memorial, Milford Street, Leighlinbridge, County Carlow.

DOWLING, CHRISTOPHER: Rank: Private. Regiment or service: Leinster Regiment. Unit: 1st Battalion. Date of death: 5 May 1915. Age at death: 24. Service No.: 9859. Born in Bagnalstown, County Carlow. Enlisted in Dublin. Killed in action.

Supplementary information: Son of Edward and Elizabeth Dowling, of 61 Francis Street, Dublin.

Grave or memorial reference: Panel 44. Memorial: Ypres (Menin Gate) Memorial in Belgium. Also listed under Bagenalstown/Fenagh on the Great War Memorial, Milford Street, Leighlinbridge, County Carlow.

DOWLING, JAMES: Rank: Lance Corporal. Regiment or service: Household Cavalry and Cavalry of the line including the Yeomanry and Imperial Camel Corps. Unit: 4th (Queen's Own) Hussars. Date of death: 26 November 1914. Service No.: 1555. Born in Rathvilly, County Carlow. Enlisted in Carlow while living in Carlow. Died. Grave or memorial reference: Panel 5. Memorial: Ypres (Menin Gate) Memorial in Belgium

Street, Bagenalstown, County Carlow. Witnesses: T.J.Waters, Corporal 5th Battalion Royal Dublin Fusiliers, Glencorse, Midlothian, Scotland.

Grave or memorial reference: Panel 144 to 145. Memorial: Tyne Cot Memorial in Belgium. Also listed under Bagenalstown/Fenagh on the Great War Memorial, Milford Street, Leighlinbridge, County Carlow.

DOWLING, MICHAEL JOHN: Rank: Private. Regiment or service: Irish Guards. Unit: 2nd Battalion. Date of death: 10 December 1917. Age at death: 31. Service No.: 6221. Born in Dublin. Enlisted in Dublin while living in Tullow, County Carlow. Died.

Supplementary information: Son of Peter and Anne Dowling, of Slaney Quarter, Tullow, County Carlow.

Grave or memorial reference: V. D. 38. Cemetery: Duisans British Cemetery, Etrun in France. Also listed under Tullow on the Great War Memorial, Milford Street, Leighlinbridge, County Carlow.

DOYLE, EDWARD: Rank: Corporal. Regiment or service: Royal Dublin Fusiliers. Unit: X Company. 1st Battalion. Date of death: 28 September 1918. Age at death: 21. Service No.: 19877. Born in Bagnalstown County Carlow Enlisted in Carlow. Killed in action.

Supplementary information: Son of Michael and Katie Doyle, of 31 Regent Street, Bagenalstown, County Carlow. Date of will: 11 March 1918. Effects and property received by: (Mother) Mrs Kate Doyle, 7 Pump

DOYLE, JAMES: Rank: Private. Regiment or service: Royal Dublin Fusiliers. Unit: 1st Battalion. Date of death: 29 March 1918. Service No.: 29389. Born in Pennsylvania, USA. Enlisted in Naas while living in Rathvilly, County Carlow. Killed in action. Grave or memorial reference: VI. A. 14. Cemetery: Epehy Wood Farm Cemetery, Epehy in France. Also listed under Rathvilly on the Great War Memorial, Milford Street, Leighlinbridge, County Carlow.

DOYLE, JAMES: Rank: Corporal. Regiment or service: London Regiment (Finsbury Rifles). Unit: 11th Battalion. Date of death: 6 May 1917. Age at death: 27. Service No.: 452121. Born in Carlow. Enlisted in London while living in London, E. C. Died of wounds.

Supplementary information: Son of Myles and Annie Doyle, of Kilmeary, Carlow. From the *Nationalist* and *Leinster Times*, May 1917:

DOYLE. —Killed in action in France on May 5th, 1917. Corporal James Doyle, 2nd Battalion, London regiment. Late of Kilmeaney, Carlow, to the inexpressible grief of his sorrowing father, brothers and sisters. Sacred Heart of Jesus have mercy on his soul. Mother of Dolors, pray for him—R. I. P.

Grave or memorial reference: III. E. 15. Cemetery: Grevillers British Cemetery, Pas-de-Calais, France. Also listed under Carlow/Graigue on the Great War Memorial, Milford Street, Leighlinbridge, County Carlow.

DOYLE, JAMES: Rank: Private. Regiment or service: Royal Dublin Fusiliers. Unit: 2nd Battalion. Date of death: 30 November 1917. Service No.: 4891. Born in Bagnalstown County Carlow. Enlisted in Naas while living in Carlow. Killed in action.

Supplementary information: Husband of Katie Doyle, of Bridewell Lane, Carlow.

Grave or memorial reference: Bay 9. Memorial: Arras Memorial in France. Also listed under Bagenalstown/ Fenagh on the Great War Memorial, Milford Street, Leighlinbridge, County Carlow.

DOYLE, JOHN: Rank: Private. Regiment or service: Royal Irish Regiment. Unit: 6th Battalion. Date of death: 3 September 1916 (CWGC, SDGW, IMR) 23 December 1916 (Great War Memorial, Milford Street, Leighlinbridge). Service No.: 2563. Born in Borris, County Carlow. Enlisted in Carlow while living in Borris, County Carlow. Killed in action.

Grave or memorial reference: Pier and Face 3A. Memorial: Thiepval Memorial in France.

DOYLE, JOHN: Rank: Fireman. Regiment or service: Mercantile Marine. Unit: SS *Lusitania* (Liverpool). The Lusitania was sunk by German Submarine U-20. Date of death: 7 May 1915. Age at death: 35.

Supplementary information: Son of Lawrence Doyle of 368, Vauxhall Rd, Liverpool and the late Ann Doyle. Born at Glynn, County Wexford.

Memorial: Tower Hill Memorial UK. Also listed under St Mullins on the Great War Memorial, Milford Street, Leighlinbridge, County Carlow.

DOYLE, JOHN: Rank: Private. Regiment or service: Royal Irish Regiment. Unit: 8th Battalion. Date of death: 21 February 1919. Age at death: 30. Service No.: 9816.

Supplementary information: Son of Martin and Mary Doyle, brother of Hugh, Patrick, and James Doyle. Listed in the 1911 census in Burren Street, Carlow. Effects and property received by: (Brother) Mr Hugh Doyle. His Nuncupative (or missing) will was witnessed by Patrick Doyle, Burren Street, Carlow.

Grave or memorial reference: I.B.34. Cemetery: Street Andre Communal Cemetery, Nord, France.

DOYLE, JOHN: Rank: Private. Regiment or service: Royal Irish Regiment. Unit: 2nd Battalion. Date of death: 27 September 1918. Service No.: 16428. Formerly he was with the Leinster Regiment where his number was 4747. Born in Carlow. Enlisted in Maryborough, Queen's County while living in Carlow. Killed in action. He is buried two graves up from Thomas Landers, a Waterford man who died on the same day in the same unit. Grave or memorial reference: I. B 17. Cemetery: Moeuvres Communal Cemetery Extension, Nord in France. Also listed under Carlow/Graigue on the Great War Memorial, Milford Street, Leighlinbridge, County Carlow.

DOYLE, JOSEPH: Rank: Private. Regiment or service: Royal Dublin Fusiliers. Unit: 8th Battalion. Date of death: 9 September 1916. Service No.: 11846. Born in Bagnalstown, County Carlow. Enlisted in Carlow while living in Bagnalstown, County Carlow. Killed in action.

Supplementary information: Date of will: 28 April 1915. Effects and property received by: (Wife) Mrs Mary Doyle, Castle Hill, Carlow.

Grave or memorial reference: XXV. K. 16. Cemetery: Serre Road Cemetery No. 2 in France. Also listed under Bagenalstown/Fenagh on the Great War Memorial, Milford Street, Leighlinbridge, County Carlow.

DOYLE, MATTHEW: Rank: Private. Regiment or service: Royal Dublin Fusiliers. Unit: 2nd Battalion. Date of death: 24 May 1915. Service No.: 5308. Born in Bagnalstown, County Carlow. Enlisted in Carlow. Killed in action.

Grave or memorial reference: Panel 44 and 46. Memorial: Ypres (Menin Gate) Memorial in Belgium. Also listed under Bagenalstown/Fenagh on the Great War Memorial, Milford Street, Leighlinbridge, County Carlow.

DOYLE, MATTHEW: Rank: Private. Regiment or service: Australian Army Medical Corps. Unit: 8th Field Ambulance. Date of death: 25 September 1917. Age at death: 29. Service No.: 10063.

Supplementary information: Son of William and Catherine Doyle, of Upper Main Street, Graiguenamanagh, County Kilkenny, Ireland. Born: Graigue, Kilkenny. Occupation on enlistment, State School Teacher. Age on enlistment: 26 years 11 months. Next of kin details: (Mother) Catherine Doyle, Uper Main Street, Graig-Na-Managh, County Kilkenny. She received a pension of 40s per fortnight from 11 December 1917. Place and date of enlistment, 2 September 1915. Townsville, Queensland. Weight, 9st 6lbs. Height, 5 feet, 7 inches. Complexion, dark. Eyes, grey. Hair, black. Died of multiple wounds received in action on the Menin Road at the 3rd Field Ambulance. The day he died was known as Black Friday. From the *Nationalist* and *Leinster Times*, 1917:

Sergeant(sic) Matthew Doyle.
The many friends of Matthew Doyle, formerly of Graiguenamanagh, who fell in action in France on September 25th, while serving with his Regiment there, will deeply regret the very sad occurrence. This young fellow was trained some years

ago for the teaching profession in this country and, having spent some time in Edenderry Boys School, he at the suggestion of his Australian friends determined to parade his calling under the Southern Cross. Getting on remarkably well in his new home, and maintaining his former prestige as a teacher with his characteristic unselfishness, he in obedience to the call of his adopted country threw up a lucrative position and in company with his brother and several other young teachers, took service in the Army Service Branch of the Australian Imperial Forces. Having spent some time in preliminary training, his unit was drafted to Egypt and after a short stay there, was subsequently ordered to the front. Here he passed through many hazardous actions, as his letters to home indicated. But alas, the end came too soon, for he fell, as he lived, trying to succour others. To his sorrowing mother, sister, and brothers the greatest sympathy is extended, while the vast circle of his relations in the Counties of Carlow, Kilkenny and Wexford, as well as in Australia, will be grieved to hear of his young life cut away so swiftly.

Grave or memorial reference: Panel 31. Memorial: Ypres (Menin Gate) Memorial in Belgium.

DOYLE, MICHAEL: Rank: Private. Regiment or service: Royal Dublin Fusiliers. Unit: 2nd Battalion. Date of death: 21 March 1918 (IMR, CWGC, SDGW) 29 March 1918 (Great War Memorial, Milford Street, Leighlinbridge, County Carlow). Age at death: 20. Service No.: 5602. Born in Carlow. Enlisted in Naas while living in Carlow. Killed in action.

Supplementary information: Son of Annie Doyle, of 5 Burrin Street, Carlow, and the late Michael Doyle.

Grave or memorial reference: Panel 79 and 80. Memorial: Pozieres Memorial in France. Also listed under Carlow/ Graigue on the Great War Memorial, Milford Street, Leighlinbridge, County Carlow.

DOYLE, MICHAEL: Rank: Private. Regiment or service: Irish Guards. Unit: 1st Battalion. Date of death: 18 May 1915. Service No.: 2575. Born in Duffrey, County Carlow. Enlisted in Dublin, County Dublin. Killed in action. Grave or memorial reference: Has no known grave but is commemorated on Panel 4. Memorial: Le Touret Memorial in France.

DOYLE, PATRICK: Rank: Private. Regiment or service: Royal Irish Regiment. Unit: 1st Battalion. Secondary Regiment: Labour Corps Secondary. Unit: transferred to (622506) 1095th Division, Employment Company. Date of death: 30 March 1919. Age at death: 37. Service No.: 9990. This man is not in any other database.

Supplementary information: Brother of James Doyle, of Bridewell Lane, Carlow.

Grave or memorial reference: F. 412. Cemetery: Kantara War Memorial Cemetery in Egypt.

DOYLE, PATRICK: Rank: Private. Regiment or service: Royal Irish Regiment. Unit: 2nd Battalion. Date of death: 12 August 1917. Service No.: 6959. Born in Bagenalstown, County Carlow. Enlisted in Dublin while living in Bagenalstown, County Carlow. Killed in action. Grave or memorial reference: I. A. 6. Cemetery: Aeroplane Cemetery, Ypres, Belgium. Also listed under Bagenalstown/Fenagh on the Great War Memorial, Milford Street, Leighlinbridge, County Carlow.

DOYLE, PHILIP: Rank: Lance Sergeant. Regiment or service: Royal Dublin Fusiliers. Unit: 1st Battalion. Date of death: 4 September 1918. Service No.: 4998. Killed in action.

Supplementary information: He won the Military Medal and is listed in the *London Gazette*. Born in Leighlinbridge, Carlow. Enlisted in Carlow while living in Leighlinbridge, Carlow. Date of will: 7 April 1918. Effects and property received by; (Father) Mrs Patrick Doyle, Leighlinbridge Dispensary, County Carlow.

Grave or memorial reference: Panel 10. Memorial: Ploegsteert Memorial in Belgium. Also listed under Leighlinbridge/Old Leighlin on the Great War Memorial, Milford Street, Leighlinbridge, County Carlow.

DOYLE, THOMAS: Rank: Private. Regiment or service: Royal Irish Regiment. Unit: 2nd Battalion. Date of death: 31 August 1918 (CWGC, SDGW, IMR) 28 September 1918 (Great War Memorial, Milford Street, Leighlinbridge). Service No.: 10882. Born in Bagenalstown, County Carlow. Enlisted in Carlow while living in Bagenalstown, County Carlow. Died of wounds, also listed in De Ruvigny's Roll of Honour as 'died (as a prisoner of war)'. Date of will: 6 August 1914. Effects and property received by; (Mother) Mrs T. Doyle, 68 Kilcarrig Street, Bagenalstown, County Carlow. Grave or memorial reference: XVIII. D. 1-16. Cemetery: Cement House Cemetery in Belgium. Also listed under Bagenalstown/Fenagh on the Great War Memorial, Milford Street, Leighlinbridge, County Carlow.

DOYLE, THOMAS: Rank: Private. Regiment or service: Irish Guards. Unit: 2nd Battalion. Date of death: 9 October 1915 (SDGW, CWGC, IMR) 8 October 1915 (Great War Memorial, Milford Street, Leighlinbridge). Age at death: 26. Service No.: 6622. Born in Hackettstown, County Carlow. Enlisted in Dublin. Killed in action.

Supplementary information: Son of James and Anne Doyle, of Ballysallagh, Hacketstown, County Carlow. Volunteered from RIC. After his death his effects and property were received by: (Mother) Mrs Anne Doyle, Ballysallagh, Hacketstown, Carlow. His will was witnessed by William Hanlon, Tubberkeen, Dungloe, County Donegal, and Lawrence Green.

Grave or memorial reference: VI. D. 21. Cemetery: Vermelles British Cemetery in France.

DRYDEN, ROBERT: Rank: Lance Corporal. Regiment or service: Royal Dublin Fusiliers. Unit: 2nd Battalion. Date of death: 24 April 1918. Age at death: 22. Service No.: 27215. Born in Thomastown, County Kilkenny. Enlisted in Carlow while living in Thomastown. Service No.: 55210. Born in Ballon, County Carlow and died in the Military Hospital, Milbank. Killed in action.

Supplementary information: Son of Alfred and Mary Dryden, of Field House, Triangle, Halifax.

Grave or memorial reference: He has no known grave but is listed on Panel 79 and 80 on the Pozieres Memorial in France. He is also commemorated on the Great War Memorial in St Canice's Cathedral, Kilkenny...'To the Glory of God and in loving memory of the following members of the Diocese of Ossory who gave their lives for their country in the Great War 1914-1918' and he is also listed under Carlow/Graigue on the Great War Memorial, Milford Street, Leighlinbridge, County Carlow.

DUNNE, JOSEPH: Rank: Private. Regiment or service: Rifle Brigade. Unit: 2nd Battalion. Date of death: 4 April 1917. Service No.: Z/2309(SDGW), Z/2300(CWGC). Born in St Mary's, County Carlow. Enlisted in Manchester while living in Salford, Lancashire. Killed in action. Grave or memorial reference: Pier and Face 16 B and 16 C. Memorial: Thiepval Memorial in France. Also listed under Carlow/Graigue on the Great War Memorial, Milford Street, Leighlinbridge, County Carlow.

DUNNE, MICHAEL: Rank: Private. Regiment or service: Royal Dublin Fusiliers. Unit: 1st Battalion. Date of death: 29 March 1918. (SDGW, IMR), between 21 March 1918 and 29 March 1918 (CWGC). Age at death: 28. Service No.: 5087. Born in Athy. Enlisted in Athy. Killed in action.

Supplementary information: Son of Edward and Margaret Dunne, of Nelson Street, Athy, County Kildare; husband of Annie Maher (formerly Dunne), of Henery Street, Graiguecullen, Carlow.

Grave or memorial reference: Panel 79 and 80. Memorial: Pozieres Memorial in France. Also listed under Carlow/Graigue on the Great War Memorial, Milford Street, Leighlinbridge, County Carlow.

DWYER, EDWARD: Rank: Private. Regiment or service: Irish Guards. Unit: 2nd Battalion. Date of death: 20 November 1916. Service No.: 9508. Born in Carlow. Enlisted in Carlow. Killed in action. From the *Nationalist and Leinster Times*, November, 1917:

DWYER—In sad and loving memory of Private Edward Dwyer, 2nd Irish Guards, killed in action in France, November 20th, 1916.

One year ago we parted, 'twas a
heavy trial to bear.
To-day it is nothing lighter. God
gives each one their share.
Your gentle face and manner are
present with us still,
But heaven for you is far better,
blessed be God's Holy Will.

Inserted by his loving parents, brothers, and sisters.

Grave or memorial reference: Pier and
Face 7D. Memorial: Thiepval Memorial
in France. Also listed under Carlow/
Graigue on the Great War Memorial,
Milford Street, Leighlinbridge, County
Carlow.

E

EGAN, THE REVEREND PIERCE JOHN: Rank: Chaplain, 4th Class. Regiment or service: Army Chaplains Department. Attached to the 1st Battalion, British West Indies Regiment. Date of death: 6 April 1916. Died (accident, illness or suicide).

Supplementary information: Husband of Jessie Helen Egan, of 7A, Spencer Road, Eastbourne.

Grave or memorial reference: Q. 568. Cemetery: Alexandria (Chatby) Military and War Memorial Cemetery in Egypt. He is also listed on the Memorial to the Royal Army Chaplains Department on the east wall of the Royal Garrison Church of All Saints in Aldershot, Hants. I cannot find any Carlow connection with this man.

ELLIOTT (OWGC) **ELLIOT** (Great War Memorial, Milford Street, Leighlinbridge), **REGINALD WILLIAM SIDNEY:** Rank: Major. Regiment or service: 7th Gurkha Rifles Date of death: 23 November 1914. Age at death: 40.

Supplementary information: Son of Mr N. G. Elliott, of Kellistown, County Carlow; husband of M. E. Elliott, of Quetta, Waltham Street, Lawrence, Berkshire. From Bond of Sacrifice, Volume 1:

...born at Johnstown House, County Carlow, on the 18th April, 1874, son of Nicholas G. Elliott, Esq., late of the 62nd regiment, and a grandson of the late Captain Sir Thomas Ross, R. N. Major Elliott went to Cheltenham College in 1887, and gained a classical scholarship there in 1888, and the Schacht German prize in 1891. he was in the College boat, and in the football XV in 1891, in which year he also passed into the R. M. C., Sandhurst, taking the seventh place. He received an unattached commission in 1893, and in the following year joined the India Army, becoming Lieutenant in 1895, Captain in 1902, and Major in 1911.

He fell at festubert on the 23rd November, 1914, while leading part of the 2nd Battalion of the 8th Gurkha Rifles in an attack to recover lost trenches.

Major Elliott married Mary Emelia, youngest daughter of the late Captain Robert H. Swinton, R. N., and left one son, Robert Allen, born may, 1906.

From De Ruvigny's Roll of Honour:

...son of Nicholas G. Elliott, late 62nd Regiment. Born at Johnstown House, County Carlow, 18-April-1874. Educated at Cheltenham College (Classical Scholar), and the Royal Military College, Sandhurst. Gazetted 2nd Lieutenant, Unattached List, 29-January-1893, being posted to the Indian Army 03-April-1896. Promoted Lieutenant, 28-April-1895, Captain, 28-January-1902, and

Major, 28-January-1911. Served with the Expeditionary Force in France and Flanders, ans was killed in action at festubert, 23-November-1914, while leading an attack. Me married Mary Emila, youngest daughter of the late Captain Robert H. Swinton, R. N., and had a son, Robert Allen, born May-1906. [This officer is not listed in IMR or ODGW.]

Grave or memorial reference: I. A. 22. Cemetery: Bethune Town Cemetery in France. Also listed under Tinryland on the Great War Memorial, Milford Street, Leighlinbridge, County Carlow.

ELMES, KING: Rank: Captain. Regiment or service: Royal Army Medical Corps. Secondary Regiment: London Regiment (Queen's Westminster Rifles). Secondary. Unit: attd. 2nd /16th Battalion. Date of death: 28 September 1918. Age at death: 25. Killed in action.

Supplementary information: Son of Mr T. and Mrs M. R. Elmes of Robinstown House, Palace East, New Ross, County Wexford.

Grave or memorial reference: I. D. 3. Cemetery: Kandahar Farm Cemetery in Belgium. Also listed under Bagenalstown/Fenagh on the Great War Memorial, Milford Street, Leighlinbridge, County Carlow.

F

FARLEY, SABINA: Rank: Matron. Regiment or service: Queen Alexandra's Imperial Military Nursing Service. Date of death: 1 June 1918. Died. From *Carlow Sentinel*, June 1918:

Roll of Honour

The death occurred at the Adelaide Hospital, Dublin, on Saturday, of Miss Sabina Farley, Q. A., Q. N. S. E., late Matron of the Military Hospital, Fermoy. Miss Farley, had see a good deal of active service. In addition to the Royal Red Cross, with which she was decorated by the King on October 24th, 1917, for her services in the present war, she also held the South African Medal and Silver Badge. Miss Farley was a native of Carlow, a sister of Mrs J. B. Quinnell, Edenburn, County Kerry, and sister-in-law of the late Mr J. G. Glover, Clerk of Carlow Union.

On Wednesday, Miss Farley's remains were interred in Mount Jerome, with full military honours. The chief mourners were; --Mr J. B. Quinnell (broher-in-law); Miss E. Quinnell (niece), Mrs Farley (aunt), Mr and Miss Farley and Mr T. Cullemore(cousins). The Matron and nursing staff of the Adelaide Hospital lined up in the hall of the hospital while the coffin was being received by the principal matron and nursing staff of King George V. Hospital, who formed in processional order and marched from the hospital to the cemetery. The pall bearers were members of the R. A. M. C., and there was a firing party of about forty men of the Royal North Lancashire Regiment, under the command of Lieutenant Talbot. The Burial Service was conducted by the Reverend Canon Jennings, M. A, and at its conclusion three volleys were fired, and the "Last Post" was sounded. Amongst the general public were—Captain J. A. Battersby, Major QW. F. Law, R. A. M. C; Mr and Mrs Telford, Miss C. T. Evans, Mr B. Whitaker, Mr Lynch. Wreaths were sent by the nursing staff, King George V Hospital; Mr and Mrs Telford, Mr and Mrs Quinnell, Major T. C. Quinnell, Captain A. Quinnell, K. L. R, and the Misses Quinnell.

From De Ruvigny's Roll of Honour:

Farley, Martha Sabina, Matron, Q. A., Q. N. S. E., Military Hospital, Fermoy. Daughter of Charles Farley, of Drogheda. Born Drogheda, 24 June 1872. Educated there, and at Dublin. Served during the South African War, 1899 to 1902 (Medal and Silver Badge), and in the European War, and died at the Adelaide Hospital, Dublin, 1-June-1918, from illness, contracted while on active service. Buried in the Mount Jerome Cemetery, Dublin. From 'Supplement to the Edinburgh Gazette, October 25, 1917, page 2236; -

Miss Martha Sabina Farley, Acting Matron, Q. A. I. M. N. S. R., Military Hospital, Fermoy, County Cork.

[Miss Farley is not listed in IMR databases. Although she is listed in the CWGC she does not have a Commonwealth War Graves head-stone but a private one. Author.]

Grave or memorial reference: 4III. 281. Cemetery; Mount Jerome Cemetery, Dublin. Also listed on a memorial in St Anne's Cathedral, Belfast.

FARRELL, EDWARD: Rank: Private. Regiment or service: Royal Irish Regiment. Unit: 2nd Battalion. Date of death: 8 September 1914. Service No.: 8879. Born in Carlow and enlisted there also. Killed in action.

Supplementary information: Husband of Mary Farrell, of Cappadeen, Ballinahinch, Newport, County Tipperary.

Cemetery: Orly-Sur-Morin Communal Cemetery in France. Also listed under Carlow/Graigue on the Great War Memorial, Milford Street, Leighlinbridge, County Carlow.

FARRELL, PATRICK: Rank: Private. Regiment or service: Connaught Rangers. Date of death: 1920. I have no information on this man. Data above is listed under Leighlinbridge/Old Leighlin on the Great War Memorial, Milford Street, Leighlinbridge, County Carlow.

Pte Fenlon, from *The Wexford War Dead.*

FENLON, HUGH: Rank: Private. Regiment or service: Labour Corps. Date of death: 28 October 1918. Service No.: 620505. Formerly he was with the Royal Dublin Fusiliers where his number was 30284. Born in Athy, County Carlow. Enlisted in Dublin while living in Kellistown, County Carlow. Died. Grave or memorial reference: C. 624. Cemetery, Enniscorthy New Catholic Cemetery, Wexford.

FENLON, JAMES: Rank: Private. Regiment or service: Royal Irish Regiment. This man is not in any of the War Dead databases. From the *Nationalist* and *Leinster Times*, June 1917:

FENLON—June 11th, 1917, at his residence, Ballyhide, Carlow, Private James Fenlon, late 4th, Hussars, after a brief illness, fortified by the rites of the Holy Catholic Church. Funeral to Killeshill on Wednesday, 13th. Sacred Heart of Jesus have mercy on him. Mary Immaculate pray for him. Inserted by his loving parents, brothers and sisters. —R. I. P.

From the *Nationalist* and *Leinster Times*, June 1918:

FENLON—First Anniversary—In sad and loving memory of Private James Fenlon, late 4th Hussars, who departed this life June 11th, 1917, at his residence, Ballyhide, Carlow, on whose soul Sweet Jesus have mercy. Our Lady of Good Counsel intercede for him.

The cold, cold hand of cruel death
Upon his young life felt.
No moon on earth we hear the
voice.
Of one we loved so well.
The sunshine of our happy home,
Will ever clouded be.
But there, O'Lord, has sent this
cross.
We bear it all for Thee.

Inserted by his sorrowing father, mother, brothers and sisters.

Grave or memorial reference: Not available. Cemetery: Killeshill.

FENLON, MATTHEW: Rank: Private. Regiment or service: Royal Inniskilling Fusiliers. Unit: 1st Battalion. Date of death: 1 February 1917. Age at death: 18. Service No.: 28036 and 3/28036. Born in Carlow. Enlisted in Carlow. Killed in action.

Supplementary information: Son of Patrick and Margaret Fenlon, of 12, Little Barrack Street, Carlow. Date of will: 13 December 1915. Effects and property received by: (Mother) Mrs Maggie Fenlon, 12 Little Barracks Street, County Carlow. Witnesses: J.J.Jones, CSM, Ebrington Barracks, Londonderry, Ireland and Sergeant J Sehaill.

Grave or memorial reference: Pier and Face 4 D and 5 B. Memorial: Thiepval Memorial in France. Also listed under Carlow/Graigue on the Great War Memorial, Milford Street, Leighlinbridge, County Carlow.

FENLON, PATRICK: Rank: Private. Regiment or service: Royal Irish Regiment. Unit: 7th (South Irish Horse). Battalion. Date of death: 21 March 1918. Service No.: 4894 and 4/894. Born in Bagenalstown, County Carlow. Enlisted in Carlow while living in Bagenalstown, County Carlow. Killed in action.

Supplementary infortmation: After his death his effects and property were received by: (Wife) Mrs Kate Fenlon, Barratt Street, Bagenalstown, County Carlow.

Grave or memorial reference: Panel 30 and 31. Memorial: Pozieres

Memorial in France. Also listed under Bagenalstown/Fenagh on the Great War Memorial, Milford Street, Leighlinbridge, County Carlow.

FENNELL, NATHANIEL: Rank: Lance Corporal/Acting Lance Corporal. Regiment or service: Military Police Corps. Unit: Mounted Police. Date of death: 21 August 1915. Service No.: 464. Born in Toronto Canada. Enlisted in Aldershot while living in Tilford. Died of wounds in Mesopotamia. From the *Nationalist and Leinster Times*, September 1915:

FENNELL—August 21ˢᵗ, 1915, at the Dardanelles, from wounds received in action, Corporal Nathaniel James Fennell, M. M. P., youngest son of the late Richard Fennell, Burrin Street, Carlow. Death of a Carlow Man.

Information has been received of the death of Corporal Nathaniel Fennell, Military Mounted Police, from wounds received in action in the Dardanelles on the 20ᵗʰ August. He was the youngest son of the late Richard Fennell, Burrin Street, Carlow, and brother of Mrs Rowe, Bagnalstown. He served in the South African war, and had his horse shot from under him, and also in the battle of Omdurman (21ˢᵗ Lancers). He volunteered again when the present war broke out, and made several applications to be sent out before he was sent to the Dardanelles, where he died as he lived, a brave soldier.

Grave or memorial reference: Panel 200 or 300 (sic). Memorial: Helles Memorial in Turkey.

FFRENCH/FRENCH, JOHN: Rank: Gunner. Regiment or service: Royal Field Artillery and Royal Horse Artillery. Unit: A Battery, 28ᵗʰ Brigade. Date of death: 28 August 1917. Service No.: 77266. Born in Carlow. Enlisted in Athy. Killed in action.

FFRENCH - In sad and loving memory of Gunner John Ffrench R. F. A., Castle Hill, Carlow. Killed in action in France, August 22nd, 1917.

Day by day we sadly miss him,
Words would fail our loss to tell,
But in heaven we hope to meet him,
Whom on earth we loved so well.

From his loving mother, brothers and sisters.

Grave or memorial reference: III. B. 9. Cemetery: Klein-Vierstraat British Cemetery in Belgium. Also listed under Carlow/Graigue on the Great War Memorial, Milford Street, Leighlinbridge, County Carlow.

FIELD, JOHN WILLIAM: Rank: Captain. Regiment or service: Royal Irish Rifles. Unit: 1ˢᵗ Battalion. Date of death: 20 September 1915 (CWGC, SDGW, IMR), 20 November 1915 (Great War Memorial, Milford Street, Leighlinbridge, County Carlow). Killed in action.

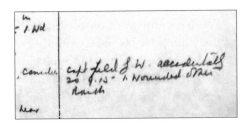

Capt. Field, section of *R.I.R. War Diary.*

Supplementary infortmation: Enlisted in the 5th Battalion Royal Irish Regiment at Camp Drinagh, Wexford on 13 June 1892 as a Private (No 3484) aged 17 years 6 months. Height 5ft 5ins, chest 33-35, weight 114lbs. Occupation on enlistment: Servant. Served in the Boer War 1901-02. Received the King's Medal with clasps for Cape Colony and the Orange Free State. Married his wife Elizabeth in Belfast on 10-December-1903. Lived at Byron Villa, Hollywood, Belfast and had 5 children. Re-enlisted in 5th Battalion Royal Irish Regiment on 13 June 1904. Character statement 'Exemplary' and 'greatly to the advantage of the battalion'. Promoted from Sergeant Major in the 4th Battalion, Royal Irish Regiment to Second Lieutenant on 20 December 1914. Joined the 1st Battalion on 11 May 1915 and promoted to Captain on 5 July 1915. He was accidentally wounded and died on 20 September 1915. At this time his wife lived at 6 Marine Parade, Hollywood and later re-married and became Mrs Elizabeth Fowles. A list of his effects included a watch, a gold ring and a French phrase book.

Grave or memorial reference: XXI. C. 6. Cemetery: Cabaret-Rouge British Cemetery, Souchez, Pas-de-Calais, France. Also listed under Carlow/ Graigue on the Great War Memorial, Milford Street, Leighlinbridge, County Carlow.

FINN, JOHN: Rank: Lance Corporal. Regiment or service: Royal Irish Regiment. Unit: 2nd Battalion. Date of death: 12 December 1914. Age at death: 19. Service No.: 10429. Born in Tullow, County Carlow. Enlisted in Bury, Lancs. while living in Salford, Lancs. Died.

Supplementary information: Born at Castlemore, County Carlow. Son of James and Margaret Finn, of 11 Meadow Road, Lower Broughton, Salford, Manchester.

Grave or memorial reference: IV. B. 17. Cemetery: Mons (Bergen) Communal Cemetery in Belgium. Also listed under Tullow on the Great War Memorial, Milford Street, Leighlinbridge, County Carlow.

FINN, PETER: Rank: Private. Regiment or service: Royal Dublin Fusiliers. Unit: 2nd Battalion. Date of death: 6 July 1915. Service No.: 5319. Born in Carlow. Enlisted in Carlow. Killed in action. Date of will: 16 January 1915. Effects and property received by: (Mother) Mrs P. Finn, Bridewell Street, Carlow. County Carlow Grave or memorial reference: Coll. grave I. D. 31. Cemetery: Bard Cottage Cemetery in Belgium. Another Carlow soldier, David Shea who was killed on the same day, with the same unit, is buried in this collective grave. Also listed under Carlow/ Graigue on the Great War Memorial, Milford Street, Leighlinbridge, County Carlow.

FISHBOURNE, CHARLES EDWARD:

Rank: Lieutenant Colonel and Temporary Lieutenant Colonel. Regiment or service: Northumberland Fusiliers. Unit: 8th Battalion. Date of death: 6 October 1916. Age at death: 47. Died of wounds.

Supplementary information: Husband of Elizabeth Leslie Shakerley (formerly Fishbourne) of Cole Allen, Cowden, Edenbridge, Kent. From *Carlow Sentinel*, October 1916:

Roll of Honour.
Lieutenant Colonel C. E. Fishbourne.
We deeply regret having to add to the long list of casualties, the name of Lieutenant Colonel C. E. Fishbourne, who died of wounds on the 6th inst; he had 24 years service, having been gazetted to 1st Battalion, Northumberland Fusiliers, "Fighting Fifth", April, 1892. He saw much active service, having been in the Nile Expedition, 1898, received medal and clasp, also Khedives medal. He then took part in the occupation of Crete; was through the whole South African campaign, being severely wounded at Belmont. For this work in the field he was awarded a Brevet majority, Queen's medal (3 clasps), King's medal (2 clasps), and was mentioned in despatches. In August, 1914, he was given command of a Battalion of the Northumberland Fusiliers, and was severely wounded at Suvla Bay landing 1915, and mentioned in despatches. On recovering he rejoined his Battalion in Egypt last February and was sent to France early in July. He was wounded about 27th September, and though at first there were hopes of his recovery he died on 6th October in France.

Lieutenant Colonel Fishbourne, who was born 1869, was the youngest and last surviving son of the late Joseph Fishbourne, of Ashfield Hall, Ballickmoyler. He leaves a widow and only son to deplore, with his other relatives, and many friends, his death while gallantly fighting in defence of King and Country.

On of his officers writes; --"Both officers and men worshipped him, and his going is not only a loss to the Battalion, but to the army. He was an ideal C. O. and we never can hope to be under anyone nearly as good."

From *The Leinster Express*, October 1916:

Lieut-Colonel C. E. Fishbourne, who died of wounds on 8th inst, had 34 years service, having been gazetted to 1st Battalion, Northumberland Fusiliers (Fighting Fifth), April 1883. He saw much active service, being in the Nile Expedition, 1885, receiving Medal and clasp, and Khedive Medal.
Roll of Honour.
Fishbourne, October 6, 1916, of wounds received in action about 27th September. Lieutenant-Col, Charles E Fishbourne, Northumberland Fusiliers, last surviving son of the late Jos. Fishbourne, Ashfield House, Ballickmoyler, Queen's County.

From the *Nationalist* and *Leinster Times*, August 1916:

Roll of Honour.

Lt-Colonel C. E. Fishbourne, who died of wounds on 6th inst., had 24 years service, having been gazetted to 1st Battalion Northumberland Fusiliers (Fighting Fifth) April 1892. He saw much active service, being in the Nile Expedition, 1898, receiving Medal and Clasp, also Khedive's Medal. He then took part in the occupation of Crete; was through the whole South African campaign, being wounded at Belmont. For his work in the field, he was awarded a Brevet Majority and Queen's Medal, three clasps; King's Medal, two clasps, and was mentioned in despatches. In August, 1914, he was given command of a Battalion of Northumberland Fusiliers, and was severely wounded at Suvla bay landing, 1915, and mentioned in despatches. On recovery he rejoined his battalion last February in Egypt, and was sent to France early in July. He was wounded about 27th September, and though at first there were hopes of his recovery, he died on 6th October, in France. Lt-Colonel Fishbourne, born 1869, was the youngest and last surviving son of the late Joseph Fishbourne, of Ashfield Hall, Ballickmoyler, Carlow. He leaves a widow and one son. One of his officers writes; -- "Both officers and men worshipped him, and his going is not only a loss to the Battalion but to the army. He was an ideal C. O., and we never can cope to be under anyone nearly as good."

Grave or memorial reference: A. 12. 3. Cemetery; St Sever Cemetery, Rouen in France. Also listed under Carlow/Graigue on the Great War Memorial, Milford Street, Leighlinbridge, County Carlow.

FISHBOURNE, DERRICK HAUGHTON GARDINER: Rank: Second Lieutenant. Regiment or service: Royal Garrison Artillery. Unit: 99th Siege Battery. Date of death: 6 May 1917. Age at death: 20. Killed in action.

Supplementary information: Son of John Gardiner Fishbourne and Sarah Elizabeth Fishbourne, of Burrin House, Carlow. From *Carlow Sentinel*, May 1917:

Roll of Honour.

2nd Lieutenant D. H. G. Fishbourne. We regret to learn that another gallant young officer closely connected with Carlow has been added to the long Roll of Honour. Second Lieutenant Derrick Haughton Gardiner Fishbourne, Royal Garrison Artillery, was killed in action on the 6th inst, in his 21st year. He was the only son of Mr and Mrs J. G. Fishbourne, bank of Ireland, Tralee, and nephew of Mr John William Haughton, J. P., Burrin House, Carlow. Lieutenant Fishbourne was educated at Russell School, Lancashire, from which he entered Trinity College, Dublin, with the view of qualifying for the Medical Profession. On the outbreak of the war he joined the T. C. D. Officer's Training Corps, obtained his commission, and went with his Regiment to France over a year ago, and fell gallantly fighting for King and Country, but to the great grief of a large circle of relatives and friends, with whom we join in heartfelt sympathy with his bereaved parents.

From De Ruvigny's Roll of Honour:

...only son of John Gardiner Fishbourne, of Tralee, Agent, Bank of Ireland, by his wife, Sarah Elizabeth, daughter of Frederick Haughton. Born Bellville, Newtown, Waterford. Educated at Castle Park, Dalkey, County Dublin, and Rossall, co. Lancaster. Was a resident student at Trinity College, Dublin. Obtained a commission, 29-December-1915. Served with the Expeditionary Force in France and Flanders, and was killed in action near Monchy 04-May-1917, while acting as sectional commander. Buried in Faubourg d'Amiens Cemetery, Arras. The General Commanding wrote; "He has shown a spirit of devotion to duty which is the true soldierly spirit which is going to win the war. His calmness and cheerfulness in the battery under fire showed courage of the highest order, which reacted on the men. He did credit to his country and his name," and his Major; "I can only assure you he is most deeply and sincerely mourned by us all, officers, N. C. O's and men, both for his cheerful spirit and keenness in everything connected with the battery." A brother officer also wrote; "I feel I have lost one of the best friends I have ever had; he was always so cheerful and brave, and was, in fact,

the life and soul of the battery. He never lost his cheerfulness under the most adverse circumstances. He has bucked me up many times by his cheery example. All the men liked him, he never lost his temper, he was always the same. He did not understand the meaning of the word 'fear'."

Grave or memorial reference: IV. G. 11. Cemetery: Faubourg D'Amiens Cemetery, Arras in France.

FITZGERALD, JAMES: Rank: Private. Regiment or service: Royal Dublin Fusiliers. Unit: 2nd Battalion. Date of death: 6 January 1915. Service No.: 9431. Born in Leighlinbridge, County Carlow. Enlisted in Carlow. Killed in action.

Supplementary information: Ward of Mrs M. Donnelly, of Coone East, Bagenalstown, County Carlow.

Grave or memorial reference: I. D. 8. Cemetery: Prowse Point Military Cemetery in Belgium. Also listed under Leighlinbridge/Old Leighlin on the Great War Memorial, Milford Street, Leighlinbridge, County Carlow.

FITZPATRICK, CHRISTOPHER JAMES: Rank: Private. Regiment or service: Irish Guards. Unit: 2nd Battalion. Date of death: 30 September 1915. Age at death: 19. Service No.: 6961. Born in Ballymore Eustace, County Kildare. Enlisted in Athy, County Kildare. Died of wounds.

Supplementary information: Son of Peter and Catherine Fitzpatrick, of Newtownbert, Athy, County Kildare.

Grave or memorial reference: IV. B. 42. Cemetery: Lillers Communal Cemetery in France.

FITZPATRICK, JAMES: Rank: Private. Regiment or service: Royal Army Medical Corps. Unit: 20th Casualty Clearing Station. Date of death: 21 August 1917. Age at death: 39. Service No.: 33817. Born in Carlow. Enlisted in Sheffield, Yorkshire. Died of wounds.

Supplementary information: Son of Michael and Mary Fitzpatrick; husband of Annie Eliza Fitzpatrick, of 24, Southern Street, Carbrook, Sheffield. Native of County Carlow.

Grave or memorial reference: IV. J. 1. Cemetery: Dozinghem Military Cemetery in Belgium. Also listed under Carlow/Graigue on the Great War Memorial, Milford Street, Leighlinbridge, County Carlow.

FITZPATRICK, PATRICK: Rank: Private. Regiment or service: 5th (Royal Irish) Lancers. Date of death: 23 June 1917(CWGC), 22 June 1917 (SDGW, IMR, Great War Memorial, Milford Street). Age at death: 34. Service No.: 3816. Born in Carlow. Enlisted in Carlow. Killed in action.

Supplementary information: Son of Daniel Fitzpatrick, of Athy Street, Carlow.

Grave or memorial reference: II. E. 19. Cemetery: Templeux-Le-Guerard British Cemetery Extension in France. Also listed under Carlow/Graigue on the Great War Memorial, Milford Street, Leighlinbridge, County Carlow.

FLEET, ALBERT GEORGE: Rank: Sergeant. Regiment or service: Royal Engineers. Date of death: 6 June 1919. Age at death: 30. Service No.: 16364. This man is not in any other database.

Supplementary information: Husband of Mary Margaret Fleet, of Hanover Mills, Carlow. Awards: DCM. From *Carlow Sentinel,* June 1919:

Military Funeral in Carlow.
  On Wednesday last Sergeant Fleet, 5th Signal Company, R. A., was buried in the New Cemetery, with military honours. Deceased was married in Carlow, and stationed here when the war broke out. He left with his regiment for the front, and while serving was awarded the D. S. M. After his return to England he succumbed to a serious attack of paralysis, and his remains were sent to Carlow by the Military Authorities. The coffin covered by the Union Jack, was borne on a gun wagon, and escorted by a firing party from the Curragh. The Reverend S Ridgeway officiated at the funeral.

Grave or memorial reference: 2. 1. 8. Cemetery: Carlow (St Mary's) Cemetery, County Carlow. Also listed under Carlow/Graigue on the Great War Memorial, Milford Street, Leighlinbridge, County Carlow.

FLEMING, THOMAS: Rank: Private. Regiment or service: Royal Irish Regiment. Unit: 1st Battalion. Date of death: 7 May 1915. Age at death: 24. Service No.: 9777. Born in St Johns,

Kilkenny. Enlisted in Carlow. Killed in action.

Supplementary information: o Born in 1891 in Maudlin Street on 7 December 1891, son of William Fleming (from Ballyhale, County Kilkenny) and Alice (*née* Tobin from Johnswell, County Kilkenny)f Railway Cottage, Carlow.. The Flemings have been traced back to at least 1766 to Newtown, Neworchard in St Johns Parish, Kilkenny City. His father was a railway ganger and milesman on the railway in Kilkenny city (on the old Waterford and Central Ireland Railway). The family moved to Railway Cottage, Carlow on Friday 2 January 1903 where William took over the railway cottage, Carlow and length of railway between milepost 53 to 56. William Fleming kept a notebook on his son's wartime adventures and other pieces of news from the front as it happened. Thomas enlisted in the 3rd Battalion (Reserve Force) of the Royal Dublin Fusiliers in Carlow and proceeded for training to Naas on Saturday 25 July 1908. His number at that time was 4840. Sailed for India on Saturday 19 November 1910 on board the SS *Dongola*. Transferred at a later time to the Royal Irish Regiment where his number changed to no 9777. His address in India was: 9777 Private Thomas Fleming, 1st RIR, Newmich, Agra, India. Thomas Fleming entered into active service in August 1914. Thomas also spent sometime in England - his address is given as 9777, A company, 2nd Royal Irish Regiment, Blackdown, Hants, England. Thomas was killed in action at Hooge, near Ypres on 7 May 1915. His father was notified by the war office on the 10 June 1915

Pte Fleming, image and information below courtesy of Gerard Fleming, (grandnephew), Dundalk.

Grave or memorial reference: Panel 33. Memorial: Ypres (Menin Gate) Memorial in Belgium. Also listed under Carlow/Graigue on the Great War Memorial, Milford Street, Leighlinbridge, County Carlow.

FLOOD, MYLES: Rank: Private. Regiment or service: Royal Dublin Fusiliers. Unit: 9th Battalion. Date of death: 9 September 1916. Age at death: 30 (should be 23, see 1911 and 1901 census). Service No.: 17402. Born in Carlow. Enlisted in Naas while living in Borris, County Carlow. Killed in action.

Supplementary information: Son of William Flood; husband of Mary Power (formerly Flood), of Burnchurch, Cuffe's Grange, County Kilkenny. From the *Nationalist* and *Leinster Times*, November 1916:

Two Brothers Killed in action.
The death in action has occurred in France of Myles and Patrick Flood (brothers). Aughmaleer(?), County Carlow. The former was killed about three weeks ago, and the latter a week back. Both were serving in the R. I. R(sic)., and their repose was prayed for at Graiguenamanagh Mass on Sunday last.

Grave or memorial reference: Pier and Face 16 C. Memorial: Thiepval Memorial in France. Also listed under Borris/Ballyellin on the Great War Memorial, Milford Street, Leighlinbridge, County Carlow.

FLOOD, PATRICK: Rank: Private. Regiment or service: Royal Dublin Fusiliers. Unit: 2nd Battalion. Date of death: 15 October 1916. Service No.: 23746. Born in Graiguenamanagh, County Kilkenny. Enlisted in Carlow while living in Borris, County Carlow. Killed in action.

Supplementary information: Brother of Myles listed above. Date of will: 6 July 1916. Effects and property received by: (Sister) Mary Flood, Ballytiglea, Borris, County Carlow. Grave or memorial reference: Pier and Face 16C. Memorial: Thiepval Memorial in France. Also listed under Borris/Ballyellin on the Great War Memorial, Milford Street, Leighlinbridge, County Carlow.

FLOOD, THOMAS: Rank: Lance Corporal. Regiment or service: Irish Guards. Unit: 2nd. Date of death: 31 July 1917. Service No.: 10901. Born in Rathvilly, County Carlow. Enlisted in Naas while living in Ticknock, County Wicklow. Killed in action. Grave or memorial reference: He has no known grave but is listed on Panel 11 on the Ypres (Menin Gate) Memorial in Belgium. Also listed under Rathvilly on the Great War Memorial, Milford Street, Leighlinbridge, County Carlow.

FLYNN, THOMAS: Rank: Private. Regiment or service: Royal Munster Fusiliers. Unit: 2nd Battalion. Date of death: 12 October 1918. Age at death: 29. Service No.: G/113. Formerly he was with the Connaught Rangers where his number was 9738. Born in Ballon, County Carlow. Enlisted in Galway. Killed in action.

Supplementary information: Husband of Julia Kiy (formerly Flynn), of 2 Yonge Park, Finsbury Park, London. Won the DCM and the Military Medal and is listed in the *London Gazette*. He was also awarded the Medal Militaire by the French Government in1916 while he was an Acting Corporal. The DCM and the Medal Militaire was presented to Corporal T. Flynn by Major General B. C. Doran, CB on 17 July 1916. From the *Nationalist* and *Leinster Times.* 1916:

Irish Valour.
The Connaught Rangers.
Kinsale, County Cork.

Sir—I wish to insert in your paper that No, 9738, Corporal Thomas Flynn, was not a Dublin man, but a native of Ballon, Tullow, County

Carlow. He has been the first County Carlow man to win the D. C. M., winning it early in the war at the battle of Neuve Chapelle; since winning the French Medaille De Military at the battle of Ypres. I am also glad to know other men from Carlow won the D. C. M., but, I think, so far, none other got that coveted French Medal. I am a Tullow man myself, and about to leave for the front in a few days time. I am sir, yours respectfully.
P. Byrne.
[P Byrne survived the war.]

Grave or memorial reference: He has no known grave but is listed on Panel 10 on the Vis-En-Artois Memorial in France. Memorial. Also listed under Ballon/Rathoe/Aghade on the Great War Memorial, Milford Street, Leighlinbridge, County Carlow.

FLYNN, THOMAS: Rank: Private. Regiment or service: Royal Dublin Fusiliers. Unit: 1st Battalion. Date of death: 15 June 1915. Service No.: 5437. Born in Leighlinbridge, Carlow. Enlisted in Leighlinbridge, Carlow. Killed in action in Gallipoli. After his death his effects and property were received by: (Mother) Mrs Annie Flynn, Rathellan, Bagenalstown, County Carlow. Grave or memorial reference: XI. C. 14. Cemetery: Twelve Tree Copse Cemetery in Turkey. Also listed under Leighlinbridge/Old Leighlin on the Great War Memorial, Milford Street, Leighlinbridge, County Carlow.

FOLEY, MICHAEL: Rank: Private. Regiment or service: Irish Guards. Unit: 1st Battalion. Date of death: 6 July 1915. Age at death: 24. Service Number: 3545. Born in Killeshin, County Carlow. Enlisted in Carlow. Died of wounds.

Supplementary information: Son of Joseph and Margaret Foley, of Aughaterry, Queen's County From the *Nationalist* and *Leinster Times,* July 1915:

FOLEY—Private Michael Foley, 1st Irish Guards, late of Chapel Street, Carlow-Graigue, agd 22 years, died of wounds received in action on the 6th day of July, 1915.

Sacred Heart of Jesus have mercy on his soul. —R. I. P.

The voice is now silent, the heart is now cold.;
The smile and welcome, that met us of old.
We miss him, and mourn him, in sorrow, unseen.
And dwell on the memory of days that have been.

Inserted by his loving parents, brothers and sisters.

Grave or memorial reference: I. D. 27. Cemetery: Chocques Military Cemetery in France.

FOLEY, MICHAEL ALPHONSUS: Rank: Lieutenant. Regiment or service: Leinster Regiment. Unit: 6th Battalion. Date of death: 25 April 1919. Died. From *Carlow Sentinel,* 10 May 1919:

Lieutenant M. A. Foley. A very deep and wide-spread regret was caused to his many relatives and friends in Carlow, his native county, by the announcement of the death of Lieutenant M. A. Foley, while serving with the Leinster Regiment in Egypt, at the age of 22. He was a son of Mr. Michael Foley, J. P. Leighlin House, and nephew the Lord Bishop of Kildare and Leighlin, and Rev. Dr. Foley, President of Carlow College. When the war broke out he was a student of the University College, Dublin.

He received his commission in 1916, and was on active service from that time until the time of his death. At Monday's meeting of Carlow Urban District Council a resolution of sympathy was passed to Mr. and Mrs. Foley, and other members of the family, and a fitting tribute paid to the memory of deceased.

Grave or memorial reference: M. 238. Cemetery: Cairo War Memorial Cemetery in Egypt. Also listed under Leighlinbridge/Old Leighlin on the Great War Memorial, Milford Street, Leighlinbridge, County Carlow.

FORBES, ARTHUR WALTER:
Rank: Lieutenant. Regiment or service: Royal Navy. Unit: HMS/M. 'H5'. HMS/M. 'H5', a British H-class submarine was rammed by the British Merchantman *Rutherglen* after being mistaken for a German Submarine. She sank with the loss of all hands. Date of death: 2 March 1918 (CWGC) 2 March 1919 (Great War Memorial, Milford Street, Leighlinbridge). Age at death: 25. Awarded the Distinguished Service Order.

Supplementary information: Son of Helen A Forbes. From *Carlow Sentinel*, March 1918:

Roll of Honour.
Lieutenant A. W. Forbes, R. N.
The official announcement that Lieutenant Arthur W Forbes, D. S. C., R. N., has been killed at sea while on active service, was received in Carlow with feelings of sincere and wide-spread regret. This gallant young officer, who was recently married, was a member of a family long and intimately connected with the county, being second son of Captain W. B. Forbes, R. N., Rathwade, Bagenalstown, with whom and the other members of the family very sincere sympathy is felt. The closing meeting of the season of the Carlow Hounds, which had been fixed for Saturday last, was abandoned as a mark of respect to the memory of deceased.

Roll of Honour.
FORBES—Lost at sea, on active service, Lieutenant Arthur W. Forbes, D. S. O., N. R. N, husband of betty Forbes (nee Sukerland(sic)), and elder son of Captain W. B. Forbes, R. N, and Mrs Forbes, Rathwade, Bagenalstown, Ireland, aged 25 years.

Grave or memorial reference: 28. He has no known grave but is listed on the Chatham Naval Memorial. A plaque commemorating the 26 crew who drowned was dedicated on Armed Forces Day 2010 in Holyhead.

FOULDS, JOHN ROBERTSON:
Rank: Private. Regiment or service: London Regiment. Unit: 15th (County of London) Battalion. PWO Civil Service Rifles. Date of death: 4 May 1918. Age at death: 19. Service No.: 535270. Born in Tipperary. Enlisted in Merthyr. Killed in action.

Supplementary information: Son of William Mason Foulds and Mary Foulds, of Cromlix Gardens, Dunblane, Perthshire.

Grave or memorial reference: X. A. 14. Cemetery: Dernancourt Communal Cemetery Extension in France. Also listed under Rathvilly on the Great War Memorial, Milford Street, Leighlinbridge, County Carlow.

FOX, JOHN: Rank: Private. Regiment or service: Royal Dublin Fusiliers. Unit: 2nd Battalion. Date of death: 8 March 1916. Service No.: 8643. Born in Ballon Hill, County Carlow. Enlisted in Carlow. Died. Grave or memorial reference: III. K. 8. Cemetery: Niederzwehren Cemetery in Germany. Also listed under Ballon/Rathoe/Aghade on the Great War Memorial, Milford Street, Leighlinbridge, County Carlow.

FRANCIS, MICHAEL: Rank: Sergeant. Regiment or service: Leinster Regiment. Unit: 6th Battalion. Date of death: 17 October 1915. Service No.: 729 and 6/729. Born in Carlow. Enlisted in Carlow. Died in Gallipoli (as recorded in SDGW). Date of will: 13 April 1915. Effects and property received by: (Wife) Mary Francis, Market Square, Carlow. From the *Nationalist* and *Leinster Times*, October 1915:

Roll of Honour.
Popular National Volunteer Dead.
His many friends in Carlow heard with deep regret of the death of Colour Sergeant Michael Francis. Sergeant Francis had served 21 years with the Leinster Regiment, after which he came back to reside in his native Carlow. He was prominently connected with the National Volunteer movement in the town from start to finish, being commander of B. Company of the Carlow Battalion. At the outbreak of the war he volunteered for active service, and eventually took part in the Dardanelles fighting with the 10th Division. In that region he contracted disease to which he succumbed last week in Netley Hospital. May he rest in peace.

Grave or memorial reference: RC. 860. Cemetery: Netley Military Cemetery, Hampshire, UK. Also listed under Carlow/Graigue on the Great War Memorial, Milford Street, Leighlinbridge, County Carlow.

FRASER, PETER: Rank: Private. Regiment or service: Australian Infantry, A. I. F. Unit: 24th Battalion. Date of death: 19 November 1916. Age at death: 23. Service No.: 880.
Supplementary information: Son of Peter and Jane Fraser, of 74, Kilcarrig

Street, Bagenalstown, County Carlow, Ireland. Born, Koratya, India where his father was serving. Occupation on enlistment, Mechanic. Apprenticed to Mr Clarke, Kilkenny. Age on enlistment: 21 years 1 months. Initially enlisted in the 20th Hussars while underage and was claimed (after 7 months) out by his mother. Suffered from dysentery during his service. Next of kin details: (Father) Peter Fraser, Royal Oak, Bagenalstown, Carlow. Place and date of enlistment: Broadmeadows, 28 April 1915. Served in Anzac, Marseilles, Alexandria, France, Belgium and London. Weight, 11st. Height, 5 feet, 10 inches. Complexion, fair. Eyes, grey. Hair, dark brown. His father and mother were each awarded a pension of 7s 6d per fortnight. 'Buried scattered graves west of Factory Conor and Luisenhof Farm Road 2¾ miles S. S. W of Bethune.' 'Actual remains unlocated.' 'His remains were interred in the A. I. F. Burial Ground, Grass Lane, Gueudecourt, but his grave has not been located. ' Grave or memorial reference: Sp. Mem. 17. Cemetery: A. I. F Burial Ground, Flers in France. Also listed under Leighlinbridge/Old Leighlin on the Great War Memorial, Milford Street, Leighlinbridge, County Carlow.

FRASER, THOMAS: See DILLON, THOMAS.

FRENCH/FFRENCH, JOHN: Rank: Gunner. Regiment or service: Royal Field Artillery and Royal Horse Artillery. Unit: A Battery, 28th Brigade. Date of death: 28 August 1917. Service No.: 77266. Born in Carlow. Enlisted in Athy. Killed in action. Grave or memorial reference: III. B. 9. Cemetery: Klein-Vierstraat British Cemetery in Belgium.

FRIZELL, RICHARD ALEXANDER: Rank: Captain/ Temporary Captain. Regiment or service: Royal Munster Fusiliers. Unit: 2nd Battalion. Date of death: 10 November-1917. Killed in action. He is listed 7 times in the 'The Biscuit Boys' section 211 'The Battle of Loos' showing his actions during September 1915. From De Ruvigny's Roll of Honour:

...only son of Richard William Bruckfiekd Frizell, of British Columbia, by his wife, Emily, daughter of Alexander Durdin, of Huntington Castle, Ireland. Born in Charlottsville, Virginia in 1894. Educated at Bedford College, was employed on the Local Government

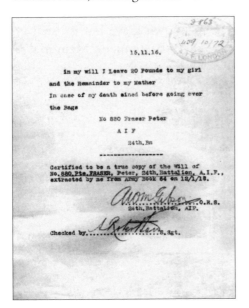

Pte Fraser, letter from records.

Board, and on the outbreak of war was acting as Secretary to the Royal Commission. Gazetted 2nd Lieutenant, the 9th (Service) Battalion, The Royal Fusiliers 28-October-1914. Promoted Lieutenant in 1915, and Captain, 28-February-1916. Served with the Expeditionary Force in France and Flanders from December-1915; was wounded at Loos in May-1916, and invalided home; transferred to the 2nd Battalion, and returned to France in December of the same year. Was reported wounded and missing after the fighting near Cambrai 10-November-1917, and is now assumed to have been killed in action on or about that date. His Commanding Officer wrote; "He gallantly led his company into action and obtained his objective; while there he was shot through the head and killed instantly, suffering no pain. The more I knew him the more I appreciated him, and I considered him the soundest company commander in the Battalion. His loss is deeply felt by everyone in the Battalion, and I am sure there is not a man in the company who would not have given his life for their leader. "

Grave or memorial reference: Panel 143 to 144. He has no known grave but is listed on the Tyne Cot memorial Memorial in Belgium. Also listed under Clonegal/Kildavin on the Great War Memorial, Milford Street, Leighlinbridge, County Carlow.

FRYER, CHARLES GEORGE: Rank: Private. Regiment or service: Australian Infantry, A. I. F. Unit: 49th Battalion. Date of death: 5 April 1917. Age at death: 27. Service No.: 5086. Born in Rockhampton/Springsure, Queensland. Enlisted 15 October 1915 in Rockhampton, Queensland, aged 26 years 3 months. Killed in action.

Supplementary information: Son of Charles George and Rosina Fryer, of Sprigshure, Queensland. I include this man as he is listed under Bagenalstown/Fenagh on the Great War Memorial, Milford Street, Leighlinbridge, County Carlow.

Grave or memorial reference: He has no known grave but is listed on the Villers-Bretonneux Memorial in France.

G

GAFFNEY, PATRICK: Rank: Private. Regiment or service: Leinster Regiment. Date of death: 18 July 1920 Service No.: 2627.

Supplementary information: Husband of E. Gaffney, of Pollerton Road, Carlow. This man is not in any other database.

Grave or memorial reference: 4. 11. 40. Cemetery: Carlow (ST. Mary's) Cemetery, County Carlow. Also listed under Carlow/Graigue on the Great War Memorial, Milford Street, Leighlinbridge, County Carlow.

GALWAY, EDWARD: Rank: Lance Corporal. Regiment or service: Royal Irish Rifles. Unit: 2nd Battalion. Date of death: 24 October 1914. Age at death: 26. Service No.: 8073. Born in Carlow. Enlisted in Carlow. Killed in action.

Supplementary information: Son of Mrs Margaret Galway, of Old Town, Leighlinbridge, County Carlow.

Grave or memorial reference: Panel 42 and 43. Memorial: Le Touret Memorial in France. Also listed under Leighlinbridge/Old Leighlin on the Great War Memorial, Milford Street, Leighlinbridge, County Carlow.

GARRETT, ARTHUR FFOLLIOTT: Rank: Major. Regiment or service: Royal Engineers. Date of death: 28 March 1920. Age at death: 45. This man is not in any other database.

Supplementary information: Son of W. R. Garrett, of Kilgarron, County Carlow; husband of Ida Garrett, of 'Courtlands', Haywards Heath, Sussex. Awards: OBE. From *Carlow Sentinel*, September 1915:

The Roll of Honour.
Major Garrett, R. E.
 We regret to notice amongst the casualties recently reported from the Dardanelles the name of Major A. FF. Garrett, R. E. Major Garrett is the youngest son of Mr W. R. Garrett of Tunbridge Wells, formerly of Kilgarron, County Carlow. He entered the R. E. in 1894, passing first out of the R. M. A., Woolwich, obtaining the Pollock gold medal and other prizes. He has twice won the Montgomery Prize for the best professional essay of the year, and during his 20 years service in India has gained great distinction as an Engineer. Major Garrett was shot through the neck, but is making a good recovery.

Grave or memorial reference: III. C. 13,. Cemetery: Mazargues War Cemetery Cemetery, Marseilles, France.

GAUSSEN, ARRATOON WILLIAM DAVID (ODGW), **GAUSSEN, WILLIAM DAVID** (CWGC, Great War Memorial, Milford Street, Leighlinbridge) **GAUSSEN, A. W. DAVID** (IMR), **D., GAUSSEN**(*Our Heroes*)**:** Rank:

Captain. Regiment or service: Highland Light Infantry. Unit: 2nd Battalion. Date of death: 17 May 1915. Age at death: 39. Killed in action.

Supplementary information: Son of David Gaussen; husband of Marguerite Gaussen. From *Our Heroes*:

. . who was killed in action in France on May 17th, belonged to an old Irish family, and had a wide circle of friends in Dublin, where for many years he was attached to the Headquarters Staff. His mother resides at Upton, Bagenalstown, and jis wife whom he leaves surviving, was Miss Marguerite Kelly, daughter of the late Judge Kely. Though only in his 40th year, Captain Gaussen had seen much active service during the operations on the North-West Frontier of India, including the attack and capture of the Tanga Pass, for which he received the Medal with clasp, and afterwards in the South African War, for his services in which he received the Queen's Medal with three clasps and the King's Medal with two clasps.

From the *Nationalist* and *Leinster Times* and the *Carlow Sentinel*, October 1914:

A Wounded Officer correspondent sends us the following particulars about Captain Gaussen who was slightly wounded recently; --

Born in July, 1875, Captain Gaussen is the third son of the late Mr David Gaussen, of Broughton Hall, Lechdale, and Gardiners Place, Dublin. He was gazetted second lieutenant in the Highland Light Infantry

in 1895, and two years later served in the operations on the North-West Frontier of India with the Malakand and Buner Field Forces. Present at the attack and capture of the Tanga Pass, he received the medal with clasp. During the campaign in South Africa Captain Gaussen was in the fighting at Paardeberg, and subsequently in the actions at Wittebergen and Witport. The Queen's medal (three clasps) and the King's medal (two clasps) were awarded him. From November, 1909, to December, 1913 this officer was attached to the General Staff of the Irish Command, with the Rank of Brigadier Major.

From the *Nationalist* and *Leinster Times*, and the *Carlow Sentinel*, May 1915:

Killed in action in Flanders.
We much regret to notice the death of Captain A. W. David Gaussen (Tod), aged 39, 2nd Highland Light Infantry, youngest son of the late David Gaussen, of Broughton Hall, Lochdale (Glos), and of Mrs Gaussen, of Upton, County Carlow. Captain Gaussen was killed in action in Flanders on Ascension Day. He was educated at Sandhurst, and distinguished himself in the Tireh Campaign (N. W. Frontier), and also in the South African War. He served as staff officer in Cork and Dublin, joining the Expeditionary Force at the commencement of the war. Wounded at the battle of the Marne he was sent home, but after a short time in hospital he returned to his regiment. In the engagement in which he met his death he was

in command of his regiment, as the Colonel was on sick leave.

Much sympathy is felt by all creeds and classes for Mrs Gaussen on the death of her brave and distinguished son. Mrs Gaussen has at all times been devoted to social and philanthropic work. Since the war broke out her desire to alleviate the sufferings of the wounded soldiers, and to provide comforts for those who are fighting for their country is nothing short of a ruling passion.

Grave or memorial reference: Panel 37 and 38. He has no known grave but is listed on the Le Touret Memorial. Also listed under Bagenalstown/Fenagh on the Great War Memorial, Milford Street, Leighlinbridge, County Carlow.

GEEHAN, PATRICK: Rank: Private. Regiment or service: Royal Irish regiment. Unit: 1st Garrison Battalion. Date of death: 8 November 1918. Age at death: 43. Service No.: 4380. Formerly he was with the Royal Inniskilling Fusiliers where his number was 12185. Born in Leinster, County Carlow (sic). Enlisted in Carlow while living in Carlow. Died in Egypt.

Supplementary information: Husband of Annie Geehan, of 36 Blenheim Street, Tyldesley, Manchester.

Grave or memorial reference: H. 57. Cemetery, Cairo War Memorial Cemetery in Egypt.

GEOGHEGAN/GEOHEGAN, MARTIN: Rank: Private. Regiment or service: Royal Irish Regiment. Unit:

6th Battalion. Date of death: 5 August 1917 Age at death: 24. Service No.: 5312. Born in Graigue, Kilkenny. Enlisted in Kilkenny. Died of wounds at home.

Supplementary information: Husband of Johannah Geoghegan, of Graiguenamanagh, County Kilkenny.

Grave or memorial reference: East of ruins. Cemetery: Tinnahinch (St Michael's) Cemetery in Carlow.

GEOGHEGAN, MARTIN: Rank: Private. Regiment or service: Royal Dublin Fusiliers. Unit: 2nd Battalion. Date of death: 27 August 1914. Age at death: 33. Service No.: 7636. Born in Carlow. Enlisted in Carlow. Killed in action.

Supplementary information: Son of Edward and Maria Geoghegan, of Bridewell Lane, Carlow.

Memorial: La Ferte-Sous-Jouarre Memorial in France. Also listed under Carlow/Graigue on the Great War Memorial, Milford Street, Leighlinbridge, County Carlow.

GIBSON, EDWARD: Rank: Sapper. Regiment or service: Corps of Royal Engineers. Unit: Royal Engineers, Command Depot, Thetford. Date of death: 1 July 1917. Age at death: 37. Service No.: 150220. Born in Carlow. Enlisted in Dublin. Died at home.

Supplementary information: Husband of Mary McMahon (formerly Gibson), of 63 Bride Street, Dublin.

Grave or memorial reference: R.C. 525. Cemetery: Grangegorman Military Cemetery in Dublin. Also listed under Carlow/Graigue on the

Great War Memorial, Milford Street, Leighlinbridge, County Carlow.

GILL, MICHAEL: Rank: Private. Regiment or service: Northumberland Fusiliers. Unit: 27th (Tyneside Irish) Battalion. Date of death: 1 July 1916. Age at death: 36. Service No.: 27/953. Born in Fonagh (sic), County Carlow. Enlisted in Sunderland. Killed in action.
Supplementary information: Son of William and Eliza Gill.
Grave or memorial reference: Pier and Face 10B, 11B and 12B. Memorial: Thiepval Memorial in France.

GLYNN, JOHN: Rank: Corporal. Regiment or service: Leinster Regiment. Unit: 2nd Battalion. Age at death: 24. Date of death: 22 August 1916. Service No.: 397. Born in Athboy, County Meath. Enlisted in Carlow. Died of wounds.
Supplementary information: Son of Robert and Mary J. Glynn, of Lismore, County Waterford. From *Munster Express:*

Killed.
Mr Robert Glynn, Castlefarm, Lismore Castle, has received notification that his son, Corporal John Glynn, of the 2nd Leinster Regiment, has died from the wounds received in action in France. Corporal Glynn, prior to the outbreak of war was a grocer's assistant employed at Cappoquin and Carlow and volunteered in response to Lord Kitchener's appeal. He was a nice-mannered and popular young

Lismore man, and his younger brother is also at the front serving with the Leinster's. Much sympathy is expressed with Mr and Mrs Glynn in their bereavement.

Grave or memorial reference: II. A. 45. Cemetery: La Neuville British Cemetery, Corbie in France. Also listed under Carlow/Graigue on the Great War Memorial, Milford Street, Leighlinbridge, County Carlow.

GOLDING, JAMES: Rank: Private. Regiment or service: Leinster Regiment. Unit: 2nd Battalion. Date of death: 15 March 1916. Service No.: 8999. Born in Graigue, County Carlow (SDGW) Graigue Queen's County (Irelands Memorial Records). Enlisted in Maryborough, Queen's County. Killed in action. In his Will, dated 21 October 1915, his effects and property were received by: (Sister) Mrs B Rowan, 9 H Edward Street, Shieffield, Yorkshire, England. Grave or memorial reference: I. J. 12. Cemetery: Menin Road South Military Cemetery in Belgium.

GOODBODY, JOHN: Rank: Private. Regiment or service: Royal Munster Fusiliers. Unit: B Company, 1st Garrison Battalion. Date of death: 30 September 1918 (CWGC, IMR, SDGW), 21 August 1915 (Great War Memorial, Milford Street, Leighlinbridge, County Carlow). Service No.: G/1480. Formerly he was with the Royal Dublin Fusiliers where his number was 13897. Born in Carlow. Enlisted in Carlow while living in Graigue, County Carlow. Died in Italy.

Supplementary information: Served in the Boer War; re-enlisted in 1914.

Grave or memorial reference: I. C. 5. Cemetery: Arquata Scrivia Communal Cemetery Extension in Italy. Also listed under Carlow/Graigue on the Great War Memorial, Milford Street, Leighlinbridge, County Carlow.

GRATTON-BELLEW, WILLIAM ARTHUR: Rank: Second Lieutenant/ Temporary Major. Royal Flying Corps. Regiment or service: Connaught Rangers. Unit: Attached to the 29th Squadron of the Royal Flying Corps. Date of death: 24 March 1917. Age at death: 23. Died of wounds.

Supplementary information: Son of Mr H. Grattan-Bellew, of Mount Bellew, County Galway. He won the Military Cross and is listed in the *London Gazette.*

Grave or memorial reference; III. C. 3. Cemetery: Avesnes-le-Comte Communal Cemetery Extension, Pas-de-Calais, France.

GREENE, MICHAEL: Rank: Private. Regiment or service: Royal Dublin Fusiliers. Unit: 2nd Battalion. Date of death: 21 March 1919 (CWGC, IMR), 21 March 1918(Noted on his will, SDGW, and the Great War Memorial, Milford Street). Age at death: 43. Service No.: 18877. Killed in action.

Supplementary information: Son of John and Elizabeth Greene, of Tullow; husband of Margaret Greene, of Bishop Street, Tullow, County Carlow. Born in Tullow, County Carlow. Enlisted in Naas

while living in Tullow. Patrick Reilly of the same unit died on the same day and is also buried in this cemetery. Date of will: 18 July 1916. Effects and property received by; (Wife) Margaret Greene Bishop Street, Tullow, County Carlow.

Grave or memorial reference: II. G. 3. Cemetery: Unicorn Cemetery, Vend'huile in France. Also listed under Tullow on the Great War Memorial, Milford Street, Leighlinbridge, County Carlow.

GRIFFIN, PETER SAMUEL: Rank: Lance Corporal. Regiment or service: Royal Inniskilling Fusiliers. Unit: 9th Battalion. Date of death: 7 May 1918. Age at death: 29. Service No.: 27636. Born in Arklow, County Wicklow. Enlisted in Enniskillen. Killed in action also listed as died of wounds received accidentally in Equalberg in France.

Supplementary information: Son of John and Sarah Griffin, of Knocknaboley, Hacketstown, County Carlow; husband of Mary Margaret Griffin, of Cappagh, Aughrim, County Wicklow.

Grave or memorial reference: I. C. 21. Cemetery: Esquelbeco Military Cemetery in France. Also listed under Hacketstown on the Great War Memorial, Milford Street, Leighlinbridge, County Carlow.

GRIFFITH, GEORGE: Rank: Private. Regiment or service: Irish Guards. Unit: 1st Battalion. Date of death: 1 November 1914. Age at death: 19. Service No.: 4457. Born in Finglas, Dublin. Enlisted Carlow, County Carlow. Killed in action.

Supplementary information: Son of James and Anne Griffith, of Rosdinig, Borris, County Carlow. Grave or memorial reference: Panel 11. Memorial: Ypres (Menin Gate) Memorial in Belgium. Also listed under Borris/Ballyellin on the Great War Memorial, Milford Street, Leighlinbridge, County Carlow.

GRIMES, WILLIAM: Rank: Scting Lance Corporal. Regiment or service: Connaught Rangers. Unit: 5th Battalion. Date of death: 21 August 1915. Age at death: 19. Service No.: 4149. Born in Carlow. Enlisted in Dublin while living in Hulme, Manchester. Killed in action in Gallipoli.

Supplementary information: Son of James Grimes, of 4 Dorset Place, Hulme, Manchester.

Grave or memorial reference: Panel 181 to 183. Memorial: Helles Memorial in Turkey. Also listed under Leighlinbridge/Old Leighlin on the Great War Memorial, Milford Street, Leighlinbridge, County Carlow.

GRIMES, WILLIAM: Rank: Private. Regiment or service: Royal Inniskilling Fusiliers. Unit: 1st Battalion. Date of death: 22 May 1915. Age at death: 28. Service No.: 9356. Born in Leighlinbridge, Carlow. Enlisted in Newry. Killed in action in Gallipoli.

Supplementary information: Brother of Matthew Grimes, of 37, Kirk Road, Litherland, Liverpool.

Grave or memorial reference: Panel 97 to 101. Memorial: Helles Memorial in Turkey.

H

HALL, WILLIAM CHARLES:
Rank: Major. Regiment or service:
Royal Irish Rifles. Date of death: 17
December 1917. Died.

Supplementary information: Son of
Major W. Hall; husband of Mrs W. Hall,
of Kellistown, Carlow. Born at Narrow-
water, County Down. From *Carlow
Sentinel*, December 1917:

> Roll of Honour.
> Hall–December 17, 1917, killed in
> bombing accident, at Newtownards,
> County Down, major Wiliam
> Charles Hall, R. I. Rifles, for-
> merly of Royal Welch Fusiliers, of
> Ballitore, County Kildare, son of
> the late Major W. J. Hal, D. L., of
> Narrow Water, County Down, aged
> 51.

From *Carlow Sentinel*, December 1917:

> Bomb Fatality in County Down.
> Death of Major W. C. Hall.
> The many Carlow and other friends
> of Major Hall, R. I. R., have heard
> with sincere regret of his sad death,
> on Tuesday last, at the age of 31, as
> the result of a bomb accident during
> practice at Newtownards, where
> he was second in command. At the
> inquest on Wednesday, touching his
> death and that of Corporal Parker,
> R. I. C., Lance Corporal Donaldson,
> a witness of the tragedy, said that as
> Parker was going to throw the bomb
> with his hand above his head there
> was a deafening report. The corporal

> immediately fell, as did Major Hall
> and 2nd Lieutenant Hull, who was
> near. Parker must have thrown hun-
> dreds of bombs at the front
> Dr E. Jameson, M. O. at the
> camp, said Parker's fatal wound
> penetrated the brain. A piece of
> shrapnel pierced Major Hall's chest,
> and curved towards the abdomen.
> Captain Clapham, bombing officer,
> said the explosion might have been
> due to a defect in the fuse or in the
> grenade. The jury found a verdict of
> accidental death.
> 2nd Lieutenant Corry and Hull,
> who were injured are progressing
> favourably.
> Major Hall was married to Olive,
> daughter of the late Sir Standish
> O'Grady Roche, Bart, Aghade
> Lodge, Tullow, with whom deep
> sympathy is felt.

Grave or memorial reference: In
Old ground, right of gate. Cemetery:
Clonallan Church of Ireland
Churchyard, County Carlow. Also listed
under Ballon/Rathoe/Aghade on the
Great War Memorial, Milford Street,
Leighlinbridge, County Carlow.

HAMILTON, JAMES: Rank: Private.
Regiment or service: Irish Guards.
Unit: 2nd Battalion. Date of death: 6
October 1915. Age at death: 22. Service
No.: 4372. Born in Carlow. Enlisted
in Dublin, County Dublin. Died of
wounds.

Supplementary information: Son of Thomas and Margaret Hamilton, of 38 Foyle Road, Fairview, Dublin.

Grave or memorial reference: IV. E. 90. Cemetery: Bethune Town Cemetery in France. Also listed under Carlow/ Graigue on the Great War Memorial, Milford Street, Leighlinbridge, County Carlow.

HAUGHNEY, CHARLES: See **HOUGHNEY, CHARLES.**

HAUGHNEY, PATRICK: Rank: Private. Regiment or service: Irish Guards. Unit: 1st Battalion. Date of death: 10 October 1917. Age at death: 20. Service No.: 11559. Died of wounds.

Supplementary information: Son of Martin Haughney, Clonbrock, Crettyard, County Carlow. Born in Doonane, Queen's County. He was 26 years old, part of the 1st Guards Brigade, 1st Guards Division. Enlisted in Edinburgh, Midlothian while living in Clonbrook, Queen's County.

Grave or memorial reference: IX. J. 19. Cemetery: Dozinghem Military Cemetery in Belgium. Also listed under Carlow/Graigue on the Great War Memorial, Milford Street, Leighlinbridge, County Carlow.

HAWE, MICHAEL: Rank: Sergeant. Regiment or service: Irish Guards. Unit: No. 1 Company. 2nd Battalion. Date of death: 27 November 1917. Age at death: 20. Service No.: 4730. Born in Bagnalstown County Carlow. Enlisted in Carlow. Killed in action.

Supplementary information: Son of James and Maria Hawe, of Leighlinbridge, County Carlow. See Cullen, John.

Grave or memorial reference: Panel 2 and 3. Memorial: Cambrai Memorial in Louveral in France. Also listed under Leighlinbridge/Old Leighlin on the Great War Memorial, Milford Street, Leighlinbridge, County Carlow.

HAWE, ROBERT: Rank: Private. Regiment or service: Royal Dublin Fusiliers. Unit: 2nd Battalion. Date of death: 31 August 1914. Age at death: 31. Service No.: 8961. Born in Leighlinbridge, County Carlow. Enlisted in Carlow. Died of wounds.

Supplementary information: Son of James and Ellen Hawe, of Leighlinbridge, County Carlow.

Grave or memorial reference: V. G. 24. Memorial: Cambrai Memorial in Louveral in France. Also listed under Leighlinbridge/Old Leighlin on the Great War Memorial, Milford Street, Leighlinbridge, County Carlow.

HAYDEN, LEO ANTHONY: Rank: 2nd Lieutenant. Regiment or service: Royal Irish Regiment. Unit: 2nd Battalion. Date of death: 14 January 1917. Died of wounds. Listed in the *London Gazette*, 24 September 1915. Grave or memorial reference: I. C. 10. Cemetery: Hazebrouck Communal Cemetery, Nord in France.

HAYDON, DANIEL: Rank: Driver. Regiment or service: Royal Dublin

Fusiliers. Unit: 1st Battalion. Date of death: 11 September 1915. Service Number: 9798. Born in Carlow Graigue, Queen's County. Enlisted in Carlow. Died in Gallipoli.

Supplementary information: Son of J. Haydon, of Milford, County Carlow. From the *Nationalist* and *Leinster Times*, May 1915:

Carlow Soldier's Narrative.
Incident of the Battle of Ypres.
Lance Corporal J. Hayden(sic), Royal Dublin Fusiliers, writing to his father in Burrin Street, Carlow, from the Mill Lane, Liverpool, gives a vivid account of the long battles raging around Ypres. He tells of the sanguinary bayonet charges, etc., and the death of his brother, Paddy. He was speaking to his brother— who had only left Cork a few days before—on a Saturday, and on the following day, Sunday, was told that he had been killed. He afterwards found his grave and placed a nice wooden cross over it, and put flowers on it. The writer was only 100 yards from his brother's grave when he got wounded. He says the poison gas had not much effect on his section of the force, and could not move them one inch, although they lost a few hundred in that particular place.

Writing to a friend in Carlow, he says that thousands have been lost in the battles around Ypres, but the Germans lost double.

Grave or memorial reference: He is commemorated on the Grangegorman (Cork) Memorial Headstones Spec. Memorial. Alternative Commemoration – He is buried in Cork Military Cemetery. Also listed under Carlow/Graigue on the Great War Memorial, Milford Street, Leighlinbridge, County Carlow.

HAYDON, PATRICK: Rank: Private. Regiment or service: Royal Dublin Fusiliers. Unit: 2nd Battalion. Date of death: 9 May 1915. Service No.: 8501. Born in Carlow. Enlisted in Carlow while living in Gorey, County Wexford. Killed in action. Grave or memorial reference: III. H. 24. Cemetery: Ypres Town Cemetery Extension in Belgium. Also listed under Carlow/Graigue on the Great War Memorial, Milford Street, Leighlinbridge, County Carlow.

HAYES, HENRY: Rank: Gunner. Regiment or service: Royal Field Artillery. Unit: 120th Battery. Date of death: 25 April 1915. Age at death: 25. Service No.: 13353. Born in Carlow. Enlisted in Carlow. Killed in action.

Supplementary information: Son of William and Elizabeth Hayes, of Henry Street, Graigue Cullen, Carlow.

Grave or memorial reference: Panel 5 and 9. Memorial: Ypres (Menin Gate) Memorial in Belgium. Also listed under Carlow/Graigue on the Great War Memorial, Milford Street, Leighlinbridge, County Carlow.

HEARNS, PATRICK: Rank: Sergeant. Regiment or service: Royal Dublin Fusiliers. Unit: 2nd Battalion. Date of death: 8 November 1920. Service No.: 7075036.

Supplementary information: Noncupative will was witnessed by (sister) Miss Mary Hearns, Dublin Road, Carlow and John Killan, RC Priest, Carlow. Effects and property received by his mother.

Grave or memorial reference: I.K.15. Cemetery: Haidar Pasha Cemetery, Turkey.

HENLEY, JOSEPH: Rank: Private, Lance Corporal. Regiment or service: Royal Irish Regiment. Unit: 1st Battalion. Date of death: 15 March 1915. Service No.: 9794. Born in Carlow. Enlisted in Carlow. Killed in action. From the *Nationalist* and *Leinster Times*, March, 1917:

HENLEY—(Second Anniversary)—In sad and loving memory of Joseph Henley, late of Montgomery Street, killed in France on the 15th March, 1915. On whose soul, Sweet Jesus, have mercy, Queen of the Most Holy Rosary, pray for him. R. I. P.

In far off France the stars are gleaming,
Gleaming on a silent grave;
There he lies sleeping, without dreaming,
One we loved, but could not save.
Two years have passed, and still we miss him,
Words can fail our loss to tell;
But again we hope to meet him,
When the days of life are fled;
And in heaven with joy to greet him,
Where no farewell tears are shed.

Inserted by his sorrowing mother and sisters.

Grave or memorial reference: Panel 33. Memorial: Ypres (Menin Gate) Memorial in Belgium. Also listed under Carlow/Graigue on the Great War Memorial, Milford Street, Leighlinbridge, County Carlow.

HENNESSY, JAMES: Rank: Private. Regiment or service: Royal Dublin Fusiliers. Unit: 2nd Battalion. Date of death: 23 December 1914. Service No.: 8922. Born in Tipperary. Enlisted in Carlow while living in Graigue, Carlow. Killed in action. Grave or memorial reference: I. C. 4. Cemetery: Prowse Point Military Cemetery in Belgium. Also listed under Carlow/Graigue on the Great War Memorial, Milford Street, Leighlinbridge, County Carlow.

HENNESSY, MURLAGH FRANCIS: Rank: Gunner. Regiment or service: Royal Marine Artillery. Unit: HMS *Lion*. Date of death: 31 May 1916. Age at death: 27. Service No.: RMA/12255. Killed in action during the Battle of Jutland.

Supplementary information: Son of Arthur Hennessy and Margeret Connors his wife, of Turbotstown, Coole, County Westmeath. Native of Newtown, Bagenalstown, County Carlow. Killed on the first day of the Battle of Jutland. Grave or memorial reference: 21. Memorial: Portsmouth Naval Memorial UK. From 'Naval Operations' by Sir Julian Corbett, 1923:

...with main and secondary armament in action the German salvoes were being delivered about every twenty seconds, and our ships too were in a forest of waterspouts. It was one of the hottest moments of the action, when every nerve had to be strained to the utmost, and Admiral Beatty, having the enemy well abaft his beam, signalled to the 13th flotilla that it seemed a good opportunity to attack. Five minutes later, while the fight still raged at its hottest, the Lion received a nearly fatal blow. A heavy shell struck Q-turret, entered the gun-house, burst over the left gun, and killed nearly the whole of the guns crews, and it was only the presence of mind and devotion of the officer of the turret, major F. J. Harvey, R. M. L. I., when almost incapacitated with a mortal wound, that saved the flagship from sudden destruction.

HEYDON, PATRICK: Rank: Private. Regiment or service: Royal Dublin Fusiliers. Unit: 1st Battalion. Date of death: 9 June 1916. Service No.: 9470. Born in Tinryland, Carlow. Enlisted in Carlow. Killed in action. Information from his noncuperative will: Effects and property received by: (Mother) Mrs County Carlow. Witnesses: Ellen Hayden, Tinnyland, Carlow, Edward Haydon, Tinnyland, Carlow, Richard P(sic). Grave or memorial reference: Pier and Face 16C. Memorial: Thiepval Memorial in France. Also listed under Tinryland on the Great War Memorial, Milford Street, Leighlinbridge, County Carlow.

HILL, JOHN STUART: Rank: Private. Regiment or service: Dorsetshire Regiment. Unit: 1st Battalion. Date of death: 14 June 1918. Service No.: 22342. Formerly he was with the DCLI where his number was 27179. Born in Carlow. Enlisted in Arlesford, Hants. Killed in action. Grave or memorial reference: III. B. 9. Cemetery: Berles New Military Cemetery in France. Also listed under Carlow/Graigue on the Great War Memorial, Milford Street, Leighlinbridge, County Carlow.

HOARE, JOSEPH: Rank: Private. Regiment or service: Irish Guards. Unit: 1st Battalion. Date of death: 5 December 1917. Service No.: 3544. Born in Killeshen, County Carlow. Enlisted in Carlow. Killed in action. Grave or memorial reference: Panel 2 and 3. Memorial: Cambrai Memorial in Louveral in France. Also listed under Carlow/Graigue on the Great War Memorial, Milford Street, Leighlinbridge, County Carlow.

HOBSON, ELIZABETH: See **HOBSON, NATHANIEL.**

HOBSON, NATHANIEL JAMES FENNEL. Rank: Lieutenant. Regiment or service: King's Liverpool Regiment. Unit: 5th Battalion. Date of death: 10 October 1918.
Supplementary inforrmation: Born in County Louth in 1881, he was a Master Baker before he obtained his commission. Drowned when the Packet

Steamship RMS *Leinster* was torpedoed and sunk by German Submarine U-123 on 10 October 1918. Medal index card shows his widow living in Wales after the war. First entered the theatre of war (France) on 7 June 1916. Mentioned twice in the *London Gazette*, issue no. 30376, supplement 11674, and no. 30753, supplement 7273. Husband of Elizabeth Mary Hobson(born 1886 in Belfast). They had two sons, Nathaniel Thomas Fennel Hobson, born in the first half of 1909, and Richard Henry Hobson, born in 1910. Medal index card shows his widow, Elizabeth Mary Hobson, living in Wales after the war. Parents: Abraham, born in Wicklow, 1837 and Elizabeth, born in Laois, 1847 during the height of the Irish famine. In 1911 they were living in Kingstown (Dun Laoghaire) County Dublin and in 1901 Cromac, County Antrim. Abraham Dobson is buried in Dunleckney Cemetery. Headstone reads:

In loving memory of Abraham Hobson, Kingstown, County Dublin, aged 84 years, and his wife Elizabeth Hobson aged 80 years, who departed this life April 9th 1921 and July 4th 1928 respectively. Also of Lieutenant N. J. Hobson, Elizabeth M Hobson and Richard H. Hobson (Dodo), son, daughter and grandson of Abraham and Elizabeth Hobson who were lost on the Leinster Oct 10th 1918.

From 'Death in the Irish Sea' by Roy Stokes:

Lieutenant Nathaniel Hobson of the 5th battalion The King's (Liverpool Regiment) had received a French decoration for his war service. He was from Kingstown, County Dublin, *Leinster's* place of departure. He has visited Kingstown to collect his ten year old son Richard and bring him back to school in Liverpool. Richard had been staying with Nathaniel's parents at 28 Northumberland Avenue, Kingstown. As Nathaniel's parents ran a school from that address, the boy had probably received some education there. Elizabeth travelled on the *Leinster* with her brother and nephew. All three were lost.

For more information see *Carloviana*, (2003) page 62; – Bagenalstown Men who died in the Great war by John Kenna. The estate of Nathaniel James Fennel Hobson of Daffodil Road, Claughton, Birkenhead totalled £218 1s 4d. His will was administered in Chester, 24 June 1919 to his wife Elizabeth Mary Hobson. His son left £233.

Grave or memorial reference: He has no known grave but is listed on the Hollybrook Memorial, Southampton, UK.

HOBSON, RICHARD THOMAS: See HOBSON, NATHANIEL.

HODGES, ALFRED G: Rank: Lance Sergeant. Regiment or service: Leinster Regiment. Unit: 6th Battalion. Date of death: 10 August 1915. Service No.: 400. Born in Carlow. Enlisted in Carlow. Died of wounds at sea.

Supplementary information: His last will and testament dated 13 April 1915.

Effects and property received by his mother, Mrs Kate Hodges, 13 Tullow Street, Carlow. Was a member of the Carlow Company of the Boy's Brigade. From the *Nationalist* and *Leinster Times*, August 1915:

Young Carlowman Killed.
Last week news reached Carlow of the death of Lance Corporal Alfred G. Hodges, of the 6th Leinster Regiment, at the Dardanelles. Young Hodges was very popular in the town, and his death at the early age of 21 is widely regretted. He was the son of the late Mr Edward Hodges, Carlow.

From the *Nationalist* and *Leinster Times*, March 1917:

Carlow Man Honoured.
Bombardier Francis Edwin Hodges, South African Heavy Artillery, eldest son of the late Edward and Mrs Hodges, Tullow Street, Carlow, has been awarded the Medaille Militaire (French Military Medal) for bravery on the field. Mrs Hodges has also two other sons serving in France, and a fourth died of wounds in action at Suvla Bay.

Francis Edwin Hodges, brother of Alfred is listed in the Supplement to the *Edinburgh Gazette*, May 3 1917. From *Carlow Sentinel*, March 1917:

French Honour for a Carlow Man.
We feel pleasure in announcing that our young townsman, Bombardier Francis Edwin Hodges, South African Infantry, has been awarded the

"Medaile Militaire" (French Military Medal) for bravery in the field—the first honour of its kind held by the Regiment, which, however, has won several other British medals. This gallant soldier is eldest son of the late, Mrs Hodges, Tullow Street, Carlow. Twpo of his brothers are serving with the colours in France, and a third died of wounds received in action at Salonika Bay, a little over a year and a half since. Mrs Hodges, who deserves well of King and Country, has been warmly congratulated on the distinguished honour conferred on her boy Bombardier.

From *Carlow Sentinel*, November 1918:

Roll of Honour.
His many friends will learn with pleasure that sergeant Edward C Hodges, 8th African Heavy Artillery, has been awarded the D. C. M., for gallantry under heavy fire. He is seconds son of Mrs Hodges, Tullow Street, Carlow, who has three other sons serving, while another son paid the supreme penalty.

Grave or memorial reference: Panel 184 and 185. Memorial: Helles Memorial in Turkey.

HOGAN, MICHAEL: Rank: Rifleman. Regiment or service: King's Royal Rifle Corps. Unit: 12th Battalion. Date of death: 3 May 1917. Service No.: 10299. Born in Leighlinbridge. Enlisted in Colchester. Died of wounds. He won the Military Medal and is listed in the *London Gazette*. Grave or memorial reference: P. I. H. 1A. Cemetery; St Sever Cemetery Extension, Rouen in France.

HOGAN, PATRICK: Rank: Private. Regiment or service: Royal Munster Fusiliers. Unit: 2nd Battalion. Date of death: 31 October 1918. Service No.: 6054. Born in St John's, Limerick. Enlisted in Ennis, County Clare while living in Limerick. Died. Patrick was an 'Old Contemptable' and embarked for France on 13 August 1914. Died as a prisoner of war at Giessen. Grave or memorial reference: XIV. D. 6. Cemetery: Cologne Southern Cemetery, in Germany. Also listed under Leighlinbridge/Old Leighlin on the Great War Memorial, Milford Street, Leighlinbridge, County Carlow.

HOGAN, WILLIAM: Rank: Trooper. Regiment or service: Household Cavalry and Cavalry of the line including the Yeomanry and Imperial Camel Corps. Unit: Household Battalion. Date of death: 22 December 1917. Service No.: 2608. Born in Kilkenny, County Kilkenny. Enlisted in London while living in London. Died of wounds.

Supplementary information: Husband of L. Hogan, of 5 Herbert Gardens, Kensal Rise, London. Grave or memorial reference: V. D. 51. Cemetery: Duisans British Cemetery, Etrun in France. Also listed under Leighlinbridge/Old Leighlin on the Great War Memorial, Milford Street, Leighlinbridge, County Carlow.

HOLDEN, JAMES: Rank: Private. Regiment or service: Royal Inniskilling Fusiliers. Unit: 7th Battalion. Date of death: 16 August 1917. Service No.: 27699. Formerly he was with the Royal Irish Regiment where his number was 11382. Born in Carlow. Enlisted in Athy while living in Carlow. Killed in action. After his death his effects and property was received by his mother, Mrs Mary A. Holden, Brown Street, Carlow. Grave or memorial reference: Panel 70 to 72 Memorial: Tyne Cot Memorial in Belgium. Also listed under Carlow/Graigue on the Great War Memorial, Milford Street, Leighlinbridge, County Carlow.

HOLLAND, JAMES: Rank: Private. Regiment or service: Royal Irish Fusiliers. Unit: 1st Battalion. Date of death: 22 April 1918. Age at death: 23. Service No.: 27777. Born in Carlow. Enlisted in Manchester while living in Dublin. Died of wounds. Grave or memorial reference: IX. A. 11. Cemetery: Boulogne Eastern Cemetery in France. Also listed under Carlow/Graigue on the Great War Memorial, Milford Street, Leighlinbridge, County Carlow.

HOLOHAN, THOMAS: Rank: Rifleman. Regiment or service: Royal Irish Rifles. Unit: 2nd Battalion. Date of death: 28 September 1916. Age at death: 19. Service No.: 7909. Born in Graigue, County Carlow. Enlisted in New Ross, County Wexford. Killed in action.

Supplementary information: Son of Matthew Holohan, of Coolroe, Graiguenamanagh, County Kilkenny.

Grave or memorial reference: Pier and Face 15 A and 15 B A. Memorial: Thiepval Memorial in France.

HOPKINS, ROBERT: Rank: Saddler-Corporal. Regiment or service: Household Cavalry and Cavalry of the line including the Yeomanry and Imperial Camel Corps. Unit: C Squadron, 3rd Dragoon Guards. Date of death: 17 November 1914. Age at death: 27. Service No.: 5987. Born in Carlow. Enlisted in Curragh Camp while living in Dublin. Killed in action.

Supplementary information: Son of Elizabeth Hopkins, of 50 Black Hall Place, Dublin, and the late James Hopkins.

Grave or memorial reference: Panel 3. Memorial: Ypres (Menin Gate) Memorial in Belgium. Also listed under Carlow/Graigue on the Great War Memorial, Milford Street, Leighlinbridge, County Carlow.

HORE, WILLIAM: Rank: Private. Regiment or service: Royal Dublin Fusiliers. Unit: 2nd Battalion. Date of death: 4 November 1920. Age at death, 32. Service No.: 8938. This man is not in any other database.

Supplementary information: Son of E. Hore, of Kilree Street, Bagenalstown, County Carlow.

Grave or memorial reference: In the South West part. Cemetery: Sleaty Old Burial Ground in County Laoise. Also listed under Bagenalstown/Fenagh on the Great War Memorial, Milford Street, Leighlinbridge, County Carlow.

HOUGHNEY/HAUGHNEY, CHARLES: Rank: Private. Regiment or service: Royal Inniskilling Fusiliers. Unit: 7th Battalion. Date of death: 31 July 1918. Age at death: 20. Service No.: 28037. Born in Carlow Grange, Queen's County. Enlisted in Carlow. Killed in action.

Supplementary information: Son of Edward and Johana Haughney, of Church Street, Graiguecullen, Carlow. In his Will, dated 22 February 1917, his effects and property were received by: (Mother) Mrs Johemia Haughney, Chuch Street, Carlow. Witnessed by: D. H. Wallace Sergeant, Ebrington Barracks, Londonderry. F. Sehill Sergeant, Ebrington Barracks, Londonderry.

Grave or memorial reference: V. E. 12. Cemetery: Valenciennes (St Roch) Communal Cemetery in France. Also listed under Carlow/Graigue on the Great War Memorial, Milford Street, Leighlinbridge, County Carlow.

HOWARD, WILLIAM: Rank: Private. Regiment or service: Royal Dublin Fusiliers. Unit: 10th Battalion. Date of death: 30 November 1917. Service No.: 29345. Born in Tinryland, County Carlow. Enlisted in Carlow. Killed in action. Byrne, Thomas, another Carlowman, died on the same day and is buried two graves down from William. Grave or memorial reference: II. F. 15. Cemetery: Croiselles British Cemetery in France. Also listed under Tinryland on the Great War Memorial, Milford Street, Leighlinbridge, County Carlow.

HOWE, JOHN GEORGE: Rank: Driver. Regiment or service: Royal Horse Artillery and Royal Field

Artillery. Unit: 75th Battery. Date of death: 24 October 1918. Service No.: 60830. Born in St Mary's, Carlow. Enlisted in Athlone, Ireland. Died in Egypt. Grave or memorial reference: Q. 13. Cemetery, Cairo War Memorial Cemetery in Egypt. Also listed under Carlow/Graigue on the Great War Memorial, Milford Street, Leighlinbridge, County Carlow.

HOWE, WILLIAM MOLYNEUX:
Rank: Air Mechanic 1st Class. Regiment or service: Royal Air Force. Unit: 18th Balloon Sect. Date of death: 26 November 1918. Age at death: 32. Service No.: 7902. This man is not in any other database.

Supplementary information: Son of John and Anna Howe. Born at Carlow.

Grave or memorial reference: II. B. 18. Cemetery: Caudry British Cemetery in France.

HOWLIN, JAMES: Rank: Private. Regiment or service: Royal Irish Regiment. Unit: 6th Battalion. Date of death: 25 December 1915. Age at death: 39. Service No.: 3/7509 and 7509. Born in St Mullins, County Carlow. Enlisted in Enniscorthy, County Wexford. Died at Sea.

Supplementary information: Son of Patrick and Stasia Howlin of Goolin, County Carlow; husband of Bridget Howlin of Grange, Rathnure, Enniscorthy, County Wexford.

Grave or memorial reference: C. 106. Cemetery: Alexandria (Chatby) Military and War Memorial Cemetery in Egypt. Also listed under St Mullins

on the Great War Memorial, Milford Street, Leighlinbridge, County Carlow.

HUGHES, EDWARD: Rank: Lance Corporal. Regiment or service: Royal Irish Regiment. Unit: 1st Battalion. Date of death: 11 April 1915. Age at death: 21. Service No.: 10287. Born in Bagenalstown County Carlow. Enlisted in Dublin. Died of wounds.

Supplementary information: Son of James and Helen Hughes, of Bagnalstown, County Carlow.

Grave or memorial reference: II. N. 45. Cemetery: Poperinghe Old Military Cemetery in Belgium. Also listed under Bagenalstown/Fenagh on the Great War Memorial, Milford Street, Leighlinbridge, County Carlow.

HUGHES, JAMES: Rank: Sergeant. Regiment or service: Royal Irish Regiment. Unit: 2nd Battalion. Date of death: 29 August 1918. Service No.: 9453. Born in Bagenalstown, County Carlow. Enlisted in Kilkenny while living in Bagenalstown, County Carlow. Killed in action. Grave or memorial reference: Pier and Face 3A. Memorial: Thiepval Memorial in France. Also listed under Bagenalstown/Fenagh on the Great War Memorial, Milford Street, Leighlinbridge, County Carlow.

HUGHES, JOHN: Rank: Private. Regiment or service: Royal Dublin Fusiliers. Unit: 8th Battalion. Date of death: 28 October 1916. Service No.: 16239. Born in Bagnalstown, County

Carlow. Enlisted in Kilkenny while living in Goresbridge, County Kilkenny. Died. Grave or memorial reference: III. A. 244. Cemetery: Bailleul Communal Cemetery Extension (Nord) in France. Also listed under Bagenalstown/Fenagh on the Great War Memorial, Milford Street, Leighlinbridge, County Carlow.

HUGHES, W. T.: Rank: Captain. Regiment or service: Indian Army Reserve of Officers. Unit: Attached to the Indian Political Department. Date of death: 8 April 1917. From the *Nationalist* and *Leinster Times*, April 1917:

The brothers and sisters of the late Captain W. T. Hughes, Clashganny House, Borris, return sincere thanks for the many kind messages of sympathy received in their sad bereavement.

From the *Nationalist* and *Leinster Times*, April 1917:

Condolence.
At a meeting of the traders of Graiguenamanagh held in the Gaelic Club, Mr P Leary presiding, the following resolutions were passed unanimously;
"That we tender to our respected and revered pastor, Reverend J.

Mooney, P. P., our sincere sympathy in the loss he has sustained in the death of his brother. "
"That we have learned with deep regret of the death at Delhi, India, of Captain W. T. Hughes, late of Clashganny, Borris, and tender our sympathy to his brothers and sisters in their sad bereavement."

Grave or memorial reference: 8. A. 22. Cemetery: Delhi War Cemetery, India.

HUTCHINSON, MARTIN: Rank: Private. Regiment or service: Irish Guards. Unit: 2nd Battalion. Date of death: 13 September 1916. Age at death: 35. Service No.: 6982. Born in Ballickmoyler, Queen's County. Enlisted in Carlow, County Carlow. Killed in action.

Supplementary information: Son of Michael Hutchinson, of Tolerton, Ballickmoyler, Carlow.

Grave or memorial reference: He has no known grave but is listed on Pier and Face 7D on the Thiepval Memorial in France. Also listed under Carlow/Graigue on the Great War Memorial, Milford Street, Leighlinbridge, County Carlow.

I

IEVERS (also listed as **JEVERS**), **EDWIN:** Rank: Private. Regiment or service: Northumberland Fusiliers. Unit: 1st/7th Battalion. Date of death: 26 October 1917. Age at death: 32. Service No.: 205130. Born in Carlow. Enlisted in Sunderland. Killed in action.

Supplementary information: Son of E. and A. Ievers of Ballyanne, New Ross, County Wexford, Husband of Gertrude Ievers of 58 Ridley Street, Southwick, Sunderland.

Grave or memorial reference: Panel 19 to 23 and 162. Memorial: Tyne Cot Memorial in Belgium. Also listed under Carlow/Graigue on the Great War Memorial, Milford Street, Leighlinbridge, County Carlow.

IEVERS, R.W. (also listed as **IVERS, WALTER ROBERT**): Rank: Private. Regiment or service: Durham Light Infantry. Unit: 10th Battalion. Date of death: 9 April 1917. Age at death: 27. Service No.: 21481. Born in Duckets Grove, County Carlow, Ireland. Enlisted in Newcastle while living in Wexford. Killed in action.

Supplementary information: Born in County Carlow. Son of Edwin and Annie Ievers of Ballyanne House, New Ross, County Wexford.

Grave or memorial reference: B. 24. Cemetery: Hibers Trench Cemetery, Wancourt in France. Also listed under Palatine/Urglin on the Great War Memorial, Milford Street, Leighlinbridge, County Carlow.

IRWIN, HERBERT QUINTUS: Rank: Captain. Regiment or service: Connaught Rangers. Unit: 1st Battalion attached to 2nd Battalion. Date of death: 26 April 1915. Age at death: 30. Killed in action.

Supplementary information: Son of the Reverend Canon Edward Irwin and Marion Irwin, of The Deanery, Elphin, County Roscommon. His medals and plaque: – '1914 Star, with clasp (Lieut., Conn. Rang); British War and Victory Medals (Captain), with related Memorial Plaque (Herbert Quintus Irwin)' were sold by | Dix Noonan Webb, a London auction house, in 2004 for £1000. The catalogue information states:

Herbert Quintus Irwin was born in May 1884, the son of the Rev. Canon Irwin of the Deanery, Elphin, County Roscommon, and was commissioned in the Connaught Rangers from the Special Reserve in May 1909.

A Lieutenant in the 2nd Battalion by the outbreak of hostilities in August 1914, he embarked for France with his unit in the middle of the same month, and would have seen extensive action in the retreat from Mons – such were the Battalion's casualties that its survivors had to be taken on the strength of the 1st Battalion that December.

Irwin's advancement to Captain appeared in The *London Gazette* in May 1915, shortly after his death in action at St Julien in the Ypres sector on 26 April.

From *Carlow Sentinel*, May 1915:

Lieutenant H. Q. Irwin
Lieutenant Herbert Quintus Irwin, 1st Battalion, Connaught Rangers, whose death we announced on Thursday, was the youngest son of the rev Canon Irwin, some time Curate of Carlow, who some weeks since was appointed Army Chaplain at the front. He was killed in action near St Julien on the 26th April. He was educated at Trinity College, Dublin, where he graduated in the year 1906. he held a commission in the 4th Battalion, Connaught rangers from 1906-1909. In May 1909 he was gazetted Second Lieutenant, 1st Battalion, Connaught Rangers, and was promoted Lieutenant in March, 1910. Having served with his battalion in India for over three years, he was transferred to the Depot, Galway, for a tour of duty for three years.

Grave or memorial reference: I. U. 23. Cemetery: La Brique Military Cemetery, No 2, in Belgium. Also listed in the 1937 reading room memorial in Trinity College, Dublin.

IRWIN, THOMAS: Rank: Private. Regiment or service: Royal Dublin Fusiliers. Unit: 1st Battalion. Date of death: 23 April 1916 (CWGC, SDGW, IMR) 23 June 1916 (Great War Memorial, Milford Street, Leighlinbridge, County Carlow). Service No.: 5728. Born in Carlow. Enlisted in Naas while living in Carlow. Died. Awarded the Crois De Guerre. Grave or memorial reference: C. 25. Cemetery: Mailly-Maillet Communal Cemetery Extension, Somme in France. Also listed under Carlow/ Graigue on the Great War Memorial, Milford Street, Leighlinbridge, County Carlow.

IVERS, WALTER ROBERT: See **IEVERS, R. W.**

J

JACOB, JAMES: Rank: Private. Regiment or service: Royal Irish Regiment. Unit: 1st Battalion. Date of death: 13 February 1915. Service No.: 10394. Born in Athlone, County Westmeath. Enlisted in Carlow while living in Bagenalstown, County Carlow. Died of wounds.

Supplementary information: Son of Mr P. Jacob, of 18, Kilcarrig Street, Bagenalstown, County Carlow.

Grave or memorial reference: C. 8. Cemetery: Dickebusch Old Military Cemetery in Belgium. Also listed under Bagenalstown/Fenagh on the Great War Memorial, Milford Street, Leighlinbridge, County Carlow.

JAFFARES/JEFFARES, RICHARD THORPE: Rank: Captain. Regiment or service: Royal Irish Rifles. Unit: 4th Battalion. attd. 2nd Battalion. Date of death: 6 October 1917. Age at death: 27. Awards: Mentioned in Despatches. Died of wounds.

Supplementary information: Son of M. H. Jeffares, of Lower Seskin, Leighlinbridge, Bagenalstown, County Carlow. Served also in German East Africa. From *Carlow Sentinel*, May 1918.

County Carlow Captain's Death.
In the matter of Captain Richard Thorpe Jeffares, deceased, Mr Little (instructed by Messrs Colfer and Son) applied to Mr Justice Madden in the High Court, on behalf of Mr John Jeffares, of Scarke House, New Ross, to admit two letters, dated respectively 10th October, 1916 and 19th July, 1917, written by the deceased, as a soldier's will, and to grant letters of administration, with the will annexed, to his client. The deceased was a son of Mr Michael H Jeffares, of Seskin, Leighlin Bridge, was a Captain in the Royal irish Rifles, and was killed in action on the 6th October, 1917. Mr John Jeffares was his uncle, and the two letters were written to him. In the first letter, the deceased stated that his army gratuity would be paid to the applicant, whom he directed to spend some of it on his brother Michael and his sister Mary. In the letter of the 19th July deceased stated that he had put his uncle John down as his next-of-Kin, and that all his army gratuity would come to him "if he went west." And he requested him to give Mick a first call or preference. Mr Justice Madden granted the application.

Grave or memorial reference: III. J. 16. Cemetery: Bethune Town Cemetery in France. Also listed under Leighlinbridge/Old Leighlin on the Great War Memorial, Milford Street, Leighlinbridge, County Carlow.

JAMES, EDWARD: Rank: Company Sergeant. Regiment or service: Royal Dublin Fusiliers. Unit: 8th Battalion. Date of death: 18 February 1915.

Service No.: 15211. Born in Carlow. Enlisted in Dublin. Died at home.

Supplementary information: Husband of L. Ramsay, of 15 Bishop Street, Dublin.

Grave or memorial reference: R.C. 584. Cemetery: Grangegorman Military Cemetery in Dublin. Also listed under Carlow/Graigue on the Great War Memorial, Milford Street, Leighlinbridge, County Carlow.

JEVERS, EDWIN: See IEVERS.

JONES, BERNARD THOMAS:
Rank: Private. Regiment or service: Northumberland Fusiliers. Unit: 4th Battalion. Date of death: 16 November 1916. Age at death: 18. Service No.: 6828(CWGC), 6988(SDGW). Born in Rathvally, County Carlow. Enlisted in Elswick, Northumberland. Died of wounds.

Supplementary information: Son of John and Caroline Jones, of Ballybit, Tullow, County Carlow. From *Nationalist* and *Leinster Times*, 1917:

JONES—November, 1916, killed in action in France, Bernard Thomas, second and dearly beloved so of John and Caroline Jones, Ballybitt, Tullow, County Carlow. Deeply mourned by his sorrowing parents, brothers and sisters and a large circle of friends.

Peace. Perfect Peace.
His warfare is o'er, his battle fought,
His victory won, though dearly bought;

His fresh young life could not be saved.
He slumbers now in a soldier's grave.

Nationalist and *Leinster Times*, November 1917.

JONES-First Anniversary. —In sad and loving memory of Bernard Thomas, second and dearly beloved son of John and Caroline M. Jones, Ballabit, Tullow, County Carlow, who was killed in action in France on November 16th, 1916, in his 19th year, deeply mourned by his sorrowful parents and sisters. Thy will be done.
Not gone from memory, nor from love,
But to our Father's home above.
Thou art gone, dear Bernard, from us,
And our hearts are sore with pain.
Oh! This earth, it would be heaven
To see your sweet face once again,
But now my son so dear and brave
Is sleeping in a foreign grave.
Inserted by his devoted father, mother, sisters and brothers.

From the *Nationalist* and *Leinster Times*, November 1918:

Jones—Second Anniversary—In sad and loving memory of our dear son, Bernard Thomas, who was killed in France, 16th November, 1916.

Not go he from memory, nor from love; but to his Father's Home above, waiting for us there.
In a glorious summer and gathered with the angels.

Shouting victory on the strand,
waiting there to meet us.
Ah Time's lingering shadows flee,
wait with songs
To greet us near the beautiful crys-
tal sea.

Inserted by his loving parents, sisters and brothers.

Grave or memorial reference: F. 16. Cemetery: Bazentin-Le-Petit Military Cemetery, Somme, France. Also listed under Rathvilly on the Great War Memorial, Milford Street, Leighlinbridge, County Carlow.

JONES, RICHARD ARTHUR:

Rank: Private. Regiment or service: Canadian Infantry (Central Ontario Regiment). Unit: 3rd Battalion. Date of death: 2 May 1915. Age at death: 20. Service No.: 9216.

Supplementary information: Son of William Empson Jones and Agnes Eva Jones, of Woodside, Hackelstown, County Carlow, Ireland. From *King's County Chronicle*, 1915:

Irish giant soldiers.
Three giant sons of Mr William A Jones, Clerk of Hacketstown Petty Sessions, have joined the Army since the outbreak of the war. They are; - Lieut. Robert, R. E., height 6ft 3 ½ inches; Corpl, W. J., North Irish Horse, height 6ft 2 ½ inches; Private Richard, Canadian Volunteers, 6ft 0 ½ inches. Their grandfather was 6ft 5inches.

The same article was published in the Kildare Observer and a similar one in the *Nationalist* and *Leinster Times*

Grave or memorial reference: Panel 18 - 24 - 26 - 30. Memorial: Ypres (Menin Gate) Memorial in Belgium. Also listed under Hacketstown on the Great War Memorial, Milford Street, Leighlinbridge, County Carlow.

JONES, RICHARD: Rank: Corporal.
Regiment or service: Royal Horse Artillery and Royal Field Artillery. Unit: S Battery. Date of death: 8 March 1916. Age at death: 29. Service No.: 50067. Born in Wicklow, Ireland. Enlisted in Dublin, Ireland. Killed in action in Mesopotamia.

Supplementary information: Son of the late Griffith and Alicia Jones. From the *Nationalist* and *Leinster Times*:

Roll of Honour.
Corporal Jones, R. H. A., Killed.
Mr Griffith Jones, ex-R. I. C., Baltinglass, received a communica- tion on Thursday from the War Office that his fourth eldest son, Corporal Richard Jones, Royal Horse Artillery, was killed in action in Mesopotamia, on the 8th March. He was attached to the "S" Battery, R. H. A., India, which was part of the Indian Expeditionary Force, sent to the Persian Gulf, when hostilities broke out with the Turks. His Company was afterwards with the army intended to capture Baghdad. The last letter received from him was dated the 20th February, giving a vivid account of the fight- ing with the Turks and Arabs, who, in his own words, received a great ham-

mering on Xmas Eve and Xmas Day. Some good friends from Bombay sent him pudding and other comforts, which were keenly enjoyed by the men belonging to his Battery, after the battle. Deceased was 29 years of age, and had been 8 ½ years in the army, 7 ½ years of which were spent in India. He was Acting Pay Sergeant for his Battery for the past 4 ½ years. Deceased had a very creditable record in the army. His death is deeply regretted by his friends and the general public in Baltinglass district.

Grave or memorial reference: He has no known grave but is listed on Panel 3 and 60 on the Basra Memorial in Iraq. Also listed under Hacketstown on the Great War Memorial, Milford Street, Leighlinbridge, County Carlow.

JONES, WILLIAM: Rank: Rifleman. Regiment or service: Rifle Brigade. Unit: 1st Battalion. Date of death: 28 March 1918. Age at death: 26. Service No.: B/201399. Born in Bagenalstown, County Carlow. Enlisted in Kilkenny while living in Bagenalstown, County Carlow. Killed in action.
Supplementary information: Son of Margaret Jones, of 46 Kilcarrig Street, Bagenaistown, County Carlow, and the late William B. Jones.
Grave or memorial reference: Bay 9. Memorial: Arras Memorial in France.

JONES, WILLIAM ROWLAND: Rank: Private. Regiment or service: Canadian Infantry (Western Ontario Regiment). Unit: 47th Battalion. Date of death: 11 November 1916. Age at death: 33. Service No.: 629884.
Supplementary information: Son of the late William Jones (Resident Magistrate), of Carlow, Ireland. From *Carlow Sentinel*, December 1916:

> Roll of Honour.
> JONES—November 11, 1916, killed in action, William Rowland (Rollo), Canadian Contingent, second son of the late William Jones, Resident Magistrate, Grosvenor, Carlow.
> Next of kin listed as (mother), Mrs M Jones, 45, Avenue D, Saskatoon. Place of birth, Portadown, Ireland. Date of birth, 30-September-1885. Occupation on enlistment, Transit Man. Place and date of enlistment, 17-June-1915, Vernon. Height, 5 feet, 9 inches. Complexion, dark. Eyes, blue. Hair, dark.

Memorial: Vimy Memorial, Pas-de-Calais, France.

JONES, WILLIAM: Rank: Rifleman. Regiment or service: Rifle Brigade. Unit: 1st Battalion. Date of death: 28 March 1918. Age at death: 26. Service No.: B/201399. Born in Bagenalstown, County Carlow. Enlisted in Kilkenny while living in Bagenalstown, County Carlow. Killed in action.
Supplementary information: Son of Margaret Jones, of 46 Kilcarrig Street, Bagenaistown, County Carlow, and the late William B. Jones Information from his last will and testament dated 2 August 1915. Effects and property was received by his mother, Mrs Margaret

Jones, Kilcarrig Street, Bagenalstown, County Carlow.

Grave or memorial reference: Bay 9. Memorial: Arras Memorial in France. Also listed under Bagenalstown/Fenagh on the Great War Memorial, Milford Street, Leighlinbridge, County Carlow.

JORDAN, EDWARD: Rank: Corporal. Regiment or service: Rifle Brigade. Unit: 7th Battalion. He was previously with the K. E. H. where his number was 1156. Date of death: 22 February 1917. Age at death: 27. Service No.: B/200715. Born in Wicklow. Enlisted in Hounslow in Middlesex while living in Holloway in Middlesex. Died.

Supplementary information: Son of Mr and Mrs Jordan, of County Carlow; husband of Edith Jordan, of 16 Scholefield Road, Upper Holloway, London.

Grave or memorial reference: I. D. 9. Cemetery: Mount Huon Military Cemetery, Le-Treport in France. Also listed under Tullow on the Great War Memorial, Milford Street, Leighlinbridge, County Carlow.

JOYCE, EDWARD: Rank: Lance Corporal. Regiment or service: King's Liverpool Regiment. Unit: 18th Battalion. Date of death: 1 July 1916. Service No.: 16825. Born in Carlow.

Enlisted in Liverpool while living in Carlow. Killed in action. Grave or memorial reference: W. V. 5. Cemetery: Danzig Alley British Cemetery Mametz in France. Also listed under Carlow/Graigue on the Great War Memorial, Milford Street, Leighlinbridge, County Carlow.

JOYCE, JOHN: Rank: Private. Regiment or service: Royal Inniskilling Fusiliers. Unit: 2nd Battalion. Date of death: 2 April 1915. Service No.: 6176. Born in Bagnalstown, County Carlow. Enlisted in Carlow. Killed in action. Grave or memorial reference: Panel 16 and 17. Memorial: Le Touret Memorial in France. Also listed under Bagenalstown/Fenagh on the Great War Memorial, Milford Street, Leighlinbridge, County Carlow.

JOYCE, MICHAEL: Rank: Private. Regiment or service: Irish Guards. Unit: 2nd Battalion. Date of death: 13 September 1916. Service No.: 9296. Born in Bagnalstown, County Carlow. Enlisted in Carlow. Killed in action. Grave or memorial reference: Pier and Face 7D. Memorial: Thiepval Memorial in France. Also listed under Bagenalstown/Fenagh on the Great War Memorial, Milford Street, Leighlinbridge, County Carlow.

K

KANE, PATRICK JOSEPH:
Rank: Private. Regiment or service:
Canadian Infantry. Unit: 53rd Battalion.
Date of death: 9 May 1916. Service
No.: 440533.

Supplementary information: Son
of Anastasia Kane, of Rivanagh,
Coolcullen, Bagenalstown, County
Carlow, Ireland. Next of kin listed as
(mother), Anastasia Kane, Rivanagh,
Culcullen, Kilkenny, Ireland. Place of
birth, County Kilkenny, Ireland. Date of
birth, 16 February 1889. Occupation on
enlistment: Locomotive fireman. Place
and date of enlistment: 17 September
1915, Camp Hughes, Manitoba. Height,
5 feet, 9½ inches. Complexion, fair.
Eyes, blue. Hair, brown.

Grave or memorial reference: A.
1. Cemetery: Greyshott (St Joseph)
Roman Catholic Churchyard,
Hampshire, UK. Also listed under
Leighlinbridge/Old Leighlin on the
Great War Memorial, Milford Street,
Leighlinbridge, County Carlow.

KANE-SMITH, JAMES: Rank:
Lieutenant. Regiment or service: Royal
Field Artillery. Unit: 110th Brigade. Date
of death: 27 May 1918. Age at death: 24.
Killed in action.

Supplementary information: Son of
Kane and Emily Kane-Smith, of Little
Moyle, Carlow. Awards: MC. An article
informing readers of his death in August
1917 was published by the *Carlow
Sentinel*:

Lieutenant J. Kane-Smith, R. F.
A. We regret to find in yesterday's
casualty list the name of Second
Lieutenant J. Kane-Smith, R. F. A.
He is son of Mr Kane J. Smith, Little
Moyle, Carlow, whose second son
also holds a commission, and is serv-
ing at the front.

From *Carlow Sentinel*, December 1914:

Promotion of a Carlow Volunteer.
Mr Kane Smith's eldest son "Jim,"
who enlisted in the "South irish
Horse" last September, has now
been gazetted to the Royal Field
Artillery, and is at present stationed
at Cahir, County Tipperary.

We congratulate our county man
on his pluck ad promotion, and hope
many others will follow his lead.

From *Carlow Sentinel*, January 1918:

Military Cross for Young Carlow
Officer.

We feel much pleasure in
announcing that Second-Lieutenant
James Kane-Smith, R. F.A., has been
awarded the M. C. for distinguished
gallantry. It is reported that when his
battery was being shelled he showed
a total disregard for his personal
safety in moving from gun-pit to
gun-pit encouraging the men. He
was in charge of the guns at the time,
and although himself wounded, by
his fearlessness and determination
he rallied the men and maintained

the accuracy of the battery. He also arranged for the wounded to be cleared before allowing his own wound to be dressed. Lieutenant Kane-Smith is a son of Mr Kane J Smith and Mrs Smith, Little Moyle, Carlow. He was well known in Carlow, where he was held in the greatest esteem for his amiability and sportsmanlike qualities.

From *Carlow Sentinel*, October 1917:

Second Lieutenant J. Kane Smith.
We feel pleasure in announcing that our young county man, Lieutenant Kane Smith, R. F. A., eldest son of Mr Kane Jane Smith Little Moyle, Carlow, has been awarded the Military Cross, which he gallantly won at Westhocke, where, although twice wounded he remained at his post. His friends have good reason to feel proud of him, as he is one of the few Carlow boys who rose from the ranks. He enlisted as private in the South Irish Horse, and shortly afterwards got his commission. His younger brother is serving with the 1st Division Canadian Field Artillery.

From *Nationalist* and *Leinster Times*, March 1918:

Military Cross Award.
T. Sec Lt. James Kane Smith, R. F. A. —When his battery was being heavily shelled he showed a total disregard for his personal safety in running from gun-pit to gun-pit, encouraging the men. He was in charge of the guns at the time, and although himself wounded, by his fearlessness and determination he rallied the men and arranged for the wounded to be cleared before allowing his own wound to be dressed, Lieutenant Kane Smith is son of Mr Kane J. Smith ad known in Carlow, where he was held in the greatest esteem for his amiability and sportsmanlike qualities.

From *Nationalist* and *Leinster Times*, June, 1918:

We heard with regret that Lieutenant "Jim" Kane Smith, M. C, son of Mr Kane Smith, Moyle, is reported missing. We sympathise with his parents in their anxiety, and we hope to hear soon a more reassuring report. "Jim" is a great favourite, and his many friends in the county will pray for his safety.

From *Carlow Sentinel*, June 1918:

We regret to find amongst the official causality list this week the death of this gallant young Carlow soldier, who was eldest son of Mr and Mrs Kane-Smith, Little Moyle. He was attached to the R. F. A., and some months back was reported wounded and missing, but hopes of recovery were entertained up to the last. He was awarded the M. C. for distinguished services, while his kind and genial disposition made him a fast favourite amongst his many friends, who mourn his loss, and sympathise deeply with his bereaved parents.

From *London Gazette*, January 1918:

For conspicuous gallantry and devotion to duty. When his battery was being heavily shelled he showed a total disregard for his personal safety in moving from gun-pit to gun-pit encouraging the men. He was in charge of the guns at the time, and although himself wounded, by his fearlessness and determination he rallied the men and maintained the accuracy of the fire of the battery. He also arranged for the wounded to be cleared before allowing his own wound to be dressed.

From *Carlow Sentinel*, September 1918:

Roll of Honour.
Corporal Bernard Kane Smith, Signal Company, Canadian Division, who was recently reported wounded, has been awarded the Military Medal for gallantry, during the big advance in September, 1918, and is again doing his "bit" at the front. We regret to learn there is not further news of his brother, Lieutenant J. Kane Smith. R. F. A., M. C., who is missing since the 27th May.

Grave or memorial reference: He has no known grave but is listed on the Soissons memorial in France.

KAVANAGH, THOMAS: Rank: Lance Corporal. Regiment or service: Royal Dublin Fusiliers. Unit: 1st Battalion. Date of death: 18 May 1918. Age at death: 25. Service No.: 5024. Born in Leighlinbridge, County Carlow. Enlisted in Carlow. Died of wounds.

Supplementary information: Son of Thomas and Julia Kavanagh, of Church Street, Leighlinbridge, County Carlow. Information from his last will and testament dated 27 July 1917. Effects and property was received by his mother, Mrs Julie Kavanagh, Church Street, Loughlin Bridge, County Carlow. Grave or memorial reference: IX. A. 71. Cemetery: Boulogne Eastern Cemetery in France. Also listed under Leighlinbridge/Old Leighlin on the Great War Memorial, Milford Street, Leighlinbridge, County Carlow.

KAVANAGH, THOMAS OSBORNE JOSEPH: Rank: Lieutenant. Regiment or service: Royal Irish Fusiliers. Unit: 3rd Battalion attached to the 1st Battalion. Date of death: 24 August 1918. Killed in action. He is listed in the supplement of the *London Gazette*, 13 December 1915. From *Kilkenny People*, August 1918:

KAVANAGH—August 24th, 1918, killed in action, Lieutenant T. O. J. Kavanagh, M. C., Royal Irish Fusiliers, aged 26 years, second son of P. J. Kavanagh, Monnacurragh House, Carlow, and Greystones, and nephew of Mr Kavanagh, Jordanstown House, Whitehall. —R. I. P.

Killed in action.
We regret to announce the death in action of Lieutenant T. O. J. Kavanagh, Royal Irish Fusiliers, who was killed while gallantly leading his men on the 24th August lst. Lieutenant Kavanagh, who was

recently presented with the Military Cross for bravery in action, was apprenticed to Mr Fotterell, solicitor, Dublin, and joined the O. T. C. at its formation. His Colonel in a letter to his relatives wrote; --"I cannot let you know how much we feel his loss. He was always wiling to do any work, particularly if it was dangerous work, and he was an officer it will be difficult to replace." Lieutenant Kavanagh was son of Mr P. J. Kavanagh, late of Monnacarragh House, Carlow, and Greystones, and nephew of Mr K. J. Kavanagh, Jordanstown House, Kilkenny.

From *Carlow Sentinel*, September 1918:

Roll of Honour.
This week's list of casualties includes the name of Lieutenant T. O. J. Kavanagh, R. I. F., formerly of Monacurragh House, Carlow, When he joined he was apprenticed to Mr J. G. Fottrell, Solicitor.

He is also listed in 'Wigs and Guns.'
Grave or memorial reference: II. A. 2. Cemetery: Bertenacre Military Femetery, Fletre, Nord in France.

KEALY, PETER: Rank: Bombardier. Regiment or service: Royal Horse Artillery and Royal Field Artillery. Unit: No. 5 'C' Reserve Brigade. Date of death: 2 April 1917. Service No.: 50790. Born in Carlow. Enlisted in Kilkenny. Died at home. Grave or memorial reference: A. 47. Cemetery: Northfleet Cemetery, Kent, UK.

KEARNEY, EDWARD: Rank: Private. Regiment or service: Royal Irish Regiment. Unit: 2nd Battalion. Date of death: 10 September 1917. Service No.: 6790. Born in Bagenalstown, County Carlow. Enlisted in Dublin while living in Bagenalstown, County Carlow. Killed in action. Grave or memorial reference: I. E. 30. Cemetery: Croiselles British Cemetery in France. Also listed under Bagenalstown/Fenagh on the Great War Memorial, Milford Street, Leighlinbridge, County Carlow.

KEATING, EDWARD: Rank: Assistant Cook. Regiment or service: Mercantile Marine Reserve. Unit: HMS *Sarnia*. Date of death: 12 September 1918. Age at death: 18. Service No.: 864594. Fleet Messenger *Sarnia* was torpedoed in the Mediterranean and sunk.
Supplementary information: Son of Julia Tobin (formerly Keating), of Chapel Street, Graigue, Cullen, Carlow, and the late John Keating.
Grave or memorial reference: 31. Memorial: Plymouth Naval Memorial UK.

HMS *Sarnia*.

KEEFE, RICHARD: See **O'KEEFE, RICHARD.**

KEEFFE, JAMES: Rank: Private. Regiment or service: Machine Gun Corps. Unit: Infantry. Date of death: 26 March 1918. Service No.: 43772. Formerly he was with the Royal Irish Regiment where his number was 4889. Born in Carlow. Enlisted in Carlow. Killed in action. Grave or memorial reference: Bay 10. Memorial: Arras Memorial in France. Also listed under Carlow/Graigue on the Great War Memorial, Milford Street, Leighlinbridge, County Carlow.

KEEGAN, JAMES: Rank: Private. Regiment or service: Highland Light Infantry. Unit: 1st Battalion. Date of death: 12 March 1915. Service No.: 11078. Born in Rathville, County Carlo(sic). Enlisted in Coatbridge, Lanarkshire while living in Glenboig, Lanarkshire. Died of wounds. Grave or memorial reference: I. B. 9. Cemetery: Merville Communal Cemetery in France. Also listed under Rathvilly on the Great War Memorial, Milford Street, Leighlinbridge, County Carlow.

KEEGAN, MICHAEL: Rank: Private. Regiment or service: Leinster Regiment. Unit: 2nd Battalion. Date of death: 22 July 1918. Service No.: 5254. Born in Carlow. Enlisted in Athy, County Kildare while living in Carlow. Died. Grave or memorial reference: V. D. 3. Cemetery: Cemetery: Valenciennes (St Roch) Communal Cemetery in France. Also listed under Carlow/Graigue on the Great War Memorial, Milford Street, Leighlinbridge, County Carlow.

KEEGAN, PETER: Rank: Rifleman. Regiment or service: London Regiment (Post Office Rifles). Unit: 8th (City of London) Battalion (Post Office Rifles). Date of death: 29 May 1916. Service No.: 3480. Enlisted in Carlow while living in Carlow. Died. Grave or memorial reference: X. F. 9. Cemetery: Cologne Southern Cemetery in Germany. Also listed under Carlow/Graigue on the Great War Memorial, Milford Street, Leighlinbridge, County Carlow.

KEHOE, JAMES: Rank: Private. Regiment or service: Royal Dublin Fusiliers. Unit: 2nd Battalion. Date of death: 16 August 1915. Service No.: 5588. Born in Dublin. Enlisted in Carlow while living in Tullow, County Carlow. Killed in action. Information from his last will and testament dated 3 May 1915: James Keogh (sic). Effects and property received: Mrs Kehoe, Church Street, Tullow, County, Carlow. Grave or memorial reference: III. B. 7. Cemetery: Sucrerie Military Cemetery, Colinclamps in France. Also listed under Tullow on the Great War Memorial, Milford Street, Leighlinbridge, County Carlow.

KEHOE, MICHAEL: Rank: Sapper. Regiment or service: Royal Engineers. Unit: Formerly he was with the Irish

Guards 170th Tunnelling Company where his number was 5328. Date of death: 3 July 1915. Age at death: 25. Service No.: 86131. Born in Carlisle in Cumberland. Enlisted in Glasgow while living in Avoca.

Supplementary information: Son of Annie Byrne (formerly Kehoe), of Shraughmore, Avoca, County Wicklow, and the late Charles Kehoe. From the *Nationalist* and *Leinster Times,* June 1916:

> Private M. Kehoe, Ballyedmond, Hackettstown, who joined the Irish Guards when war broke out, was killed on July 3rd, 1915, while working a machine gun covering the retreat of his company.

He is also listed in *The Wicklow War* Dead.
Grave or memorial reference: A. 17. Cemetery: Cambrin Military Cemetery in France.

KEHOE, NICHOLAS: Rank: Private. Regiment or service: Irish Guards. Unit: 3rd Battalion. Date of death: 6 March 1918. Service No.: 7585.

Supplementary information: Son of Mr N. Kehoe, of Leighlinbridge, Carlow. This man is not in any other database.

Grave or memorial reference: South of Church. Cemetery: Ballyknocken Church of Ireland Churchyard, Carlow. Also listed under Leighlinbridge/Old Leighlin on the Great War Memorial, Milford Street, Leighlinbridge, County Carlow.

KELLY, DENIS: Rank: Private. Regiment or service: Royal Army Service Corps. Date of death: 11 January 1919 (CWGC) 11 January 1916 (Great War Memorial, Milford Street, Leighlinbridge, County Carlow). Age at death: 36. Service No.: R/384059. This man is not in any other database. Grave or memorial reference: 4. 11. 11. Cemetery: Carlow (ST. Mary's) Cemetery, County Carlow.

KELLY, JAMES: Rank: Private. Regiment or service: Royal Dublin Fusiliers. Unit: 1st Battalion. Date of death: 1 March 1917. Age at death: 21. Service No.: 5574. Born in Dublin. Enlisted in Carlow while living in Tullow, County Carlow. Killed in action.

Supplementary information: Son of Mr and Mrs James Kelly, of Old Chapel Lane, Tullow, County Carlow. Information from his last will and testament dated 19 May 1915. Effects and property was received by his father, Mr James Kelly, Chapel Lane, Tullow, County Carlow.

Grave or memorial reference: Pier and Face 16 C. Memorial: Thiepval Memorial in France. Also listed under Tullow on the Great War Memorial, Milford Street, Leighlinbridge, County Carlow.

KELLY, JAMES: Rank: Private. Regiment or service: Royal Munster Fusiliers. Unit: 2nd Battalion. Date of death: 23 December 1916. Service No.: 6927. Formerly he was with the Royal Army Service Corps where his number was R/4/089319. Born in Ballon, County Carlow. Enlisted in Carlow while living in Ballon, County Carlow.

Died. Grave or memorial reference: IV. E. 4. Cemetery: Dernancourt Communal Cemetery Extension in France. Also listed under Ballon/Rathoe/Aghade on the Great War Memorial, Milford Street, Leighlinbridge, County Carlow.

KELLY, JOHN: Rank: Private. Regiment or service: Royal Dublin Fusiliers. Unit: 1st Battalion. Date of death: 3 September 1916. Age at death: 19. Service No.: 5809. Born in Ballyconnell, County Wicklow. Enlisted in Naas while living in Tullow, County Carlow. Killed in action.

Supplementary information: Son of Mary Kelly, of Ballygalduff, Tobinstown, Tullow, County Callow, and the late Daniel Kelly.

Grave or memorial reference: He has no known grave but is listed on Pier and Face 15 A on the Theipval Memorial in France. Also listed under Carlow/Graigue on the Great War Memorial, Milford Street, Leighlinbridge, County Carlow.

KELLY, PATRICK: Rank: Private. Regiment or service: Royal Dublin Fusiliers. Unit: 2nd Battalion. Date of death: 1 July 1916. Age at death: 43. Service No.: 18666. Born in Carlow. Enlisted in Grimsby while living in Carlow. Killed in action.

Supplementary information: Husband of Mary Edith Kelly, of 51A, Cottage, Back Market Place, Cleethorpes, Grimsby. Served in the Boer War and was wounded. From the *Nationalist* and *Leinster Times*, August 1916:

KELLY—July 1st, 1916, died of wounds received in action in France, No 18666, Private P. Kelly, 2nd battalion, R. D. F., eldest son of Mrs Kelly, Pollerton Road, Carlow. Deeply regretted by his sorrowing mother and children. May the Lord have mercy on his soul—R. I. P.

Eternal honour give him. Hail and farewell to those who died in that full splendour of heroic pride, that we might live."
With thee were the dreams of my first early love.
Every thought of my reason was thine;
In my last humble Spirit above.
Thy name shall be mingled with mine.

Inserted by his loving mother.

From the *Nationalist* and *Leinster Times*, June 1917:

KELLY-First Anniversary of Private P. Kelly, 18656, 2nd Battalion, Royal Irish Fusiliers, who was reported killed in action on the 1st July, at the Battle of the Somme, in France, while fighting for the rights of Humanity. It was God's Will he should pay the great sacrifice, and lay down his life for his Brethren. He is deeply regretted by his sorrowing mother and orphaned children. May he rest in Peace, Amen.
In Memoriam.

The year has grown in tumult and in strife since that far day,

When thou wast cast to everlasting
life across death's way.
Does thy dear spirit at war's horrors
fret,
Or is it bound in peace eternal, do
the dead forget.
When peace they've found, do
dreams of all the mem'ried, part the
world above.
Wing soft their way to whisper thee
at last their living love.
It is a mystery, we can but pray for
our dear dead.
We cannot pierce the dark dividing
way, where souls have fled,
But with the memory of cherished
years build we a shrine,
And set above our tributes and our
tears its light divine.

Inserted by his ever loving mother, Mrs M.
Kenny, 12, Pollerton Road, Carlow.

(See KENNY, MICHAEL JOSEPH.)

Grave or memorial reference:
Pier and Face 16 C. Memorial:
Thiepval Memorial in France. Also
listed under Carlow/Graigue on the
Great War Memorial, Milford Street,
Leighlinbridge, County Carlow.

KELLY, THOMAS: Rank: Gunner.
Regiment or service: Royal Garrison
Artillery. Unit: 4th Siege Battery. Date of
death: 5 January 1917. Age at death: 33.
Service No.: 79335. Born in Leighton
Bridge, County Carlow. Enlisted in
Norwood, Surrey while living in
Wilesden, Middlesex. Killed in action.
Supplementary information: Son of John
and Mary Kelly, of Milford, County

Carlow; husband of Emily E. Kelly, of 16
Offerton Avenue, Normanton, Derby.
Grave or memorial reference:
XXVI. A. 4. Cemetery: Delville Wood
Cemetery, Longueval in France. Also
listed under Leighlinbridge/Old
Leighlin on the Great War Memorial,
Milford Street, Leighlinbridge, County
Carlow.

KEMPSTON, ROBERT JAMES:
Rank: Lieutenant. Regiment or serv-
ice: Royal Dublin Fusiliers. Unit: 2nd
Battalion. Date of death: 24 May 1915.
Killed in action. Grave or memorial ref-
erence: Panel 44 and 46. Memorial: Ypres
(Menin Gate) Memorial in Belgium.
Also listed under Clonegal/Kildavin on
the Great War Memorial, Milford Street,
Leighlinbridge, County Carlow.

KENNEDY, THOMAS: Rank: Private.
Regiment or service: Royal Dublin
Fusiliers. Unit: 1st Battalion. Date of death:
4 January 1916. Service No.: 19914. Born
in Bagnalstown, County Carlow. Enlisted
in Carlow. Died at Sea. Information
from his last will and testament dated
20 November 1915. Effects and property received: (Mother) if not deceased
then (Father) 70 Kilcarrig Street,
Bagenalstown, County Carlow. Grave or
memorial reference: Panel 190 to 196.
Memorial: Helles Memorial in Turkey.
Also listed under Bagenalstown/Fenagh
on the Great War Memorial, Milford
Street, Leighlinbridge, County Carlow.

KENNY, C: Rank: Guardsman.
Regiment or service: Irish Guards. Unit:

2nd Battalion. Date of death: 16 October 1919. Service No.: 4954. This man is only listed in the CWGC database.

Supplementary information: Husband of M. Kenny, of Eagle Hill Lane, Hacketstown, County Carlow.

Grave or memorial reference: RC. 681. Cemetery: Grangegorman Military Cemetery in Dublin.

KENNY, MICHAEL JOSEPH: Rank: Private. Regiment or service: Irish Guards. Unit: 1st Battalion. Date of death: 29 June 1916. Age at death: 22. Service No.: 4608. Born in Carlow. Enlisted in Carlow. Died of wounds. Information from his last will and testament dated 5 August 1914. Effects and property received: (Mother) Mary Kenny, Pullerton Road, Carlow.

Supplementary information: Son of Joseph and Mary Kenny, of 12 Pollerton Road, Carlow. From the *Nationalist* and *Leinster Times,* July 1916:

KENNY—Private Michael Joseph Kenny, aged 22 years, No 4608, 1st Battalion, Irish Guards, who died on 28th June, 1916, from wounds received whilst doing his duty in the first line trenches in France, where he served for 1 year and 10 months.

From the *Nationalist* and *Leinster Times,* June 1917:

KENNY—First Anniversary of private M. J. Kenny, No 4608, 1st battalion, Irish Guards, who died from wounds received while doing his duty in the first line trenches in

France. He was shot by a hidden foe, a cowardly sniper, who took him unawares, and fatally wounded him in the springtime of his manhood, at the age of 22. He lingered a few days, and died on the 28th June, 1916, fully conscious and hopeful for the fight of Humanity. After receiving the last rites and Sacraments of his Church from the hands of the Rev. F. M. Browne and Captain Frank. L. French, Priest and Chaplain, he fervently kissed and gazed on the Cross, the emblem of his faith, as his spirit took its flight to the God of Love to rest in peace for everyone. Amen.

Oh, faithful Cross, Oh, noblest tree
In all our woods there's none like
Thee;
No earthly groves, nor shady bowers,
Produce such leaves, such fruit, such
flowers.
How sweet the nails, how sweet the
wood,
That bore a weight so sweet and
good;
Sing, Oh my soul, devoutly sing.
The glorious laurels of our King.
Sing of the triumph, victory, gained
on the Cross
Erected high where man Redeemer
yields his breath,
And dying, conquers hell and death.
Oh, my boy, my pride and glory.
Is one numbered with the slain.
On earth no more I will behold him
But I hope that in heaven we'll meet
again.

Inserted by his sorrowing and ever loving mother, Mrs M. Kenny, No 12, Pollerton Road Carlow.

Pte Kenny's headstone.

(See **KELLY, PATRICK.** Rank: Private. Service No.: 18666.)

Grave or memorial reference: VIII. B. 26A. Cemetery: Lijssenthoek Military Cemetery in Belgium. Also listed under Carlow/Graigue on the Great War Memorial, Milford Street, Leighlinbridge, County Carlow.

KENNY, PATRICK: Rank: Private. Regiment or service: Connaught Rangers. Unit: 1ˢᵗ Battalion. Date of death: 8 October 1917. Service No.: 5823. Born in Carlow. Enlisted in Carlow while living in Carlow. Died in India. Brother of Michael Kenny above. Information from his last will and testament dated 27 June 1916.

Effects and property received: (Mother) Mary Kenny, Potterton Road, Carlow. Witnessed by H.W.Biddulph, Major, 4ᵗʰ Connaught Rangers. Grave or memorial reference: He has no known grave but is listed on Face E of the Kirkee 1914-18 Memorial in India. Also listed under Carlow/Graigue on the Great War Memorial, Milford Street, Leighlinbridge, County Carlow.

KEHOE, JAMES: See **KEOGH, JAMES.**

KEOGH, T: Rank: Gunner. Regiment or service: Royal Field Artillery. Date of death: 13 October 1920. Age at death: 35. Service No.: 12063.

Supplementary information: This man is not in any other database. Son of the late Timothy Keogh; husband of Annie Keogh, of Tower View, Glencormac, Bray, County Wicklow. Born at Tullow, County Carlow.

Grave or memorial reference: C. A. 35. Cemetery: Acton Cemetery UK.

KEPPEL, JOHN MERCIER: Rank: Private. Regiment or service: Royal Dublin Fusiliers. Unit: 10ᵗʰ Battalion. Date of death: 26 March 1918. Age at death: 41. Service No.: 25352. Born in Dublin. Enlisted in Dublin. Killed in action.

Supplementary information: Son of the late John and Caroline Keppel, of Graigue Hill House, Carlow.

Grave or memorial reference: Panel 79 and 80. Memorial: Pozieres Memorial in France. Also listed under Carlow/Graigue on the Great War Memorial,

Milford Street, Leighlinbridge, County Carlow.

KIDD, SYDNEY GEORGE: Rank: Boy 1st Class. Regiment or service: Royal Navy. Unit: HMS *Viknor*. Date of death: 13 January 1915(CWGC, IMR) 13 October 1915 (Great War Memorial, Milford Street, Leighlinbridge). Age at death: 17. Service No.: J/28053. *Viknor* was an armed Merchant Cruiser. She struck a sea mine off Tory Island and went down with all 295 crew. There were no survivors.

Supplementary information: Born in Bagenalstown. Son of Frederick and Sarah Anne Kidd, of Bagenalstown, County Carlow.

Grave or memorial reference: 8. Memorial: Portsmouth Naval Memorial UK. Also listed under Bagenalstown/Fenagh on the Great War Memorial, Milford Street, Leighlinbridge, County Carlow.

KIERNAN, MICHAEL: Rank: Corporal. Regiment or service: Royal Dublin Fusiliers. Unit: 2nd Battalion. Date of death: 24 May 1915. Service No.: 7683. Born in Caragh, County Kildare. Enlisted in Naas while living in Carlow. Killed in action. Grave or memorial reference: Panel 44 and 46. Memorial: Ypres (Menin Gate) Memorial in Belgium. Also listed under Carlow/Graigue on the Great War Memorial, Milford Street, Leighlinbridge, County Carlow.

KINSELLA, JOHN: Rank: Driver. Regiment or service: Corps of Royal Engineers. Unit: 254 Tunnelling Company. Date of death: 30 January 1916. Service No.: 33220. Born in Graiguenamanagh, County Carlow. Enlisted in London. Died at sea.

Supplementary information: Son of Mrs Margaret Kinsella, of High Street, Graiguenamanagh, County Kilkenny.

Grave or memorial reference: Chatby Memorial in Egypt.

KIRKHAM, WILLIAM LABAN: Rank: Second Lieutenant. Regiment or service: Royal West Kent Regiment. Unit: 9th Battalion. Date of death: 21 October 1916. Age at death, 22. Born in Borris, County Carlow. Died of wounds received in action.

Supplementary information: Son of Mr and Mrs J. Kirkham, of Kinlough, Cong, County Mayo.

Grave or memorial reference: II. A. 25. Cemetery: Contay British Cemetery, Somme, France.

KIRWAN, PATRICK: Rank: Able Seaman. Regiment or service: Royal Navy. Unit: HMS/M 'E14' (Submarine). Date of death: 28 January 1918. Age at death: 23. Service No.: J/11213. Submarine E14 was on a mission from Corfu to the Dardanelles to sink the Turkish Battleship *Goeben* which had already been damaged by seamines and run aground. By the time E14 arrived at the Dardanelles *Goeben* had been refloated and towed away. E14 ran aground and was destroyed by the Turkish Navy and shore based artillery. All the officers were killed and those of the crew that survived were taken prisoner by the Turks. The submarine Commander was posthumously awarded the Victoria Cross, the second Victoria Cross awarded to a Commander of E14.

Supplementary information: Son of John and Annie Kirwan of Bolacrean, Gorey, County Wexford.

Grave or memorial reference: 27. Memorial: Plymouth Naval Memorial UK.

L

LACEY(SDGW, IMR, CWGC) **LACY** (Great War Memorial, Milford Street, Leighlinbridge), **JAMES**: Rank: Private/Lance Corporal. Regiment or service: Royal Irish Regiment. Unit: 6th Battalion. Date of death: 9 September 1916. Service No.: 11264. Born in Carlow Graigue, Carlow. Enlisted in Carlow while living in Clongrennon, Carlow. Killed in action. Grave or memorial reference: Pier and Face 13 A. Memorial: Thiepval Memorial in France. Also listed under Leighlinbridge/Old Leighlin on the Great War Memorial, Milford Street, Leighlinbridge, County Carlow.

LA TOUCHE, AVERELL (ODGW, Great War Memorial, Milford Street, Leighlinbridge). **DIGGES LA TOUCHE, AVERELL** (CWGC) **LA TOUCHE, AVERELL *DIGGS*** (IMR) **AVERELL DIGGES LA TOUCHE** (*Our Heroes*): Rank: Lieutenant. Regiment or service: Royal Irish Rifles. Unit: 5th Battalion attached to 2nd Battalion. Date of death: 25 September 1915. Age at death: 30. Killed in action.

Supplementary information: Son of Major Everard N. and Mrs Clementine Digges La Touche, of 56 Highfield Road, Rathgar, Dublin. From *Our Heroes*:

...killed in action 25th last in France. He was youngest and only surviving son of Mrs E. N. Digges La Touche and the late Major E. N. Digges La Touche, Bengal Infantry and Assam Commission. He was educated at Bedford Grammar School, and afterwards entered the College of Science, Dublin. When the war broke out he immediately volunteered and got a commission in the 5th Royal Irish Rifles, and left for the front on June 21st. He was attached to the 2nd Royal Irish Rifles.

From *Carlow Sentinel*, September 1915:

Lieutenant A. Diggs La Touche. Lieutenant Averell Digges La Touche, reported killed in action in France, between the 25th and the 27th of September, was the youngest son of Mrs E. N. Digges La Touche, Bengal Infantry, and Assam Commission. He was 30 years of age, and volunteered from Carlow immediately the war broke out. He got a commission in the 5th Royal Irish Rifles, and as stationed at Belfast and Holywood Barracks, and went to the front on the 21st of June. He was a well known golfer on the Carlow and other links, was a semi-finalist for Irish Close Championship in 1906 and 1911, and tied for scratch prize in the Irish Open Amateur Championship in 1908. His elder and only brother, Second Lieutenant the Rev Dr Evererard Digges La Touche, 6th Reinforcement, 2nd Battalion, Australian Imperial Force, was also killed in action on August 6th at the

Dardanelles. On going to the front, Lieutenant A. Digges La Touche was attached to the 2nd Battalion Royal Irish Rifles, which regiment was commanded in South Africa by his uncle, Lieutenant Colonel Eagar, who died there of wounds received at Stormberg.

Grave or memorial reference: Panel 40. He has no known grave but is listed on the Ypres (Menin Gate) Memorial in Belgium. Also listed under Leighlinbridge/Old Leighlin on the Great War Memorial, Milford Street, Leighlinbridge, County Carlow.

LAWLESS, WILLIAM: Rank: Sapper. Regiment or service: Corps of Royal Engineers. Unit: 80th Field Company. Date of death: 21 September 1918. Service No.: 40932. Born in Carlow. Enlisted in Carlow. Killed in action. Information from his last will and testament dated 18 March 1917. Effects and property received: (sister) Fannie Lawless, Centaur Street, Tullow, Carlow. Grave or memorial reference: V. L. 6. Cemetery: Peronne Communal Cemetery Extension in France. Also listed under Carlow/Graigue on the Great War Memorial, Milford Street, Leighlinbridge, County Carlow.

LAWLOR, LAURENCE: Rank: Private. Regiment or service: Leinster Regiment. Unit: 2nd Battalion. Date of death: 9 June 1917 Service No.: 3412. Born in Tullow, County Carlow. Enlisted in Maryborough, Queen's County. Killed in action.

Supplementary information: Father of Katie Lawlor, of Upper Augha, Bagenalstown, County Carlow.

Grave or memorial reference: Panel 44. Memorial: Ypres (Menin Gate) Memorial in Belgium. Also listed under Leighlinbridge/Old Leighlin on the Great War Memorial, Milford Street, Leighlinbridge, County Carlow.

LAWLOR, MICHAEL: Rank: Private. Regiment or service: Royal Dublin Fusiliers. Unit: 1st Battalion. Date of death: 15 August 1915. Service No.: 19178. Born in Carlow. Enlisted in Glasgow. Killed in action. Grave or memorial reference: VII. F. 12. Cemetery: Twelve Tree Copse Cemetery in Turkey. Also listed under Carlow/Graigue on the Great War Memorial, Milford Street, Leighlinbridge, County Carlow.

LAWRENCE, WILLIAM: Rank: Private. Regiment or service: Royal Dublin Fusiliers. Unit: 8th Battalion. Date of death: 27 April 1916. Age at death: 28. Service No.: 24563. Born in Hacketstown, County Carlow. Enlisted in Dublin while living in Moyne, County Wicklow. Killed in action.

Supplementary information: Son of Thomas Lawrence, of Slieverue, Ballinglen, County Wicklow.

Grave or memorial reference: He has no known grave but is listed on Panel 127 to 129 on the Loos Memorial in France. Also listed under Hacketstown on the Great War Memorial, Milford Street, Leighlinbridge, County Carlow.

LEAKES/LEEKES, JOSEPH: Rank: Private. Regiment or service: Royal Irish Regiment. Unit: 1st Battalion. Date of death: 10 May 1915. Age at death: 24. Service No.: 10185. Born in Bagenalstown, County Carlow. Enlisted in Kilkenny while living in Shankill, County Kilkenny. Killed in action.

Supplementary information: Son of James and Maria Leakes, of Shankill, Whitehall, County Kilkenny.

Grave or memorial reference: Panel 33. Memorial: Ypres (Menin Gate) Memorial in Belgium. Also listed under Bagenalstown/Fenagh on the Great War Memorial, Milford Street, Leighlinbridge, County Carlow.

LECKY, JOHN RUPERT FREDERICK: Rank: Captain. Regiment or service: Royal Fusiliers. Unit: 7th (Special Reserve)Battalion, attached to 2nd Battalion(9th Foot), Norfolk Regiment. Date of death: 28 September 1915. Age at death: 30. Killed in action.

Supplementary information: Son of John Rupert Robert and Florence Lecky, of Ballykealey, County Carlow. Also served in France with 4th Battalion. Royal Fusiliers. From *Our Heroes*:

… was killed in action in the Persian Gulf operations, was the only son of Mrs Rupert Lecky and the late Mr. J. Rupert Lecky, of Ballykealey, Tullow, County Carlow. He was educated at Elstree, Harrow, and was a member of the Middle Temple. Captain Lecky joined the 7th Battalion, Royal Fusiliers in 1896, and on the outbreak of the war he went to the front, attached to the 4th Battalion, Royal Fusiliers, in November, 1914. On December 14th he was wounded, and on the 16th obtained his Captaincy. At the beginning of May last he left for the Persian Gulf, was in the battle of Nasayral and was killed in action at the taking of Kut el Amara in September last. Captain Lecky was High Sheriff of Carlow in 1912, and is succeeded to the family estate by his uncle, Colonel F. Beauchamp Lecky, D. S. O.

From *Carlow Sentinel*, September 1915:

Captain J. R. F. Lecky.
We learn with sincere regret that Mrs Lecky, BallyKealy, Carlow has received a telegram announcing that her only son, Captain John Ropery Lecky, Royal Fusiliers, attached to the 2nd Norfolks, has been killed in the Persian Gulf campaign. Captain Lecky, who was in his 31st year, was only son of the late Mr Rupert Lecky, and some months since was home slightly wounded. He served as High Sheriff of Carlow in 1914, and represented one of the oldest county families, deriving originally from Stirlingshire, and being in possession of Carlow estate for over 300 years. He was highly popular, and his death will be specially mourned in the Ballon and adjoining districts, where deep sympathy is felt with his bereaved mother, and other relatives.

From the *Nationalist* and *Leinster Times*, October 1915:

A gloom was cast over Ballon and the surrounding district on Tuesday evening when it became known that Captain J. R. F. Lecky, Ballykealy, had been killed in action at the Persian Gulf. Deceased was deservedly popular among all classes in his native district, and deep sympathy is felt with the mother of deceased in her great bereavement. The late Mr Lecky was for some time on active service in Flanders where he was severely wounded. After recovering he joined the Expeditionary force in the Persian Gulf, which only recently gained a victory over the Turks, and in which action Mr Lecky probably lost his life.

From the *Nationalist* and *Leinster Times*, October 1915:

Last week the death of Captain J. R. F. Lecky was briefly announced in our columns. The deceased, who was the only son of Mr Lecky, Ballykealy, County Carlow, was killed in the battle of Kut-el-Amara, one of the most important engagements in the Persian Gulf campaign. Captain Lecky was only in his thirty first year, and only few months ago was home slightly wounded. He acted as High Sheriff for County Carlow two years ago. Th family have been in County Carlow for over three centuries, originally coming from Stirlingshire. In the Ballon district Captain Lecky was deservedly popular, and deep sympathy is being extended to his widowed mother. Amongst other names recently mentioned in the Roll of Honour were Captain Hon. C. M. B. Ponsonby, second son of the Earl and Countess of Bessborough; also Lieutenant and Digges-La-Touche, who volunteered from Carlow at the outbreak of the war.

From De Ruvigny's Roll of Honour:

...only son of the late John Rupert Robert Lecky, of Ballyhealey, Tullow, 8th Hussars, by his wife, Florence Mary (Ardoyne Glebe, Tullow, County Carlow), daughter of the Rev. F. H. Snow Pendleton, Rector of St Sampson's, Guernsey. Born Fenny Bentley, near Ashbourne. County Derby, 3 April 1885. Educated at Elstree, Harrow, and privately. Was a member of the Middle Temple, and Fellow of the Meteorological Society; High Sheriff of Carlow 1912. Joined the Royal Hussars as 2nd Lieutenant in May-1905, and retired in July, 1914, but immediately rejoined on the outbreak of war; was promoted Captain 16-December following. He went to France, attached to the 4th Royal Fusiliers, November-1914. Was wounded twice, the second time in action near Westutre, 14-December and invalided. Left for the Persian Gulf, attached to the 2nd Norfolks early in May. Took part in the taking of Nasiriyeh, and was killed in action at Saffa on the Tigris, 28 Sept 1915, during the taking of Kut-el-Amara. Buried where he fell.

Grave or memorial reference: Panel 10. Memorial: Basra Memorial in Iraq. Also listed under Ballon/Rathoe/Aghade on

the Great War Memorial, Milford Street, Leighlinbridge, County Carlow.

LECKY-PIKE, ROBERT MAXWELL: See **PIKE, ROBERT MAXWELL.**

LENNON, JOHN: Rank: Private. Regiment or service: Connaught Rangers. Unit: 2nd Battalion. Date of death: 14 September 1914. Service No.: 8300. Born in Carlow. Enlisted in Carlow while living in Carlow. Killed in action. Listed in De Ruvigny's Roll of Honour with no new information. Grave or memorial reference: I. G. 6. Cemetery: Vailly British Cemetery in France. Also listed under Carlow/Graigue on the Great War Memorial, Milford Street, Leighlinbridge, County Carlow.

LENNON, MURTAGH: Rank: A/C. S. M. Regiment or service: Royal Dublin Fusiliers. Unit: 9th Battalion. Date of death: 10 September 1916 (SDGW, CWGC, IMR) 25 September 1915 (Great War Memorial, Milford Street, Leighlinbridge). Age at death: 41. Service No.: 15729. Born in Hackettstown, County Carlow. Enlisted in Dublin while living in Norbury. Killed in action.
Supplementary information: Husband of Georgina E. Lennon, of 24, Dalmeny Avenue, Norbury, London. Native of Dublin. Won the DCM.
Grave or memorial reference: XI. F. 8. Cemetery: Guards Cemetery, Lesboeufs in France.

LEONARD, PATRICK: Rank: Private. Regiment or service: Royal Dublin Fusiliers. Unit: 2nd Battalion. Date of death: 29 April 1915. Service No.: 7982. Born in Athy, County Kildare. Enlisted in Naas while living in Athy. Died of wounds. Grave or memorial reference: Panel 44 and 46. Memorial: Ypres (Menin Gate) Memorial in Belgium.

LEONARD, THOMAS: Rank: Private. Regiment or service: Royal Dublin Fusiliers. Unit: 2nd Battalion. Date of death: 26 February 1915. Age at death: 18. Service No.: 11734. Born in Rathvilly, County Carlow. Enlisted in Naas while living in Rathvilly. Killed in action.
Supplementary information: Son of Mary Leonard, of Broughillstown, Rathvilly, County Carlow.
Grave or memorial reference: I. E. 2. Cemetery: Prowse Point Military Cemetery in Belgium. Also listed under Rathvilly on the Great War Memorial, Milford Street, Leighlinbridge, County Carlow.

LOWRY, JOSEPH: Rank: Private. Regiment or service: Royal Defence Corps. Unit: 3rd Battalion. Age at death: 60. Date of death: 23 February 1919. Service No.: 6292. This man is only listed in the CWGC database.
Supplementary information: Served in the Egyptian Campaign (1882-89). 30 years' service. Born at Carlow. Grave or memorial reference: EB. 106. Cemetery: Cardiff (Cathays) Cemetery, Glamorganshire, UK.

LYNCH, JAMES: Rank: Private. Regiment or service: Royal Irish Regiment. Unit: 2nd (Home Service) Garrison. Battalion. Date of death: 23 May 1918. Service No.: 2G/2780(CWGC) 2780(SDGW). Born in Kilkenny. Enlisted in Carlow while living in Kilkenny. Died at home. Formerly he was with the Leinster Regiment where his number was 3765. Grave or memorial reference: In north-east part. Cemetery: Kilkenny (St John) Catholic Churchyard, Kilkenny. Also listed under Leighlinbridge/Old Leighlin on the Great War Memorial, Milford Street, Leighlinbridge, County Carlow.

LYONS, PATRICK: Rank: Private. Regiment or service: Royal Dublin Fusiliers. Unit: 8th Battalion. Date of death: 8 August 1917. Service No.: 10155. Born in Tullow, County Carlow. Enlisted in Carlow. Died of wounds. From the *Nationalist* and *Leinster Times*, August 1917:

> LYONS—On August 8th, at Station Hospital, France, died of wounds received in action, Patrick J Lyons, R. D. F., late of 56 Clarence Street and formerly of Ballymurphy,

Pte Lyons' headstone.

Tullow. Sacred Heart of Jesus have mercy on his soul—R. I. P.

Grave or memorial reference: XVII. D. 11A. Cemetery: Lijssenthoek Military Cemetery in Belgium. Also listed under Tullow on the Great War Memorial, Milford Street, Leighlinbridge, County Carlow.

M

MACDOWELL, CHARLES MICHAEL VERE: Rank: Captain. Regiment or service: Black Watch (Royal Highlanders). Unit: 6th (Perthshire) Battalion (Territorial) (SDGW) 1/6th Battalion (CWGC). Date of death: 28 April 1917. Age at death: 19. Died of wounds.

Supplementary information: Son of Lieutenant Colonel Charles Carlyle Macdowell, CMG, DSO, (RFA), of Montgomery House, Carlow From *Carlow Sentinel*, December 1918:

Roll of Honour.
Lieutenant Colonel. C. C. Macdowell, D. F. C., (Major Reserve of Officers, Royal Artillery). Son of the late C. W. Macdowell, M. D., of Otter Holt, Carlow, has been appointed in the recent King's Birthday Honours, a companion of the order of St Michael and St George, for his services in the final advance at Mons where he commanded four brigades of Artillery. Colonel Macdowell after serving in the early days of the war, as second-in-command of the 6th Battalion, Royal Highlanders (The Black Watch) through the battles of Festubert and Neuve Chapelle, 1915, was selected to command the 281st Brigade, R. F. A., 1 November, 1915, and has continued in command of this brigade on the Western Front since that date. The D. S. O., was awarded to him for his service in the battle of the Somme. He commanded a group pf artillery in all the great battles of the years 1916, 1917, 1918, including Arras, Cambrai, Vimy Ridge, Ypres, Langumark, Bapaume, St Quentin, and Mons. Colonel Macdowell's eldest son, Captain C. M. V. Macdowell, died of wounds received at Gavrelle during the first battle of Arras, 1917, after serving with the famous 51st (highland) Division in France since early in 1915, he was only 19 ½ years, when he was killed.

Grave or memorial reference: VII. A. 6. Cemetery: Boulogne Eastern Cemetery in France.

MAGEE (SDGW, CGWC, IMR), **McGEE** (Great War Memorial, Milford Street, Leighlinbridge, County Carlow.), **ADAM:** Rank: Private. Regiment or service: Royal Dublin Fusiliers. Unit: 1st Battalion. Date of death: 9 May 1915. Service No.: 10030. Born in Craigue, Queen's County. Enlisted in Carlow while living in Craigue. Killed in action in Gallipoli. Grave or memorial reference: He has no known grave but is listed on Panel 190 to 196 on the Helles Memorial in Turkey.

MAGUIRE, THOMAS: Rank: Gunner. Regiment or service: Royal Garrison Artillery. Date of death: 10 March 1919. Service No.: 8570. Born in Carlow. Died in Karachi, India. Grave or memorial reference: Karachi 1914–1918 War Memorial in Pakistan.

MAHER, JOHN: Rank: Private. Regiment or service: Royal Dublin Fusiliers. Unit: 2nd Battalion. Date of death: 20 March 1916. Age at death: 21. Service No.: 5650. Born in Carlow. Enlisted in Carlow. Killed in action.

Supplementary information: Son of Mr and Mrs T. Maher of Pretoria Road, Carlow.

Grave or memorial reference: XIV. A. 2. Cemetery: Bienvillers Military Cemetery in France. Also listed under Carlow/Graigue on the Great War Memorial, Milford Street, Leighlinbridge, County Carlow.

MAHER, MICHAEL: Rank: Lance Corporal. Regiment or service: Royal Dublin Fusiliers. Unit: 2nd Battalion. Date of death: 16 August 1917. Age at death: 26. Service No.: 9824. Born in Carlow. Enlisted in Naas while living in Carlow. Killed in action.

Supplementary information: Foster son of John and Katherine Ryan, of Upper Pollerton Road, Carlow.

Grave or memorial reference: Panel 144 to 145. Memorial: Tyne Cot Memorial in Belgium. Also listed under Carlow/Graigue on the Great War Memorial, Milford Street, Leighlinbridge, County Carlow.

MAHON, WILLIAM: Rank: Lance Corporal. Regiment or service: Leinster Regiment. Unit: 2nd Battalion. Date of death: 12 August 1915. Service No.:

9967. Born in Dublin. Enlisted in Drogheda, County Louth. Killed in action. Grave or memorial reference: II. D. 27. Cemetery: Birr Cross Roads Cemetery in Belgium. Also listed under Tullow on the Great War Memorial, Milford Street, Leighlinbridge, County Carlow.

MANGAN, FRANCIS: Rank: Sapper. Regiment or service: Corps of Royal Engineers. Unit: 56th Field Company (Royal Engineers). Date of death: 16 June 1915 (CWGC, SDGW, IMR), 16 September 1915 (Great War Memorial, Milford Street, Leighlinbridge, County Carlow). Service No.: 22503. Born in Arklow, County Wicklow. Enlisted in Manchester while living in Bagenalstown, County Carlow. Killed in action. From Kilkenny Journal and the *Nationalist* and *Leinster Times*, July 1915:

Killed at the Front.
The many friends of John(sic) Mangan, Bagnalstown, will regret to hear of his death at the early age of twenty years. He joined the army about three years ago and was at the front since the outbreak of the war. [The is no John Mangan in the 1911 census in Bagenalstown but there is a Francis Mangan, aged 17 listed there.]

Grave or memorial reference: Enclosure No. 2 IV. B. 4. Cemetery, Bedford House Cemetery in Belgium and listed under Bagenalstown/Fenagh on the Great War Memorial, Milford Street, Leighlinbridge, County Carlow.

McASSEY, MICHAEL: Rank: Private. Regiment or service: Devonshire Degiment. Unit: 1st Battalion. Date of death: 14 April 1918. Service No.: 31207. Formerly he was with the 2nd Dragoon Guards (Queen's Bays) where his number was 20304. Born in Leighlin Bridge, County Carlow. Enlisted in Aldershot while living in Leighlin Bridge. Killed in action. Grave or memorial reference: Panel 3. Memorial: Ploegsteert Memorial in Belgium. Also listed under Leighlinbridge/Old Leighlin on the Great War Memorial, Milford Street, Leighlinbridge, County Carlow.

McASSEY, MICHAEL: Rank: Private. Regiment or service: Devonshire Regiment. Unit: 9th Battalion. Date of death: 7 May 1917. Age at death: 30. Service No.: 43240. Born in Carlow, Ireland. Enlisted in Plymouth while living in Yelverton, Devon. Killed in action.

Supplementary information: Son of Abraham and Sarah Jane McAssey, of Graigue Hill, Carlow. From the *Nationalist* and *Leinster Times*, May 1917:

McASSEY—Killed in action, instantaneously, during an attack on a German line, Private M. McAssey, 3rd Devon Regiment, second youngest son of Abraham McAssey, Graigue Hill, Carlow.
Thy will be done.

Safe in the arms of Jesus
Safe on his gentle breast
There by his love o'er shaded

Calmly thy soul shall rest.
Inserted by his sorrowing father,
brothers and sisters

Grave or memorial reference: Bay 4. Memorial: Arras Memorial in France. Also listed under Carlow/Graigue on the Great War Memorial, Milford Street, Leighlinbridge, County Carlow.

McCOMBE, ALBERT: Rank: Private. Regiment or service: Canadian Infantry (Alberta Infantry). Unit: 31st Battalion. Date of death: 15 September 1916. Age at death: 34. Service No.: 434797. Born in Mountrath, Queen's County, Ireland. Date of birth: 5th August 1882.

Supplementary informtation: Son of John McCombe, Agency House, Athboy, County Meath. Place and date of enlistment: Calgary, Alberta, 4 July 1915. Occupation on enlistment: Storekeeper. Height, 5 feet, 7½ inches. Complexion, fair. Eyes, blue. Hair, fair.

Grave or memorial reference: He has no known grave but is listed on the Vimy Memorial, Pas-de-Calais, France. Also listed under Clonegal/Kildavin on the Great War Memorial, Milford Street, Leighlinbridge, County Carlow.

McCORMACK, MICHAEL: Rank: Private. Regiment or service: Royal Dublin Fusiliers. Unit: 2nd Battalion. Date of death: 5 July 1916. Service No.: 17002. Born in Rathdrum, County Wicklow. Enlisted in Cork while living in Bagnalstown. Killed in action. Information from his last will and testament dated 2 June 1915. Effects and property received: (Wife)

Mrs Kathleen McCormack, Kilcarrig Street, Bagenalstown, County Carlow. Grave or memorial reference: He has no known grave but is listed on Pier and Face 16 C on the Theipval Memorial in France. Also listed under Bagenalstown/Fenagh on the Great War Memorial, Milford Street, Leighlinbridge, County Carlow.

McCORMACK, PIERCE: Rank: Private. Regiment or service: Irish Guards. Unit: 2nd Battalion. Date of death: 8 March 1915 (CWGC), 8 May 1915 (War Memorial, Milford Street, Leighlinbridge, County Carlow). Age at death: 23. Service No.: 7533. This man is not in SDGW or IMR)

Supplementary information: Son of John McCormack, of 7 High Street, Bagenalstown, County Carlow.

Grave or memorial reference: N. 173108. Cemetery: Brompton Cemetery, London and listed under Bagenalstown/Fenagh on the Great War Memorial, Milford Street, Leighlinbridge, County Carlow.

McCOWAN: See **McGOWAN, EDWARD.**

McCUDDEN, JAMES THOMAS BYFORD: Rank: Major. Regiment or service: Royal Air Corps. Unit: 60th Squadron. Date of death: 9 July 1918. Age at death: 23.

Supplementary information: Awarded VC, DSO and Bar, MC and Bar, MM, Croix de Guerre (France). Son of Amelia E. McCudden, of 'Pitlochry', 37 Burton Road, Kingston-on-Thames, and the late William McCudden. His brothers William T. J. McCudden and John Anthony McCudden also fell. From *London Gazette*, No. 30604, 29 March 1918:

For most conspicuous bravery, exceptional perseverance, keenness and very high devotion to duty. Captain McCudden has at the present time accounted for 54 enemy aeroplanes. Of these 42 have been definitely destroyed, 19 of them on our side of the lines. Only 12 out of the 54 have been driven out of control. On two occasions he has totally destroyed four two-seater enemy aeroplanes on the same day, and on the last occasion all four machines were destroyed in the space of 1 hour and 30 minutes. While in his present squadron he has participated in 78 offensive patrols, and in nearly every case has been the leader. On at least 30 other occasions, whilst with the same squadron, he has crossed the lines alone, either in pursuit or in quest of enemy aeroplanes. The following incidents are examples of the work he has done recently: – On the 23rd December, 1917, when leading his patrol, eight enemy aeroplanes were attacked between 2. 30 p. m. and 3. 50 p. m. Of these two were shot down by Captain McCudden in our lines. On the morning of the same day he left the ground at 10.50 and encountered four enemy aeroplanes; of these he shot two down. On the 30th January, 1918, he, single-handed, attacked five enemy scouts, as a result of which two were destroyed. On this occasion he only returned home when the enemy scouts had been driven far east: his Lewis gun ammunition was all finished and the belt of his Vickers gun had broken. As a patrol leader he has at all times shown the utmost gallantry and skill, not only in the manner in which he has attacked and destroyed the enemy, but in the way he has during several aerial flights protected the newer members of his flight, thus keeping down their casualties to a minimum. This officer is considered, by the record which he has made, by his fearlessness, and by the great service which he has rendered to his country, deserving of the very highest honour.

From *Carlow Sentinel*, January 1918:

Captain McCudden's Feats.
Great Carlow Air Fighting Family.
Captain T. B. McCudden, M. C, R. F. C, who has brought down 37 German aeroplanes, is a son of Mr W. H. McCudden, a Carlow born man, long a warrant-officer in the R. E., whose father and grandfather had also been soldiers. Captain McCudden is not yet 23, and was born in Chatham. He had 3 undecisive fights with the famous German airman Immelman, to whom he paid generous tribute.

His elder brother, Flight-Sergeant W. T. McCudden, was killed while flying at Gosport, in 1915. Another brother, Second Lieutenant J. A. McCudden, has already brought down several German machines, while the youngest of the family is already, at the age of 16, in the Air Service.

Grave or memorial reference: B. 10. Cemetery: Wavans Briish Cemetery, Pas-de-Calais, France. He is also listed on the Carlow Great War Memorial, Milford Street, Leighlinbridge, County Carlow.

McCUDDEN, JOHN ANTHONY: Rank: Second Lieutenant. Regiment or service: Royal Flying Corps. Unit: 84th Squadron. Date of death: 18 March 1918. Age at death: 20. He won the Military Medal and is listed in the *London Gazette*. Killed in action.

Supplementary information: Son of Amelia Emma McCudden, of 'Pitlochry', 37 Burton Road, Kingston-on-Thames and the late William Henry McCudden. His brothers James Thomas Byford McCudden and William T. J. McCudden also fell.

Grave or memorial reference: III. D. 4. Cemetery: St Souplet British Cemetery in France. He is also listed on the Carlow Great War Memorial, Milford Street, Leighlinbridge, County Carlow. Also listed under Carlow/Graigue on the Great War Memorial, Milford Street, Leighlinbridge, County Carlow.

McCUDDEN, WILLIAM: Rank: Sergeant. Regiment or service: Royal Flying Corps. Unit: 13th Squadron. Date of death: 2 May 1915. Age at death: 24. Service No.: 61

Supplementary information: Son of Amelia E. McCudden, of 'Pitlochry',

37 Burton Road, Kingston-on-Thames, and the late William Henry McCudden. His brothers James Thomas Byford McCudden and John Anthony McCudden also fell.

Grave or memorial reference: CC. 959. Cemetery: Chatham (Maidstone Road) Cemetery, Kent. He is also listed on the Carlow Great War Memorial, Milford Street, Leighlinbridge, County Carlow.

McCULLOGH, JOHN: Rank: Corporal. Regiment or service: Royal Dublin Fusiliers. Unit: 1st Battalion. Date of death: 4 October 1917. Service No.: 18288. Born in Tullow, County Carlow. Enlisted in Carlow. Killed in action. Grave or memorial reference: Panel 144 to 145. Memorial: Tyne Cot Memorial in Belgium. Also listed under Tullow on the Great War Memorial, Milford Street, Leighlinbridge, County Carlow.

McDONALD, JAMES: Rank: Gunner. Regiment or service: Royal Horse Artillery and Royal Field Artillery. Unit: 30th Division Ammunition Col. Date of death: 19 April 1916. Age at death: 18. Service No.: 100549. Born in Coolkenno, County Wicklow. Enlisted in Naas, Ireland. Died. Son of Edward and Annie McDonald, of Tulloclay, Tullow, County Carlow. From the *Nationalist* and *Leinster Times*, May 1916:

Roll of Honour.
McDONALD—Killed in France, Gunner James McDonald, 3rd Section, 30th D. C. M., (sic) son of Edward McDonald, Tullowclay, Tullow. —R. I. P.

From the *Nationalist* and *Leinster Times*,. May 1916:

Tullowclay Man's Death in France.
Mrs McDonald, Tullowclay, has received the following letter from "Somewhere in France," April 22nd, 1916:

Dear Mrs McDonald and family— It is with the deepest regret I write these few words to inform you of the death of your son. He was only amongst us a few days, but during that time, we found him a cheerful comrade. He was buried in the village graveyard with full military honours, the local Catholic Padre officiating. It was a most touching incident, and a lot of the villagers attended and showed deep sympathy, They presented a beautiful wreath, as also the officers and non-coms, and men of the No 3 section, to which he had been attached when the sad accident took place. I am enclosing your son's cap badge, which you will no doubt like to keep as a memento of him who came out to do his duty to his King and Country, and who made the supreme sacrifice. I will now close, assuring you of the deepest sympathy of behalf of his comrades in your sad bereavement.
Corporal, J. Kenyon.

No 3 Section, 30 DRC, BEF Grave or memorial reference: South. 3 U. 6 East. Cemetery: Argoeuves Communal

Cemetery in France. Also listed under Tullow on the Great War Memorial, Milford Street, Leighlinbridge, County Carlow.

McDONALD, WILLIAM: Rank: Private. Regiment or service: Royal Irish Regiment. Unit: 2nd Battalion. Date of death: 15 July 1916. Service No.: 11031. Born in Carlow. Enlisted in Carlow. Killed in action. Effects and property received by: (Brother) John McDonald, 5 Granby Row, Carlow. Will witnessed by: (Mother) Bridget McDonald, William Haughton, J.P. for County Carlow. Grave or memorial reference: Pier and Face 3A. Memorial: Thiepval Memorial in France. Also listed under Carlow/Graigue on the Great War Memorial, Milford Street, Leighlinbridge, County Carlow.

McDONNELL, JAMES: Rank: Private. Regiment or service: Royal Dublin Fusiliers. Unit: 6th Battalion. Date of death: 9 August 1915. Age at death: 35. Service No.: 13099. Born in Dublin. Enlisted in Dublin while living in Leighlinbridge, County Carlow. Killed in action in Gallipoli.
Supplementary information: Husband of Annie McDonnell, of Ballyknockan, Leighlinbridge, County Carlow.
Grave or memorial reference: Panel 190 to 196. Memorial: Helles Memorial in Turkey. Also listed under Leighlinbridge/Old Leighlin on the Great War Memorial, Milford Street, Leighlinbridge, County Carlow.

McGEE, ADAM: See **MAGEE, ADAM.**

McCOWAN (C W G C) **McGOWAN** (SDGW, IMR, Great War Memorial, Milford Street, Leighlinbridge, County Carlow), **EDWARD:** Rank: Private. Regiment or service: Connaught Rangers. Unit: 1st Battalion. Date of death: 17 July 1915. Service No.: 5220. Born in Carlow. Enlisted in Liverpool while living in Castlebar, County Mayo. Killed in action.
Supplementary information: Son of Mr E. McCowan, of Sallagher, Ross West, Castlebar, County Mayo.
Grave or memorial reference: V. A. 14. Cemetery: Royal Irish Rifles Graveyard Laventie in France. Also listed under Carlow/Graigue on the Great War Memorial, Milford Street, Leighlinbridge, County Carlow.

McKENNA, EDWARD: Rank: Private. Regiment or service: Royal Irish Fusiliers. Unit: 1st Battalion. Date of death: 14 April 1918. Age at death: 24. Service No.: 41762. Born in Omagh, County Tyrone. Enlisted in Carlow. Killed in action. Formerly he was with the Royal Army Service Corps where his number was S/4/094647.
Supplementary information: Son of Edward and Minnie McKenna, of Tallow Street, Carlow.
Grave or memorial reference: Panel 140 to 141. Memorial: Tyne Cot Memorial in Belgium. Also listed under Carlow/Graigue on the Great War Memorial, Milford Street, Leighlinbridge, County Carlow.

McKENNA, JAMES: Rank: Private. Regiment or service: Leinster Regiment. Unit: 2nd Battalion. Date of death: 10 November 1914. Age at death: 21. Service No.: 9508. Born in Enniskillen, County Armagh. Enlisted in Carlow. Killed in action.

Supplementary information: Son of Edward and Minnie McKenna, of 49 Tallow Street, Carlow, Republic of Ireland.

Grave or memorial reference: 2. E. 2. Cemetery: Canadian Cemetery No. 2 Neuville-Street Vaast in France. Also listed under Carlow/Graigue on the Great War Memorial, Milford Street, Leighlinbridge, County Carlow.

McLINTOCK, JOHN LAWRIE (CWGC, ODGW), **RONALD** (Great War Memorial, Milford Street, Leighlinbridge): Rank: Lieutenant. Regiment or service: Royal Flying Corps. Unit: 19th Squadron. Date of death: 26 February 1918. Killed in action. Grave or memorial reference: He has no known grave but is listed on the Memorial. Arras Flying Services Memorial, Pas-de-Calais, France. Also listed under Leighlinbridge/Old Leighlin on the Great War Memorial, Milford Street, Leighlinbridge, County Carlow.

McLOUGHLIN, CHARLES: Rank: Rifleman. Regiment or service: King's Royal Rifle Corps. Unit: 2nd Battalion. Date of death: 20 August 1916 (CWGC, SDGW), 10 August 1916 (Great War Memorial, Milford Street, Leighlinbridge). Age at death: 30. Service No.: R/10459. Born in Carlow.

Enlisted in London while living in Carlow. Killed in action.

Supplementary information: Son of Charles and Catherine McLoughlin, of Bagenalstown, County Carlow. From the *Nationalist* and *Leinster Times*, September 1916:

McLOUGHLIN—Killed in action, August 20th, Charlie, Lewis machine Gun Section, K. R. R. C., son of Charles McLoughlin, Kilree Street, Bagenalstown. Sacred Heart of Jesus, have mercy on him. —R. I. P.

Grave or memorial reference: Pier and Face 13 A and 13 B. Memorial: Thiepval Memorial in France. Also listed under Bagenalstown/Fenagh on the Great War Memorial, Milford Street, Leighlinbridge, County Carlow.

McMAHON, AUGUSTA MARY: Rank: Mechanic Driver. Regiment or service: Women's Legion, attached to the Army Service Corps. Unit: Date of death: 28 October 1918. Grave or memorial reference: About 5 yards south of the Church. Cemetery: Killeshin Church of Ireland Churchyard in County Laois. She is also listed on the Carlow War Memorial. Also listed under Carlow/Graigue on the Great War Memorial, Milford Street, Leighlinbridge, County Carlow.

McNALLY, JOHN: Rank: Private. Regiment or service: Royal Dublin Fusiliers. Unit: C Company. 2nd Battalion. Date of death: 28 June 1915. Age at death: 43. Service No.: 19512.

Born in Leighlinbridge, County Carlow. Enlisted in Naas while living in Leighlinbridge, County Carlow. Killed in action.

Supplementary information: Husband of Mary McNally, of Rathoman, Leighlinbridge, Bagenalstown, County Carlow.

Grave or memorial reference: Panel 44 and 46. Memorial: Ypres (Menin Gate) Memorial in Belgium. Also listed under Carlow/Graigue on the Great War Memorial, Milford Street, Leighlinbridge, County Carlow.

McNALLY, THOMAS: Rank: Private. Regiment or service: Royal Dublin Fusiliers. Date of death: 28 June 1915. Age at death: 43. The only information I have found on this man comes from his inscription under Leighlinbridge/Old Leighlin on the Great War Memorial, Milford Street, Leighlinbridge, County Carlow.

McNALLY, THOMAS: Rank: Private. Regiment or service: Royal Dublin Fusiliers. Unit: 2nd Battalion. Date of death: 28 April 1915. Age at death: 21. Service No.: 5765. Born in Carlow. Enlisted in Naas while living in Carbury, County Kildare. Killed in action.

Supplementary information: Son of Mrs Mary McNally, of Drihid, Carbury, County Kildare.

Grave or memorial reference: Panel 44 and 46. Memorial: Ypres (Menin Gate) Memorial in Belgium. Also listed under Carlow/Graigue on the Great War Memorial, Milford Street, Leighlinbridge, County Carlow.

MEANEY, EDWARD: Rank: Sergeant. Regiment or service: Australian Infantry, AIF Unit: 3rd Battalion. Date of death: 4 October 1917. Age at death: 29. Service No.: 2646.

Supplementary information: Son of Edward and Anne Meaney, of Leighlin Bridge, County Carlow, Ireland. Born, Glebe, Sydney. Occupation on enlistment, Baker. Age on enlistment: 28 years 3 months. Apprenticiship: 4 years. Next of kin details: (father) Edward Meaney, Church Street, Leighlinbridge, County Carlow. Originally he listed his brother Jeremiah as NOK but changed it later. His personal effects were sent to Anne Meaney of the same address. Place and date of enlistment: Liverpool, N. S. W. 6 June 1915. Weight, 164lbs. Height, 5 feet, 8½ inches. Complexion, fair. Eyes, blue. Hair, fair. Wounded in action in France, July 1916, gunshot to the head and neck. Admitted to 8th General Hospital, Rouen. Transferred by hospital ship *St Patrick* bound for to the War Hospital in Graylingwell, Chichester and Parkhouse, Wareham, England. Admitted there with shell wound to face and throat. Returned to Etaples, France after treatment on April 1917. Rejoined his Battalion in May 1917. Promoted to Sergeant in July 1917. Buried in a temporary grave in Passchendale and exhumed later.

Grave or memorial reference: XLI. A. 24. Cemetery: Tyne Cot Cemetery in Belgium. Also listed under Leighlinbridge/Old Leighlin on the Great War Memorial, Milford Street, Leighlinbridge, County Carlow.

Sgt Meaney, Will.

MEANEY, JAMES: Rank: Private. Regiment or service: Shropshire Light Infantry. Unit: 2nd Battalion. Date of death: 12 April 1915. Age at death: 25. Service No.: 9267. Born in Dublin. Enlisted in Hereford while living in Clonmelch, County Carlow. Killed in action.

Supplementary information: Son of the late Martin and Anne Meaney.

Grave or memorial reference: Panel 47 and 49. Memorial: Ypres (Menin Gate) Memorial in Belgium. Also listed under Carlow/Graigue on the Great War Memorial, Milford Street, Leighlinbridge, County Carlow. Also listed under Leighlinbridge/Old Leighlin on the Great War Memorial, Milford Street, Leighlinbridge, County Carlow.

MERCER, SAMUEL ALEXANDER: Rank: Corporal and Acting Corporal. Regiment or service: Royal Engineers. Unit: Inland Water Transport. Date of death: 22 May 1918. Age at death: 29. Service No.: WR/552234 and also down as 168453. Born in Gorey, County Wexford. Enlisted in Gorey, County Wexford. Died in Mesopotamia.

Supplementary information: Son of George and Anna Mercer. of Gorey. County Wexford.

Grave or memorial reference: I. T. 21. Cemetery: Basra War Cemetery in Iraq. Also listed under Carlow/Graigue on the Great War Memorial, Milford Street, Leighlinbridge, County Carlow.

MILLS, MARTIN: Rank: Private. Regiment or service: Leinster Regiment. Unit: 1st Battalion. Date of death: 12 May 1915. Age at death: 23. Service No.: 9772. Born in Carlow. Enlisted in Carlow. Killed in action.

Supplementary information: Son of the late Mr and Mrs J. Mills, of Carlow.

Grave or memorial reference: Panel 44. Memorial: Ypres (Menin Gate) Memorial in Belgium. Also listed under Carlow/Graigue on the Great War Memorial, Milford Street, Leighlinbridge, County Carlow.

MITCHELL, HERBERT (CWGC) **ROBERT** (SDGW, IMR) **JOSEPH, ROBERT HERBERT J.** (Great War Memorial, Milford Street, Leighlinbridge, County Carlow): Rank: Corporal. Regiment or service: Royal Irish Regiment. Unit: (1597) 7th (South Irish Horse) Battalion. Date of death: 30 November 1917. Age at death: 23. Service No.: 25610. Born in Tullow, County Carlow. Enlisted in Dublin while living in Tullow, County Carlow. Killed in action.

Supplementary information: Son of Joseph and Mary Mitchell, of Tullowland, Tullow, County Carlow. From *Nationalist* and *Leinster Times*, December, 1917:

Mitchell–November 30th, killed in action, Corporal H. J. Mitchell (Bert) South Irish Horse, youngest and dearly loved son of Joseph and Mrs Mitchell, Tullowland, Tullow.

Grave or memorial reference: II. B. 13. Cemetery: Croisilles British Cemetery in France. Also listed under Tullow on the Great War Memorial, Milford Street, Leighlinbridge, County Carlow.

MOLLOY, JAMES: Rank: Private. Regiment or service: Leinster Regiment. Unit: 2nd Battalion (SDGW), 7th Battalion (CWGC & SDGW). Date of death: 3 September 1916. Service No.: 4979. Born in Carlow. Enlisted in Naas, County Kildare. Killed in action. This man is listed twice in Soldiers Died in the Great War where his battalion is shown as 2nd and 7th. All other details are the same. Grave or memorial reference: Pier and Face 16. Memorial: Thiepval Memorial in France. Also listed under Carlow/Graigue on the Great War Memorial, Milford Street, Leighlinbridge, County Carlow.

MONKS, WILLIAM: Rank: Private. Regiment or service: Royal Dublin Fusiliers. Unit: 8th Battalion. Date of death: 30 August 1917. Age at death: 37. Service No.: 28261. Born in Carlow. Enlisted in Carlow. Killed in action.
Supplementary information: Son of James and Mary Monks, of Staplestown Road, Carlow; husband of Bridget Monks, of Canal Side, Athy, County Kildare. From the *Nationalist* and *Leinster Times*, September 1918:

MONKS—First Anniversary—In sad ad loving memory of private Williak Monks, Staplestown Road, killed in action in France, August 30th, 1917. Sweet Jesus have mercy on his soul—R. I. P.

In far of France the stars are gleaming,
Gleaming on a silent grave,
Where he lies sleeping without dreaming.
One loved we loved but could not save.

Inserted by his loving wife and child, father, brothers and sisters.

Grave or memorial reference: I. G. 22. Cemetery: Croisilles British Cemetery in France. Also listed under Carlow/Graigue on the Great War Memorial, Milford Street, Leighlinbridge, County Carlow.

MOORE, CHRISTOPHER: Rank: Private. Regiment or service: Royal Dublin Fusiliers. Unit: 1st Battalion. Date of death: 1 March 1917. Service No.: 5617. Born in Leighlinbridge, County Carlow. Enlisted in Carlow while living in Leighlinbridge, Carlow. Killed in action. Information from his last will and testament dated 5 September 1916. Effects and property received: (Mother) Mrs Mary Moore, Chapel Street, Leighlin Bridge, County Carlow. Grave or memorial reference: Pier and Face 16C. Memorial: Thiepval Memorial in France. Also listed under Carlow/Graigue on the Great War Memorial, Milford Street, Leighlinbridge, County Carlow. Also listed under Leighlinbridge/Old Leighlin on the Great War Memorial, Milford Street, Leighlinbridge, County Carlow.

MOORE, THOMAS: Rank: Private. Regiment or service: Royal Dublin Fusiliers. Unit: 1st Battalion. Date of death: 4 October 1917. Age at death: 22. Service Number: 19712. Born in Arles, Queen's County. Enlisted in Carlow whileliving in Ballickmoyler, Queen's County. Killed in action.

Supplementary infortmation: Son of Daniel Moore, of Rushes, Ballickmoyler, Queen's County Grave or memorial reference: Panel 144 to 145. He has no known grave but is listed on the Tyne Cot Memorial in Belgium. Also listed under Carlow/Graigue on the Great War Memorial, Milford Street, Leighlinbridge, County Carlow.

PRIVATE WILLIAM MOORE.
Royal Irish Regiment,

Pte Moore.

MOORE, WILLIAM: Rank: Private. Regiment or service: Royal Irish Regiment. Unit: 1st Battalion. Date of death: 21 November 1916. Age at death: 23. Service No.: 10534. Born in Bride Street, Wexford. Enlisted in Wexford while living in Bagenalstown, County Carlow. Killed in action in Salonika.

Supplementary information: Son of the late Laurence and Anastatia Moore. From an article in the *People*, 1915:

> Private James Moore, Selskar Street, Wexford, 2nd Battalion, Royal Irish Regiment, is in hospital suffering from a bullet wound in the right leg. Private Moore has been on active service in France since the outbreak of the war. He has another brother, William, also in the firing line.

(See James Moore, No 10370 in the *The Wexford War Dead*.)

Grave or memorial reference: He has no known grave but is listed on the Doiran Memorial in Greece. Also listed under Bagenalstown/Fenagh on the Great War Memorial, Milford Street, Leighlinbridge, County Carlow.

MORAN, JOHN: Rank: Private. Regiment or service: Royal Irish Regiment. Unit: 2nd Battalion. Date of death: 18 July 1918. Age at death: 18. Service No.: 6951. Born in Carlow Craigue, County Carlow. Enlisted in Kilkenny while living in Carlow. Died of wounds.

Supplementary information: Son of James and Bridget Moran, of 6 Sleaty Street, Carlow. Information from his last will and testament dated 5 April 1918. Effects and property received: (Mother) Mrs B Moran, 6 Slatey Street, Leighlin Bridge, County Carlow. Witnessed by J. Redmond, CQMS, 4th Battalion, Royal Irish Regiment, Queenstown, R. Burns, CSM, 4th Battalion.

Grave or memorial reference: III. D. 14. Cemetery: Bagneux British Cemetery, Gezaincourt in France. Also listed under Carlow/Graigue on the Great War Memorial, Milford Street, Leighlinbridge, County Carlow.

MORAN, MICHAEL: Rank: Private. Regiment or service: Irish Guards. Unit: 1st Battalion. Date of death: 18 May 1915. Service No.: 1934. Born in Leighlinbridge, County Carlow. Enlisted in Wicklow. Killed in action. Grave or memorial reference: Panel 4. Memorial: Le Touret Memorial in France. Also listed under Carlow/Graigue on the Great War Memorial, Milford Street, Leighlinbridge, County Carlow. Also listed under Leighlinbridge/Old Leighlin on the Great War Memorial, Milford Street, Leighlinbridge, County Carlow.

MORAN, PATRICK: Rank: Private. Regiment or service: Royal Dublin Fusiliers. Unit: 1st Battalion. Date of death: 3 April 1918. Service No.: 9502. Born in Carlow. Enlisted in Naas while living in Carlow. Killed in action. Grave or memorial reference: Panel 79 and 80. Memorial: Pozieres Memorial in France. Also listed under Carlow/Graigue on the Great War Memorial, Milford Street, Leighlinbridge, County Carlow.

MORGAN, PATRICK: Rank: Private. Regiment or service: Royal Irish Regiment. Unit: 1st Battalion. Date of death: 30 December 1917. Service No.: 1997. According to 'Soldiers Died in the Great War' and 'Ireland's Memorial Records' Patrick was born in Dublin, however, an article by John Kenna in *Carlowviana* page 64 in 2003 claims that he was born in Kilcarrig. Enlisted in Dublin. Died at sea. Grave or memorial reference: He has no known grave but is listed on the Chatby Memorial in Egypt.

MORRIS, ARTHUR RUSSELL: Rank: Private. Regiment or service: Princess Patricias Canadian Light Infantry (Eastern Ontario Regiment). Date of death: 8 May 1915. Age at death: 22. Service No.: 51344.

Supplementary information: Son of J. R. Russel and Annie F. Morris. Killed in action. From an article in the *Enniscorthy Guardian*:

> Private Arthur Russell Morris of Princess Patricias Canadian Light Infantry, has been killed in action. He was son of Mr Joseph R Morris, Somerville, Wexford and was only 21 years of age.

From *Carlow Sentinel*, May 1915:

> Killed in action in France on May 8, 1915, Arthur Russell Morris, Patricias Canadian Light Infantry, elder son of Mr Joseph Russell Morris, Summerville, Wexford (formerly of Carlow), aged 21 years.

Having spent 2 ½ years in Canada, at the outbreak of the war he resigned a good position in the bank there and joined the colours. On the completion of his training in England he left Southampton for France on the 29th of April, and was killed on the 8th of May.

Supplementary infortmation: Next of kin listed as J. R. Morris, Sommerville, Wexford, Ireland. Place of birth: Wexford, Ireland. Date of birth: 27 October 1893. Occupation on enlistment: Bank clerk. Place and date of enlistment: 17 December 1914, Winnipeg. Height, 5 feet, 11 inches. Complexion, dark. Eyes, brown. Hair, black.

Grave or memorial reference: Panel 10. Memorial: Ypres (Menin Gate) Memorial in Belgium.

MORTON, WILLIAM: Rank: Private. Regiment or service: Royal Dublin Fusiliers. Unit: 6th Battalion. Date of death: 8 October 1918. Service No.: 30931 (SDGW) 630931 (CWGC). Formerly he was with the Army Service Corps where his number was S/4/094698. Born in Kilkenny, County Kilkenny. Enlisted in Carlow. Killed in action. Information from his last will and testament dated 30 June 1915. Effects and property received: (Wife) Mrs Margaret Morton, 1 Charlotte Street, Carlow. Grave or memorial reference: G. 7. Cemetery: Beaurevoir British Cemetery in France.

MULHALL, PATRICK: Rank: Private. Regiment or service: Royal Dublin Fusiliers. Unit: 1st Battalion. Date of death: 14 January 1917. Age at death: 23. Service No.: 12132. This man is not in any other database.

Supplementary information: Son of David and Mary Mulhall, of Bridewell Street, Carlow. Died of wounds received in Gallipoli. His brother John, who also served in the Great War, died in 1941 while serving with the 77th Light Anti Aircraft Regiment of the Royal Artillery. He is buried beside him. From *Carlow Sentinel*, January 1917:

The "Last Post" for a Carlow Soldier. On Wednesday afternoon the funeral took place, with military honours, of Corporal Patrick Mulhall, son of Mr David Mulhall, Carlow. Long before the outbreak of war he enlisted in the Irish Rifles, and was bought out by his parents, but on "Kitchener's Army" being enrolled, he promptly joined the 1st Dublins, and was speedily at the brunt of the battle at the eastern front. On the 7th August, 1915, he fell in a fierce engagement at Heli Babi, having been shot through the spine and otherwise wounded with shrapnel. He was surgically treated in military hospitals abroad and at home, and about four months ago, was discharged as incurable, and then returned to his home, where kind friends had provided for him an invalid chair and other comforts, but he lingered on in great suffering until death compassionately came to his relief. His funeral was attended by bearer and firing parties of the Northumberland Hussars, under command of Captain Barnsdale, and followed to its last resting place in

The Graves by a large gathering of relatives and friends. The coffin was borne from the hearse by the military, and after the grave side service had been performed by Reverend Father Lynrin, Adm, three vollies were fired, and the buglers of the Regiment sounded the solemn "Last Post." His bereaved parents desire, through our columns, to return their sincere thanks to the many friends (who provided comforts during his closing months), including clergy and doctors, the ladies of the Red Cross Committee, and others, who paid their tribute of respect and esteem for the brave soldier who died in defence of King and country.

Grave or memorial reference: On North-East boundary. Cemetery: Carlow Old Cemetery, Carlow. Also listed under Carlow/Graigue on the Great War Memorial, Milford Street, Leighlinbridge, County Carlow.

MULHALL, THOMAS: Rank: Private. Regiment or service: Leinster Regiment. Unit: 2nd Battalion. Date of death: 19 January 1918. Age at death: 45. Service No.: 3832. This man is not in any other database.

Supplementary information: Son of David and Mary Mulhall, of Bridewell Street, Carlow; husband of T. Mulhall, of Brewery Lane, Carlow.

Grave or memorial reference: In south-east corner. Cemetery: Carlow Old Cemetery, Carlow. Also listed under Carlow/Graigue on the Great War Memorial, Milford Street, Leighlinbridge, County Carlow.

MULLEE, PETER: Rank: Sapper. Regiment or service: Royal Engineers. Unit: 26th Field Company. Date of death: 9 April 1916. Age at death: 32. Service No.: 18342. Born in Rathvilly, County Carlow. Enlisted in Naas while living in Rathvilly. Killed in action. Information from his last will and testament dated 11 March 1916. Effects and property received: (Mother) Mrs B. Mullee, Rathvilly, County Carlow.

Supplementary information: Son of John and Bessie Mullee, of Bough, Rathvilly, County Carlow, Ireland. From the *Nationalist* and *Leinster Times*, May 1916:

Roll of Honour.
MULLEE-Killed in action in France, Peter Mullee, Royal Engineers, only and very dearly loved son of John and Elizabeth Mullee, Rathvilly. Sacred Heart of Jesus, have mercy on him.

In far off France, the stars are gleaming
Gleaming on a silent grave;
There he lies sleeping, without dreaming
One we loved, but could not save.

Grave or memorial reference: Plot 2. Row B. Grave 3. Cemetery: Ferme-Olivier Cemetery in Belgium. Also listed under Rathvilly on the Great War Memorial, Milford Street, Leighlinbridge, County Carlow.

MULLERY, PATRICK: Rank: Company Quartermaster Sergeant. Regiment or service: Labour Corps. Unit: 733rd Company. Date of death: 20

November 1917. Service No.: 125321. Formerly he was with the Liverpool Regiment where his number was 8946. Born in Graigue, Queen's County. Enlisted in Warrington in Lancashire while living in Liverpool. Died. Grave or memorial reference: XXX. M. 8. Cemetery: Etaples Military Cemetery in France. Also listed under Carlow/Graigue on the Great War Memorial, Milford Street, Leighlinbridge, County Carlow.

MURPHY, DANIEL: Rank: Lance Corporal. Regiment or service: Royal Dublin Fusiliers. Unit: 1st Battalion. Date of death: 5 November 1915. Age at death: 23. Service No.: 9957. Born in Borris, County Carlow. Enlisted in Naas while living in Borris, County Carlow. Killed in action in Gallipoli.

Supplementary information: Son of Daniel and Ellen Murphy, of Knocksquire, Borris, County Carlow.

Grave or memorial reference: II. G. 5. Cemetery: Azmak Cemetery, Suvla in Turkey. Also listed under Borris/Ballyellin on the Great War Memorial, Milford Street, Leighlinbridge, County Carlow.

MURPHY, EDWARD: Rank: Private. Regiment or service: Household Cavalry and Cavalry of the line including the Yeomanry and Imperial Camel Corps. Unit: Corps of Dragoons, 4th Reserve Regiment Dragoons, also listed as 6th Dragoon Guards (Carabiners). Date of death: 28 July 1917. Service No.: 5807. Born in Leighlenbridge, Bognalstown (sic).

Enlisted in Carlow while living in Kilnana, County Carlow. Died at home. Grave or memorial reference: 602. Cemetery: Curragh Military Cemetery, Kildare. Also listed under Leighlinbridge/Old Leighlin on the Great War Memorial, Milford Street, Leighlinbridge, County Carlow.

MURPHY, EDWARD: Rank: Private. Regiment or service: Cheshire Regiment. Unit: 13th Battalion. Date of death: 26 October 1916. Service No.: 32589. Formerly he was with the Irish Guards where his number was 8602. Born in Bagenalstown, County Carlow. Enlisted in Stockport, Cheshire. Died of wounds. Grave or memorial reference: V. E. 14. Cemetery: Puchevillers British Cemetery in France. Also listed under Bagenalstown/Fenagh on the Great War Memorial, Milford Street, Leighlinbridge, County Carlow.

MURPHY, JAMES: Rank: Private. Regiment or service: Royal Irish Regiment. Unit: 2nd Battalion. Date of death: 19 October 1914. Service No.: 8156. Born in Bagenalstown, County Carlow. Enlisted in Carlow. Killed in action. Grave or memorial reference: Panel 11 and 12. Memorial: Le Touret Memorial in France. Also listed under Bagenalstown/Fenagh on the Great War Memorial, Milford Street, Leighlinbridge, County Carlow.

MURPHY, JAMES: Rank: Private. Regiment or service: Royal Irish Regiment. Unit: 2nd Battalion.

Date of death: 24 May 1915. Age at death: 50. Service No.: 6699. Born in Bagenalstown County Carlow. Enlisted in Clonmel while living in Bagenalstown County Carlow. Killed in action.

Supplementary information: Son of Thomas Murphy and Margaret Morrissey, his wife; husband of Mary Murphy, of 5 Hotel Street, Bagenalstown, County Carlow.

Grave or memorial reference: Panel 33. Memorial: Ypres (Menin Gate) Memorial in Belgium. Also listed under Bagenalstown/Fenagh on the Great War Memorial, Milford Street, Leighlinbridge, County Carlow.

MURPHY, JAMES: Rank: Private. Regiment or service: Royal Inniskilling Fusiliers. Unit: 2nd Battalion. Date of death: 1 November 1914. Age at death: 42. Service No.: 6177. Born in Bagnalstown County Carlow. Enlisted in Carlow. Killed in action.

Supplementary information: Son of John and Kate Murphy, of Killree Street, Bagenalstown; husband of Mary Murphy, of 3 Philip Street, Bagenalstown, County Carlow.

Grave or memorial reference: Panel 5. Memorial: Ploegsteert Memorial in Belgium. Also listed under Bagenalstown/Fenagh on the Great War Memorial, Milford Street, Leighlinbridge, County Carlow.

MURPHY, JOHN: Rank: Private. Regiment or service: Royal Dublin Fusiliers. Unit: 1st Battalion. Date of death: 25 September 1916. Age at death: 20. Service No.: 4589. Born in Fullow(sic), County Carlow. Enlisted in Carlow. Died of wounds in Gallipoli. Grave or memorial reference: II. H. 14. Cemetery: Hill 10 Cemetery, in Turkey. Also listed under Tullow on the Great War Memorial, Milford Street, Leighlinbridge, County Carlow.

MURPHY, JOHN: Rank: Private. Regiment or service: Leinster Regiment. Unit: D Company 6th Battalion. Date of death: 11 August 1915. Age at death: 39. Service No.: 877. Born in Carlow. Enlisted in Carlow. Killed in action in Gallipoli.

Supplementary information: Son of James and Mary A. Murphy, of Barrack Street, Carlow; husband of Sarah Murphy, of 14, Little Barrack Street, Carlow. Served in the Boer War.

Grave or memorial reference: Panel 184 and 185. Memorial: Helles Memorial in Turkey. Also listed under Carlow/Graigue on the Great War Memorial, Milford Street, Leighlinbridge, County Carlow.

MURPHY, JOHN: Rank: Corporal. Regiment or service: Royal Dublin Fusiliers. Unit: 2nd Battalion. Date of death: 23 October 1916. Age at death: 19. Service No.: 43037. Formerly he was with the Royal Irish Regiment where his number was 9775. Born in Borris, County Carlow. Enlisted in Wexford while living in Ballycullane, County Kildare. Killed in action.

Supplementary information: Son of Joseph Murphy (Stationmaster), of Ardfert Station, County Kerry; husband of Norah Murphy, of Borris, County Carlow.

Grave or memorial reference: Panel 44 and 46. Memorial: Ypres (Menin Gate) Memorial in Belgium. Also listed under Borris/Ballyellin on the Great War Memorial, Milford Street, Leighlinbridge, County Carlow.

MURPHY, JOHN JOSEPH: Rank: Private. Regiment or service: Royal Irish Rifles. Unit: 2nd Battalion. Date of death: 15 September 1914. Age at death: 22. Service No.: 9849(SDGW), 9819(CWGC). Born in Rathvilly, County Carlow. Enlisted in Belfast while living in Kill O'Grange, Dublin. Killed in action.

Supplementary information: Son of Michael and Anastasia Maria Murphy, of 1 Distillery Road, Clonliffe, Dublin.

Grave or memorial reference: Memorial: La Ferte-Sous-Jouarre Memorial in France. Also listed under Rathvilly on the Great War Memorial, Milford Street, Leighlinbridge, County Carlow.

MURPHY, JOSEPH: Rank: Private. Regiment or service: Royal Dublin Fusiliers. Unit: 2nd Battalion. Date of death: 5 August 1917. Age at death: 23. Service No.: 43036. Formerly he was with the Royal Irish Regiment where his number was 11131. Born in Carlow. Enlisted in Carlow. Killed in action.

Supplementary information: Son of Michael and Anne Murphy, of Pollerton Road, Carlow. Information from his informal last will and testament dated 21 March 1917. Effects and prop-

erty received; (Mother) Ann Murphy, Pollerton Road, Carlow.

Grave or memorial reference: A. 11. Cemetery: Potijze Chateau Lawn Cemetery in Belgium. Also listed under Carlow/Graigue on the Great War Memorial, Milford Street, Leighlinbridge, County Carlow.

MURPHY, MICHAEL: Rank: Private. Regiment or service: Irish Guards. Unit: 1st Battalion. Date of death: 27 September 1918. Age at death: 32. Service No.: 12428. Born in Myshall, County Carlow. Enlisted in Dublin while living in Myshall, County Carlow. Killed in action.

Supplementary information: Husband of Mary Anne Murphy, of Myshall, Bagenalstown, County Carlow.

Grave or memorial reference: I. B. 9. Cemetery: Sanders Keep Military Cemetery, Graincourt-Les-Havrincourt in France. Also listed under Myshall on the Great War Memorial, Milford Street, Leighlinbridge, County Carlow.

MURPHY, MICHAEL: Rank: Rifleman. Regiment or service: Royal Irish Rifles. Unit: A Company. 1st Garrison Battalion. Date of death: 11 June 1916. Age at death: 42. Service No.: G/377. Formerly he was with the Royal Munster Fusiliers where his number was 22563. Born in Dublin. Enlisted in Dublin. Died at home.

Supplementary information: Son of Patrick and Ellen Murphy, of Carlow, Republic of Ireland; husband of the late Ellen Murphy. Buried in Ranikhet New Cemetery.

Private Myles Murphy, Clonegal (Irish Guards) was killed in action on Oct. 23.

Pte Murphy.

Grave or memorial reference: Face 23. Memorial: Madras 1914-1918 War Memorial, Chennai, India. Also listed under Carlow/Graigue on the Great War Memorial, Milford Street, Leighlinbridge, County Carlow.

MURPHY, MYLES JOSEPH: Rank: Private. Regiment or service: Irish Guards. Unit: 1st Battalion. Date of death: 23 October 1915. Age at death: 28. Service No.: 5402. Born in Clonegal, County Wexford. Enlisted in Dublin, County Dublin while living in Johnstown, County Wexford. Killed in action.

Supplementary information: Son of James and Bridget Murphy of Johnstown. Clonegal, County Wexford. From *Enniscorthy Guardian:*

It was with sad regret the news was heard in Clonegal of the death of

Private Myles Murphy, Irish Guards, who was killed in action by a shell on October 23. The gallant young Guardsman had been through several engagements with his company, 1st Irish Guards; of which Lieutenant M. O'Leary, V. C., was Sergeant, and the late Father Gwynne was chaplain. His mother Mrs James Murphy has received many expressions of sympathy in her severe loss, chief amongst them being the deep sympathy of the King and Queen and Lord Kitchener, The Army Service Council, and also Father Knapp, who fortified him with the last rites of the Roman Catholic Church.

Not only was he a member of the National Volunteers, Clonegal, and the local Gaelic Football Club, but also a member of the St Brigid's Fife and Drum Band, Clonegal. He was through the battle of Festubert, Bethune, Givenchy and the bloody battle of Ritcheburg. The gallant young Guardsman sleeps to-day the sleep of the brave in a French Military Cemetery, and may he rest in peace.

From the *Nationalist* and *Leinster Times*, November 1915:

County Carlow Soldier Dead.
The many friends and comrades will learn with deep regret and sorrow of the death of Private Myles Murphy, Irish Guards, who was killed with a shell on October 23rd, in France. He had previously been twice wounded, but returned to the trenches from a Convalescent Camp at Boulogne. He was a brave

Irish Soldier, and had been through several severe engagements under Sergeant Michael O'Leary, and by his bravery and daring won the compliments of his sergeants, officers and comrades. Knowing no fear, he still upheld his old reputation of Myles the Slasher, as he was commonly known to his comrades. He enlisted on September, 1914, and has been in the firing since February. As a national Volunteer, a member of Clonegal football team, St Brigid's Fife and Drum Band, he had the respect, confidence and love of all who knew him. His mother, Mrs J. Murphy, Johnstown, Clonegal, has received many tokens of sympathy in her sad bereavement from Their Majesties the King and Queen, Lord Kitchener, the Army Service Council, and also from his Chaplain, reverend Father Knapp, who fortified him with the rites of the Roman Catholic Church previous to his death. The gallant young Guardsman sleeps to-day the sleep of the brave in a French Military Cemetery. May he rest in peace.

Grave or memorial reference: I. H. 1. Cemetery: Vermelles British Cemetery in France. Also listed under Clonegal/Kildavin on the Great War Memorial, Milford Street, Leighlinbridge, County Carlow.

MURPHY, PATRICK: Rank: Lance Corporal. Regiment or service: Royal Irish Regiment. Unit: 6th Battalion. Date of death: 13 August 1917. Service No.: 6584. Born in Borris, County Carlow.

Enlisted in Kilkenny while living in Borris, County Carlow. Killed in action. Formerly he was with the Royal Field Artillerywhere his number was 466.

Supplementary information: Son of Mrs E. Bolger, of Ballicorey, County Carlow. Grave or memorial reference: VI. G. 12. Cemetery: Tyne Cot Cemetery in Belgium. Also listed under Borris/Ballyellin on the Great War Memorial, Milford Street, Leighlinbridge, County Carlow.

MURPHY, RICHARD VICTOR: Rank: Acting Sergeant. Regiment or service: Royal Dublin Fusiliers. Unit: 1st Battalion formerly 7th Battalion. Date of death: 29 March 1918. Age at death: 32. Service No.: 14200. Born in Ballinrea, County Carlow. Enlisted in Dublin while living in Gowran, County Kilkenny. Killed in action.

Supplementary information: Son of the late William Alexander and Sarah Murphy: husband of Alice Mary Murphy. A Civil servant (Registry of Titles, Dublin).

From De Ruvignys Roll of Honour:

…son of the late William Alexander Murphy, by his wife, Sarah (-) (Gouran, County Kilkenny. Born at Ballinree, Borris, County Carlow, 28 February 1886. Educated at Kilkenny College School, Portarlington and Mountjoy School, Dublin. Was a Civil Servant, Land Registry of Ireland. Eblisted 14 September 1914. Served with the Mediterranean Expeditionary Force at Gallipoli from August-1915, and subsequently with the Serbian Army. Was invalided home in July 1916. On recovery proceeded to France, and was killed in action at Morlincourt, 26 May 1918. He married at the Parish Church, Gouran, Alice Mary, daughter of the Reverend Henry Hare, of Dublin.

Grave or memorial reference: Panel 79 to 80. Memorial: Pozieres Memorial in France. Also listed under Bagenalstown/ Fenagh on the Great War Memorial, Milford Street, Leighlinbridge, County Carlow.

MURPHY, THOMAS: Rank: Gunner. Regiment or service: Royal Garrison Artillery. Unit: 152nd Anti Aircraft Section. Date of death: 14 July 1918. Age at death: 30. Service No.: 39710. Born in Borris, County Carlow. Enlisted in Cork while living in Upper Borris. Killed in action. Information from his last will and testament dated 17 July 1915. Effects and property received: Mrs Annie Murphy, Upper Borris, County Carlow.

Supplementary information: Son of Michael and Annie Murphy, of Court Square, Stradbally, Queen's County Native of Borris, County Carlow.

Grave or memorial reference: K. 53. Cemetery: Jerusalem War Cemetery, Israel. Also listed under Borris/Ballyellin on the Great War Memorial, Milford Street, Leighlinbridge, County Carlow.

MURPHY, WILLIAM JOSEPH: Rank: Captain. Regiment or service: Royal Dublin Fusiliers. Unit: 9th

Battalion. Age at death: 36. Date of death: 9 September 1916. Awards: Mentioned in Despatches. Killed in action.

Supplementary information: Son of Edward and Mary Murphy, of Tullow, County Carlow. Joined Cadet Corps, Leinster Regiment., November 1914; appointed Lieutenant 9th Dublins, December 1914, and Capt., March, 1915. From *Carlow Sentinel*, September 1916:

Roll of Honour.
Captain William Murphy.
We regret to add to the long list of fatalities the name pf another gallant young Carlow Officer, Captain William Murphy, 9th Royal Dublin Fusiliers, who fell mortally wounded whilst leading his men at the brilliant capture of Ginchy, on the 9th inst. He was only son of the late Mr William Murphy and Mrs Murphy, Kill House, Tullow, County Carlow. Full of pluck and daring, and a good all-round sportsman, he joined the ranks two years ago, and gained speedy and well-earned promotion. His death is very deeply deplored, and especially in his native town, where he was a fast favourite, and enjoyed the good will and esteem of all classes of the community, who tender to his esteemed mother (at present on a visit in Australia with her only other child, a married daughter) heartfelt sympathy in her great bereavement. In Captain Murphy we mourn the loss of a greatly esteemed personal friend.

From the *Nationalist* and *Leinster Times*, September 1916:

Captain William Murphy, 9th, R. D. F.

With the greatest sorrow we chronicle this week the death of Captain W. Murphy, who was killed in action either at Ginchy or Guillemont, on 9th inst. Like many another brave Irish soldier he died while bravely leading his men with the dash so characteristic of the Irish officer.

The late Captain Murphy, was a son of the late Mr Edward Murphy, Tullow, the eldest brother of Father Arthur Murphy, C. C., and Dr Murphy of Naas. He was a well known sporting figure in County Carlow, and in 1906 was Captain of the County Rugby Football Club, and probably one of the best players in the United Kingdom.

"Bill"—as he was called—was extremely popular, not only amongst his sporting confreres, but with the public generally, owing to his amiability and other good qualities. In 1908 he left for Australia and began farming there on a large scale and with great success. About the time the war started he was home on holidays, and a few months after the outbreak he joined a cadet corps as a private. Captain Murphy, it may be said, entered the army from purely national motives like the late Tom Kettle, young Sheehy and others. He believed in the wisdom of Mr Redmond's policy and acted accordingly. Having spent some nine months training in County Cork, during which period he reached the rank of Sergeant Major, he received his Lieutenancy, and was transferred to the Royal Dublin Fusiliers, the regiment of his liking. Subsequently he was promoted Captain, and there was every likelihood of further honours. Providence, however, willed otherwise, and Captain Murphy has gone down to a grave of honour after doing what he considered his duty to his country. To the family and relatives we tender our condolences.

From the *Nationalist* and *Leinster Times*, November 1915:

Captain M(sic). J. Murphy, Tullow and Kill, has just visited his home before starting to take his place with his company of the Dublin Fusiliers in the trenches.

From *Carlow Sentinel*, September 1916:

In Memoriam.
Captain "Bill" Murphy, R. D. F.
Killed in action 9th, Sept, 1916.

He died as a true-hearted soldier,
And paid the last forfeit to Right,
He sleeps the calm sleep of a hero
With the boys whom he led in the
fight.
Our Captain—beloved, is departed,
He's gone to His Home in the West,
And we pray that our hero is happy
With God and his comrades at rest.
We envy your lot as a soldier
Asleep on the blood-sodden plain
Enshrined in our History's pages
On the roll of the brave Irish slain
Our patriotism we sang not in
sorrow

For Ireland you died in the strife
You followed the dictates of con-
science
To the victors-the Kingdom of Life.

James D McCarthy.

Grave or memorial reference: Sp. Mem. 4. Cemetery: Guillemont Road Military Cemetery, Guillemont, France.

MURPHY, WILLIAM: Rank: Private. Regiment or service: Royal Dublin Fusiliers. Unit: 4th Battalion. Date of death: 22 May 1916. Age at death: 36. Service No.: 26079. Born in Clough, County Kilkenny Enlisted in Athy while living in Crettyard, County Carlow. Died at home.

Supplementary information: Husband of Alice Murphy, of Crossard, Wolfhill, Athy.

Grave or memorial reference: C 3. Cemetery: Ballyglass Cemetery, County Westmeath. Also listed under Carlow/Graigue on the Great War Memorial, Milford Street, Leighlinbridge, County Carlow.

N

NEALE, WILLIAM ALBERT: Rank: Corporal. Regiment or service: Wiltshire Regiment. Unit: 2nd Battalion. Date of death: 21 March 1918. Age at death: 23. Service No.: 26848. Formerly he was with the Royal Sussex Regiment where his number was 5798. Born in Crettyard, County Carlow. Enlisted in Canterbury, Kent. Born in Crettyard, County Carlow. Killed in action.

Supplementary information: Son of Mrs Sarah Jane Neale, of Crettyard House, Crettyard, Carlow, and the late Leeson Neale.

Grave or memorial reference: Panel 64. Memorial: Pozieres Memorial in France. Also listed under Carlow/Graigue on the Great War Memorial, Milford Street, Leighlinbridge, County Carlow.

NEILL, THOMAS: Rank: Gunner. Regiment or service: Royal Garrison Artillery. Unit: 3rd Siege Battery. Date of death: 13 May 1917. Age at death: 39. Service No.: 22974. Born in Graigue, Carlow. Enlisted in Carlow. Died of wounds. From the *Nationalist and Leinster Times*, May 1917:

NEILL—Killed in action on May 13th, 1917, Tom Neill, Gunner, in the Royal Garrison Artillery, after 20 years service, son of Timothy Neill, Carlow Graigue; to the grief of his sorrowful wife, father, brothers and sisters. Sacred Heart of Jesus have mercy on his soul. —R. I. P.

Grave or memorial reference: II. C. 47. Cemetery: Highland Cemetery, Roclincourt, Pas-de-Calais, France.

NEILL, WILLIAM: Rank: Private. Regiment or service: Royal Munster Fusiliers. Unit: C Company, 2nd Battalion. Date of death: 21 March 1918. Service No.: 18188. Formerly he was with the Royal Dublin Fusiliers where his number was 26608. Born in Tullow, County Carlow. Enlisted in Dublin while living in Dublin. Killed in action.

Supplementary information: Husband of Christina A. Neill, of 5 Church Place, Rathmines, Dublin.

Grave or memorial reference: I. A. 12. Cemetery: Ste. Emilie Valley Cemetery, Villers-Faucon, Somme, France. Also listed under Tullow on the Great War Memorial, Milford Street, Leighlinbridge, County Carlow.

NEVIN, MICHAEL: Rank: Corporal. Regiment or service: Royal Munster Fusiliers. Unit: 1st Battalion. Date of death: 2 September 1918. Age at death: 21. Service No.: 18093. Formerly he was with the Royal Dublin Fusiliers where his number was 8798. Born in Close Sutton, County Carlow. Enlisted in Carlow while living in Close Sutton, County Carlow. Killed in action.

Supplementary information: Brother of John Nevin, of Closutton, Leighlinbridge, Bagenalstown, County Carlow.

Grave or memorial reference: II. C. 4. Cemetery: St Martin Calvaire British Cemetery, St Martin-Sur-Cojeul in France. Also listed under Leighlinbridge/Old Leighlin on the Great War Memorial, Milford Street, Leighlinbridge, County Carlow.

NICHOLLS, WILLIAM THOMAS: Rank: Private. Regiment or service: Royal Dublin Fusiliers. Unit: 8th Battalion. Date of death: 11 August 1918. Service No.: 10441. Born in Sheffield. Enlisted in Naas while living in Carlow. Killed in action. Grave or memorial reference: Panel 44 and 46. Memorial: Ypres (Menin Gate) Memorial in Belgium.

NICHOLSON, WILLIAM: Rank: Private. Regiment or service: Royal Dublin Fusiliers. Unit: 1st Battalion. Date of death: 11 April 1918. Service No.: 28033. Born in Carlow. Enlisted in Manchester while living in Tullow, County Carlow. Died of wounds. Information from his last will and testament dated 12 January 1917. Effects and property received: (Sister) Mrs Alice Nicholson, John Street, Tullow, County Carlow. Grave or memorial reference: P. IX. H. 8B. Cemetery: St Sever Cemetery Extension, Rouen in France. Also listed under Tullow on the Great War Memorial, Milford Street, Leighlinbridge, County Carlow.

NOBLETT, EDWARD WILLIAM: Rank: Private. Regiment or service: Cheshire Regiment. Unit: 1st Battalion.

Date of death: 14 April 1918. Age at death: 27. Service No.: 51255. Formerly he was with the Royal Army Service Corps where his number was R/4/0/66936. Born in Kiledmond, Carlow, Ireland. Enlisted in Bristol while living in Carnew, Ireland. Died of wounds.

Supplementary information: Son of Edward and Mary Noblett, of 147, The Mount, Belfast.

Grave or memorial reference: V. A. 45. Cemetery: Longuenesse (St Omer) Souvenir Cemetery in France. Also listed under Borris/Ballyellin on the Great War Memorial, Milford Street, Leighlinbridge, County Carlow.

NOLAN, CHRISTOPHER: Rank: Private. Regiment or service: Royal Dublin Fusiliers. Unit: 1st Battalion. Date of death: 24 April 1917 Service No.: 26105(CWGC), 28105(SDGW). Born in Carlow Graigue, County Carlow. Enlisted in Carlisle while living in Carlow Graigue, County Carlow. Killed in action.

Supplementary information: Son of John Nolan, of Chapel Street, Graiguecullen, County Carlow.

Grave or memorial reference: Bay 9. Memorial: Arras Memorial in France. Also listed under Carlow/Graigue on the Great War Memorial, Milford Street, Leighlinbridge, County Carlow.

NOLAN, EDMOND/EDMUND, W: Rank: Private. Regiment or service: Royal Dublin Fusiliers. Unit: 7th Battalion. Date of death: 2 March 1917. Service No.: 16858. Born in Carlow. Enlisted in Dublin while living in

Carlow. Died in the Balkans(SDGW).
From *Carlow Sentinel*, March 1917:

Roll of Honour.
NOLAN—On March 2nd, 1917, at King George V. Hospital, Dublin, E. W. Nolan, "Pals" Battalion, R. D. Fusiliers, from malaria contracted o active service, eldest son of Mrs and the late Dr Joseph J. Nolan, Tullow, --R. I. P.

From the *Nationalist* and *Leinster Times*, October 1915:

In Servia.
Amongst those now serving with the forces in Servia are... Private Eddie Nolan, son of the late Dr Nolan, Tullow.

Nationalist and *Leinster Times*, March 1917.

The death of Private Eddie Nolan, Pals Battalion, R. D. F, has evoked very deep regret in Baltinglass district. Deceased was a son of the late Dr J. J. Nolan, Tullow, and a nephew of Mr William. J. Kelly, J. P., Talbotstown. Deceased joined the colours shortly after the outbreak of the war, and contracted malaria while on active service, which ultimately brought about his early demise. The large and representative funeral at Tullow on Sunday was a fitting tribute to the esteem in which deceased was held.

From *Carlow Sentinel* and the *Nationalist* and *Leinster Times*, March 1917:

Roll of Honour.
We regret to announce the death of Mr E. W. Nolan, which sad event took place on Friday of last week, and whose remains were interred in Rathoe on Sunday. At the outbreak of the ar, Mr Nolan joined the "Pals" Battalion R. D. F., and took part in the historic but disastrous landing at Suvla Bay, where so many of his brave countrymen fought their last fight, and in which engagement he was wounded. He subsequently took part in the campaign in Salonika, where he contracted malaria, and was invalided home, but from which he never quite recovered. At the time of his death he had been recommended for a Commission, and remarked to a friend, who happened to meet him, a few days before the sad event, that he was glad to have won it. Mr Nolan was a well-known horseman, and as a prominent follower of the Carlow Hounds and the winner of many Point-to-Point Races, will long be remembered.

We desire to join the sincere and widespread expressions of condolence with the members of his family in their deep bereavement.

Grave or memorial reference: South west of the church. Cemetery: Rathtoe Catholic Churchyard, County Carlow. Also listed under Ballon/Rathoe/Aghade on the Great War Memorial, Milford Street, Leighlinbridge, County Carlow.

NOLAN, EDWARD: Rank: Private. Regiment or service: Royal Dublin

Fusiliers. Unit: 2nd Battalion. Date of death: 18 October 1918. Age at death: 33. Service No.: 12311. Born in Bagnalstown, County Carlow. Enlisted in Naas while living in Bagnalstown, County Carlow. Killed in action.

Supplementary information: Son of Margaret Nolan. Grave or memorial reference: III. C. 11. Cemetery: Highland Cemetery, Le Cateau in France. Also listed under Bagenalstown/Fenagh on the Great War Memorial, Milford Street, Leighlinbridge, County Carlow.

NOLAN, JAMES: Rank: Private. Regiment or service: Royal Irish Regiment. Unit: 2nd Battalion. Date of death: 21 March 1918. Service No.: 11110. Born in Bagenalstown, County Carlow. Enlisted in Kilkenny while living in Townduff, County Carlow. Killed in action. Information from his Nuncupative (or missing) will.Effects and property received: (Mother) Mrs Anne Nolan, c/o Mrs Kerr, Killedmond, Borris, County Carlow. Witnessed by (sisters and brothers) Margaret 11 years, Kate 16 yrs, and Thomas 13 years. Grave or memorial reference: Panel 30 and 31. Memorial: Pozieres Memorial in France. Also listed under Bagenalstown/Fenagh on the Great War Memorial, Milford Street, Leighlinbridge, County Carlow.

NOLAN, JAMES: Rank: Private. Regiment or service: Royal Dublin Fusiliers. Unit: 6th Battalion. Date of death: 4 October 1917. Age at death: 19. Service No.: 19448. Born in Tullow, County Carlow.

Supplementary information: Son of James and Sarah Nolan, of Tullowland, Tullow, County Carlow. Enlisted in Naas while living in Carlow. Died in Egypt. Information from his last will and testament dated 20 March 1917. Effects and property received: (Mother) Mrs Sarah Nolan, Tullowland, Tullow, County Carlow. The *Nationalist* and *Leinster Times*, October 1917:

NOLAN—Pte James Nolan, 19, 448, 6th Royal Dublin Fusiliers, Tullowland, Tullow, joined the army at the outbreak of the war, went to the Dardanelles, got enteric fever, came home, went to France, was wounded twice, and landed in Salonika 17th March, 1917, and died of euraemia, October 4th, 1917, at Alexandria. On whose soul Sweet Jesus have mercy. —R. I. P.
Inserted by his loving parents, sisters and brother.

Grave or memorial reference: C. 34. Cemetery: Alexandria (Hadra) War memorial Cemetery in Egypt. Also listed under Tullow on the Great War Memorial, Milford Street, Leighlinbridge, County Carlow.

NOLAN, LAWRENCE: Rank: Private. Regiment or service: Royal Inniskilling Fusiliers. Unit: 1st Battalion. Date of death: 31 December 1916. Service No.: 28106. Born in Killeshin, Queen's County. Enlisted in Carlow. Died of wounds at home. Grave or memorial reference: In the south west part. Cemetery: Sleaty Old Burial Ground, County Laois. Also listed under Carlow/Graigue on the Great War Memorial, Milford Street, Leighlinbridge, County Carlow.

NOLAN, MICHAEL: Rank: Private. Regiment or service: Highland Light Infantry. Unit: 16th (Service) Battalion (2nd Glasgow). Date of death: 1 July 1916. Service No.: 3275. Born in Carlow. Enlisted in Glssgow. Killed in action. Grave or memorial reference: Pier and Face 15 C. Memorial: Thiepval Memorial in France. Also listed under Carlow/Graigue on the Great War Memorial, Milford Street, Leighlinbridge, County Carlow.

NOLAN, PATRICK: Rank: Private. Regiment or service: Royal Dublin Fusiliers. Unit: 1st Battalion. Date of death: 7 March 1917. Age at death: 21. Service No.: 21565. Born in Close Tullow, County Carlow. Enlisted in Naas while living in Tullow, County Carlow. Died of wounds.

Supplementary information: Son of John and Ellen Nolan, of Mill Street, Tullow, County Carlow.

Grave or memorial reference: III. C. 47. Cemetery: Grove Town Cemetery, Meaulte, France. Also listed under Tullow on the Great War Memorial, Milford Street, Leighlinbridge, County Carlow.

NOLAN, PATRICK: Rank: Private. Regiment or service: Royal Dublin Fusiliers. Unit: 2nd Battalion. Date of death: 26 December 1916. Age at death: 29. Service No.: 22296. Born in Tullow, County Carlow. Enlisted in Naas while living in Tullow. Killed in action.

Supplementary information: Son of Patrick and Margery Nolan, of Ardristan, Tullow, County Carlow. Information from his last will and testament dated 1 February 1916. Effects and property received: (Sister) Mrs Bridget Nolan, Ardristan, Tullow, County Carlow.

Grave or memorial reference: N. 39. Cemetery: Kemmel Chateau Military Cemetery in Belgium. Also listed under Tullow on the Great War Memorial, Milford Street, Leighlinbridge, County Carlow.

NOLAN, PATRICK: Rank: Private. Regiment or service: Irish Guards. Unit: 2nd/2nd Battalion. Date of death: 3 July 1916 (CWGC) 2 July 1916 (SDGW, IMR, Great War Memorial, Milford Street, Leighlinbridge). Age at death: 22. Service No.: 8541. Born in Banalstown County Carlow. Enlisted in Dublin while living in Banalstown(sic) County Carlow. Killed in action.

Supplementary information: Son of Thomas Nolan, of Slyguff, Bagenalstown, County Carlow, and the late Mary Nolan. From the *Nationalist* and *Leinster Times*, April 1917:

NOLAN—Reported Missing the 2nd July, 1916, now reported killed. P. J. Nolan, 2nd Battalion, Irish Guards, second son of Thomas Nolan, Slyguff, Bagenalstown.

Grave or memorial reference: V. A. 28. Cemetery: Poelcapelle British Cemetery in Belgium. Also listed under Bagenalstown/Fenagh on the

Great War Memorial, Milford Street, Leighlinbridge, County Carlow.

NOLAN, PATRICK: Rank: Private. Regiment or service: Royal Munster Fusiliers. Unit: 1st Battalion. Date of death: 21 August 1915. Age at death: 20. Service No.: 10504. Born in Ballon, County Carlow. Enlisted in Naas while living in Ballon, County Carlow. Killed in action in Gallipoli. Formerly he was with the Lancers of the line where his number was 6104.

Supplementary information: Son of John and Mary Nolan, of Ballinvalley, Ballan, County Carlow.

Grave or memorial reference: Panel 185 to 190. Memorial: Helles Memorial in Turkey. Also listed under Ballon/Rathoe/Aghade on the Great War Memorial, Milford Street, Leighlinbridge, County Carlow.

NOLAN, PETER: Rank: Private. Regiment or service: Royal Irish Regiment. Unit: 1st Battalion. Date of death: 24 April 1915. Service No.: 9778. Born in Close Tullow, County Carlow. Enlisted in Carlow. Killed in action.

Supplementary information: Son of James and Margaret Nolan, of Market Square, Carlow. From the *Nationalist* and *Leinster Times*, May 1915:

Nolan—On April, 24th, 1915, Private P. Nolan, 1st Royal Irish Regiment, and late of Pollerton Road, Carlow.
In far off France, the stars are gleaming,
Gleaming o'er a silent grave;
There he lies sleeping, without dreaming.

One we loved, but could not save.
Inserted by his fond aunt and cousins—R. I. P.

Grave or memorial reference: Panel 33. Memorial: Ypres (Menin Gate) Memorial in Belgium. Also listed under Carlow/Graigue on the Great War Memorial, Milford Street, Leighlinbridge, County Carlow.

NOLAN, PROB JAMES JOSEPH: Rank: Surgeon. Regiment or service: Royal Naval Volunteer Reserve. Unit: HMS *Candytuft*. Date of death: 18 November 1917. Age at death: 21. This man is not in any other database.

Supplementary information: Son of Joseph J. Nolan MD and Christina M. Nolan, of 'St Edwards', Adelaide Street, Kingstown. Native of Carlow. 'Candytuft' was torpedoed and sunk.

Grave or memorial reference: 24. Memorial: Plymouth Naval Memorial UK.

NOLAN, STEPHEN: Rank: Private. Regiment or service: Leinster Regiment. Unit: 1st Battalion. Date of death: 14 February 1915. Service No.: 10155. Born in Tullowbeg, County Carlow. Enlisted in Maryborough. Killed in action. Grave or memorial reference: Panel 44. Memorial: Ypres (Menin Gate) Memorial in Belgium. Also listed under Tullow on the Great War Memorial, Milford Street, Leighlinbridge, County Carlow.

NOLAN, THOMAS: Rank: Private. Regiment or service: Royal Dublin

Fusiliers. Unit: 10th Battalion. Date of death: 23 March 1918. Age at death: 33. Service No.: 22297. Born in Tullow, County Carlow. Enlisted in Carlow while living in Tullow, County Carlow. Killed in action. Information from his last will and testament dated 11 April 1916. Effects and property received: (Sister) Mrs Bridget Nolan, Ardristan, Tullow, County Carlow. Brother of Patrick (22296) above.

Supplementary information: Son of Patrick Nolan, of Ardristan, Tullow, County Carlow.

Grave or memorial reference: I. C. 8. Cemetery: Ennemain Communal Cemeteryu Extension, Somme, France. Also listed under Tullow on the Great War Memorial, Milford Street, Leighlinbridge, County Carlow.

NORRIS, THOMAS: Rank: Private. Regiment or service: Irish Guards. Unit: 1st Battalion. Date of death: 6 November 1914. Age at death: 23. Service No.: 3647. Born in Newtownbarry, County Kilkenny. Enlisted in Dublin, County Dublin. Killed in action.

Supplementary information: Son of William and Anne Norris of Kilbranish, Newtownbarry, County Wexford.

Grave or memorial reference: Panel 11. Memorial: Ypres (Menin Gate) Memorial in Belgium. Also listed under Clonegal/Kildavin on the Great War Memorial, Milford Street, Leighlinbridge, County Carlow.

O

O'BRIEN, ANDREW: Rank: Rifleman. Regiment or service: South African Mounted Rifles. Unit: 5th. Date of death: 5 April 1915. Age at death: 31. Service No.: 1988.

Supplementary information: Son of Patrick and Mary O'Brien, of The Parade, Bagnalstown, County Carlow, Ireland.

Grave or memorial reference: A/C. by Spec. Mem. Cemetery: Windhoek Old Municipal Cemetery in Namibia.

O'BRIEN, DANIEL: Rank: Private. Regiment or service: Labour Corps. Unit: 17th Company. Date of death: 28 April 1918. Service No.: 364525. Born in Malahide, Dublin. Enlisted in Dublin while living in Bagenalstown, County Carlow. Died of wounds. Grave or memorial reference: II. A. 4. Cemetery: Arneke British Cemetery in France. Also listed under Bagenalstown/Fenagh on the Great War Memorial, Milford Street, Leighlinbridge, County Carlow.

O'BRIEN, THOMAS: Rank: Private. Regiment or service: Leinster Regiment. Unit: 1st Battalion. Date of death: 28 April 1915(IMR, CGWC, SDGW), 28 May 1915 (Great War Memorial, Milford Street). Service No.: 3713. Born in Carlow. Enlisted in Maryborough, Queen's County. Killed in action. From the *Nationalist* and *Leinster Times*, May 1915:

Carlow Soldier's Death.

Mrs O'Brien, Green Lane, Carlow, has received the following letter, under date of April 29th, from Sergeant Major, J. Matthews, 1st Leinster Regiment, B. E. Force, 82 Brigade; --"I deeply regret to announce that No 3713, Private Tom O'Brien, of my company, was killed in action on yesterday by shell fire. His death was very much regretted by his comrades. He died as a brave Irish soldier, keeping up the traditions of his country and the British Army. On behalf of the Officers, N. C. O's, and men of A Company, we extend to you our deepest sympathy in this your great loss."

Grave or memorial reference: Panel 44. Memorial: Ypres (Menin Gate) Memorial in Belgium. Also listed under Carlow/Graigue on the Great War Memorial, Milford Street, Leighlinbridge, County Carlow.

O'BRIEN, WILLIAM: Rank: Rifleman. Regiment or service: London Regiment (Post Office Rifles). Unit: 2nd/8th Battalion. Date of death: 30 October 1917. Age at death: 19. Service No.: 371350. Born in Fenagh, County Carlow. Enlisted in Bagenalstown County Carlow. Killed in action.

Supplementary information: Son of Thomas and Elizabeth O'Brien, of Barrett Street, Bagnalstown, County Carlow. Information from his informal will dated 9 January 1917. Effects and property received: (Mother) Mrs Elizabeth O'Brien, 18 Barrett Street, Bagenalstown, County Carlow. Witnessed by Richard O'Keeffe, Dublin Road, Carlow, and Patrick Hennessey, Lower Green.

Grave or memorial reference: Panel 150 to 151. Memorial: Tyne Cot Memorial in Belgium. Also listed under Bagenalstown/Fenagh on the Great War Memorial, Milford Street, Leighlinbridge, County Carlow.

O'CONNELL, ROBERT: Rank: Private. Regiment or service: Royal Dublin Fusiliers. Unit: 1st Battalion. Date of death: 25 April 1915. Service No.: 9908. Born in Bagnalstown, County Carlow. Enlisted in Carlow. Killed in action in Galipoli. He has no known grave but is listed on the Special Memorial, B, 73. V Beach Cemetery in Turkey. Also listed under Bagenalstown/Fenagh on the Great War Memorial, Milford Street, Leighlinbridge, County Carlow.

O'DONNELL, THOMAS HENRY: Rank: Private. Regiment or service: Australian Infantry, AIF. Unit: 50th Battalion. Age at death: 27. Date of death: 28 September 1917. Service No.: 6183. Killed in action.

Supplementary information: Son of Thomas Henry and Elizabeth Mary O'Donnell. Native of Tullow, County Carlow, Ireland. Born, Carlow, Ireland. Occupation on enlistment: Bank Clerk. Age on enlistment: 25 years 9 months. Embarked for the battlefields aboard the *Afric*. Place and date of enlistment,

29 September 1916 at Adalaide, South Australia. Weight, 141lbs. Height, 5 feet, 10 ½ inches. Complexion, fair. Eyes, blue. Hair, brown. From *Carlow Sentinel*, May 1915:

These verses (says the "Irish Times") have come to us from Gallipoli. They were written by John P. O'Donnell, Machine Gun Section, 1st Australian Expeditionary Force, who has been at the front since the landing at Anzac in April. Mr O'Donnell is a native of Carlow.

The ghastly moon goes creeping
Across old Seddal Bar,
The sobbing wind goes whispering
Its mournful news afar.
The stars look down upon the land,
The white mist covers all
Those gallant hearts who shed their
blood
And heard their country's call.

Oh! Many a home is desolate,
And many a heart is sore,
Away beneath the Southern Cross,
That far Australian shore.
Their loved ones lie a-sleeping now,
Where Grecian heroes lie;
The same pale moon looks down at
them,
The same stars in the sky.

The teamster cracks his rawhide
thong,
The horses strain anew.
Old Mulga Bill comes rattling in,
As only he can do.
Mick Flannagan's Bar is chock-a-
block,
For half the town is there,

The latest list of casualties
Is spread upon a chair.

A cheery word to Mrs F.,
A nod to lanky Mick;
He shoves his way across the bar,
To where the crowd is thick.
A whisper circles round the place,
The men fall back a pace;
He slowly scans the long, long list,
Until he find the place.

No need to ask for news of him,
The only son he had;
Killed at the front, not twenty yet,
Why! He was but a lad.
A score of hands stretch out to grasp.
He sways, and almost falls;
Then slowly leaves the crowded place,
And heeds not all their calls.

So many another heart is sad
Through all that peaceful land.
The touch of "German Culture" now
Is felt on every hand.
Their fame shall live unsullied,
through ages yet to be;
Those gallant dead in lonely graves
Across the Aegean Sea.

The writer of the above pathetic
lines is a son of Mr T. O'Donnell,
manager of the National bank,
Carlow. He was slightly wounded at
the dardanelles, and afterwards erro-
neously reported as missing. Two
interesting letters from him have
been published in our columns. —
Ed. C. S.
Australian Contingent at the
Dardanelles.
Letter from a Carlow Volunteer.
Writing from the Clan Magillvray

Hospital Ship, Alexandria, on 29th
April, Mrs O'Donnell, National
Bank, Carlow, has received the fol-
lowing; --

Dearest Mater—I suppose you
are all anxious to know how your
soldier boy is. Well, I'm not dead
yet, not by a bit! But have been
wounded, shpt through the side. The
bullet came clean round the shoulder, making a deep flesh wound, and
so preventing me using the rifle for
a day or so.

I am a present at the above
address, as was to be sent to hospital, but owing to a wireless request-
ing all men who could manage to
get around at all to reinforce, myself
and about thirty others on board are
going straight back again voluntarily.
It will take us two days to get there,
and as we are two days on board we
will be pretty fit again by that.
You have seen the papers by now,
so no need to give you much information with regard to fight, except
to say the Australians have covered
themselves with glory, though at a
great sacrifice.

I believe there is only 15% fighting strength of our Brigade left, and
the other Brigade suffered heavily
too, at least those that landed on
that eventful Sunday. Three landings were made on the Peninsula
altogether—the French on one side
(extreme left), English on the right
somewhere, and Australians and
new Zealanders in centre.

We left Lemnos Island 9 a Greek
possession), which we had occupied
for 7 weeks, and on Sunday morning
about 2 a. m. our battalion put out

on a torpedo destroyer for our destination. We were supposed to land under cover of darkness, I think, but it was daybreak when we arrived. The destroyer ran up as close as she could and we slipped out boats and made for the beach. The enemy were on a cliff 100ft high, and entrenched well. They kept up a terrific fire on us—machine guns, shrapnel, and rifle. A number of our fellows never reached the shore, and were swept out to sea, their boat having been hit by shrapnel. We could see the first two companies that landed fix bayonets and get ready to charge. With the exception of one or two we reached the shore all right, though the fire was terrible (the Turks are rotten shots), and jumped into the water, which was in most cases neck deep, and rushed to the beach. No time to write more. The ship is sailing for the Dardanelles.

Jack.

From the *Nationalist* and *Leinster Times*, October 1917:

Pte Tom O'Donnell.

With feelings of sincere regret we announce the death of Private T. H. O'Donnell, National Bank, Carlow. He was killed in battle in France on September 28th, death being instantaneous. News to hand goes to show that he was on fatigue duty at about 10 p. m., when a shell exploded some fifty yards away. Portion of the shell struck him in the breast and arm, The letter home—from a comrade—states that there was a smile on poor O'Donnell's face as he lay on the stretcher, he having been laughing and joking when the missile struck him. After several unsuccessful attempts at enlisting in Australia he finally succeeded and arrived in England in January last with the 5th Battalion Australian Infantry. He had nearly completed his twenty seventh year. To his bereaved parents and other members of the family we tender our sympathy. R. I. P.

His older brother, John Patrick also served in the Australian Army in the Great War, was wounded in 1915 but survived the war. From *Carlow Sentinel*, October 1917:

Private "Tom" O'Donnell.

...Mr MrGrath next proposed a vote of sympathy with Mr T. H. McDonnell and family. He regretted very heartily that the occasion arose to move this vote of sympathy to one whom he had known as a mere child, a boy, a young man, able and willing to defend the rights of liberty and justice. No doubt he was only one of the many who had fallen in this cruel war from their own district, The Council were painfully aware of what gaps had been made in their midst and what sorrow had been brought to many a home within the last three years by reason of this war...

Roll of Honour
Private T. H. O'Donnell, Australian Expeditionary Force.

We learned with deep regret of the death in action of "Tom" O'Donnell, son of T. H. O'Donnell National Bank, Carlow. In a private letter from a dear friend and comrade to his bereaved parents, it appears the gallant lad was on fatigue duty. He was laughing and joking, as was his wont, with the boys, when a German shell burst near by. A splinter hit him on the chest, and he quickly passed peacefully away with a genial smile on his lips. It is a consolation to his afflicted parents that he died nobly doing his duty. He, like his twin brother, "Jack", who has been in the thick of the fighting for two years and a half, and never got a scratch, joined the Australian forces last February. On reaching England deceased had a few days leave in Carlow, where he became invalided through mumps, contracted in the transport, and developed while on leave. On recovering, he went to Salisbury training camp, and was on active service only a few short weeks, when the end of which he had a premonition come. He was a fine type of young man, standing over 6ft 1in, and a great favourite with his many friends in Carlow, who knew him as child, school boy, and youth, and to whom he endeared himself by his genial with and loving characteristics. The sympathy of the town and count go wholeheartedly to his parents in their sorrow. They are, we know, proud of their brave and gallant boy who died that we might live. R. I. P.

At the monthly meeting of the Committee of management of the Carlow Lunatic Asylum on Wednesday, a resolution of sympathy was passed to Mr O'Donnell and family in their great bereavement.

From *Carlow Sentinel*, May 1917:

The Sunken Road.
The following lines, suggested by a scene witnessed after one of their battles, were written by J. P. O'Donnell, 10th Brigade, 1st Australian Imperial Force, son of Mr T. H. O'Donnell, National Bank House, Carlow; --

Cold and biting the winter wind,
Pale the moon in a misty sky,
The sombre elms with ghostly sigh.
Whisper a tale to the moon.
White the road, of a chalky soil,
Mud and debris of horrid war,
Scattered along to the ancient ruin.
Where all through the night in straggling groups.
The weary soldiers toil.
Broken and spent with the hopeless task,
Cursing anon but grim withall
Up and down through the misty night,
Past the Corner of Dead Man's Hall.
Through and fro with their burdens quiet.
Listening perhaps to a comrade's call.
Crackle and whistle across the fields,
Down the road where the elms sigh,
The vicious bullets fall.
Pause a moment a figure there,
Last of a group on a night fatigue,
Gasps and clutches at isty air,
Falls at the Corner of Dead Man's Hall
Comrades pass with their burdens quiet,
Glance at the white and motionless form.
See the face with its boyish smile,

Curly looks in the raven hair;
See the red of his life blood run,
Over the breast in a pale Moon's glare.
Some poor mother in God's own
    Land,
Back where the almond and wattle
    bloom,
Wakes in the night in the darkened
    room,
Whispers a word for her boyish son.
Over there where the angry night,
Huge the secret she'll know too soon.
Down the road where the elms sigh.
Past the Corner of dead Man's Hall;
The wintry wind goes whispering by
At those who have answered The
    Lord's Last Call.

In a letter to his parents, the writer of the foregoing says; --

"At present we are on a different front, and have left the Somme and incidentally many brave lads behind us. Not long before we left that familiar countryside and impressive ceremony was held at Poziers in the centre of that historic ground where so many of our lands fell—the flower of Australia. It was a matter, of course, that the survivors of that engagement on the first anniversary should march ten good miles and true there and ten back in very wet weather; but to pay a tribute to such brave fellows it was done cheerfully. Many Generals were present, and numerous 'lean ways' with red caps, including some French officers and the Skipper, general Birdwood. The graveyard was not very big, and most of the crosses were erected for men who had fallen around that district, but not actually buried on this spot.

The main feature of the ceremony was the unveiling of a great wooden cross mounted on a solid cement foundation with inscription; 'Erected in memory of our comrades who lost their lives in the taking of the village of Pozieres, july 21st-23rd, by the members of the first Australian Division. ' A great Australian flag enveloped the structure from top to bottom, which on the loosening of a string slipped to the ground like clock-work. After a brief service the 'Last Post' was blown by massed bugles, and so we left them there, brave and generous fellows, many of them owning vast stretches of country in the land they left, which they willingly forfeited for a wooden cross in France. On the march home we passed the old first line of captured trenches on our right, which lay in a little hollow covered with little crosses which must have been erected there on spots where the bodies were buried. The gentle slope leading down was covered with them too, even the parapets of the trenches up to the last objective. All that remains of the village of Poziers now is a giant tree trunk, the last of what was once a pretty little village of peaceful inhabitants.

From *Carlow Sentinel*, October 1917:

Roll of Honour.
O'Donnell—September 28, 1917, killed in action in his 27th year, Private Thomas H. O'Donnell, South African Infantry, son of T. H. O'Donnell, Manager, National bank, Carlow.

From the *Nationalist* and *Leinster Times*, May 1915:

Carlow Man with the Australians Private Jack O'Donnell, of the Australian Contingent, writes as follows to his friends in Dublin. It may be mentioned that he threw up a lucrative position in Australia to respond to the call of the Empire for men. He is an old Blackrock College boy, and a son of Mt T. H. O'Donnell, manager, National Bank, Carlow:

"Clan Magillivray" Hospital Ship. Alexandria, 29th April, 1915.

I suppose you are all anxious to know how your soldier boy is. Well, I'm not dead yet, not by a bit, but have been wounded, shot through the side. The bullet came clean through the shoulder making a deep flesh wound, and so preventing me using my rifle for a day or so. I am at present at above address, and was to be sent to hospital, but pwing to a wireless which requested all men who could manage to get around at all to reinforce, myself and about thrity others on board are going straight back again, voluntarily. It will take us two days to get there, and as we are two days on board we will be, most of us, pretty fit again by that.

You must have seen the papers by now, so no need to give you much information with regard to fight, except to say the Australians have covered themselves with glory.

I believe there is only a percentage of fighting strength of our brigade left, and the other brigade suffered heavily toom at least those that landed on that eventful Sunday. Three landings were made on the peninsula altogether—the French on one side (extreme left), English on the right somewhere, and Australians and New Zealanders in centre. We left Lemnos Island (a Greek possession) which we had occupied for seven weeks, and on Sunday morning about 2 a. m., our Battalion put out on a torpedo destroyer for our destination. We were supposed to land under cover of darkness, I think, but it was daybreak when we arrived. The destroyer ran up as close as she could, and we slipped out boats and made for the beach. The enemy were on a cliff about 100 feet high, and entrenched well. They kept up a terrific fire on us—machine guns, shrapnel and rifle. Some of our fellows never reached the shore and were swept out to sea, their boats having been hit by shrapnel. We could see the first two companies that landed fix bayonets and get ready to charge. With the exception of one or two we reached the shore all right, though the fire was terrible (the Turks are rotten shots), and jumped into the water, which was in most cases neck deep, and rushed on to the beach. My rifle got choked with sand straight.

No time to write more. Jack
[John Patrick O'Donnell was a brother of Thomas Henry O'Donnell.]

O'Donnell, Will.

Grave or memorial reference: Sp. Mem. No. 4. Cemetery: Aeroplane Cemetery in Belgium. Also listed under Tullow on the Great War Memorial, Milford Street, Leighlinbridge, County Carlow.

O'DONNELL, THOMAS: Rank: Private. Regiment or service: Leinster Regiment. Unit: 2nd Battalion. Date of death: 26 October 1917. Service No.: 5343. He is also listed on the Blackrock Roll of Honor: -'National Bank House, Carlow, County Carlow. Blackrock College (1906-1908). Killed in action at age 26 on the 26th October 1917 at Passchendale during the 3rd Battle of Ypres.' Enlisted in Carlow while living in Carlow. Died. From *Carlow Sentinel*, February 1915:

Carlow Volunteers at the Front.
We feel pleasure in ------ another to the list of young Carlow men who have volunteered for serv-

ice at the front in defence of king and Country, in the person of Mr T. H. O'Donnell, Jnr ("Tom", son of Mr T. H. O'Donnell, manager of the National Bank, Carlow. Following the example of his twin brother "Jack" (both brothers holding lucrative positions in Austrlia), who is now serving with the South Australian contingent in Egypt, Tom has joined the Fourth South Australian contingent. We warmly congratulate both young townsmen on their pluck and patriotism, and trust that the "fortunes of war" may prove favourable until "peace with honour" ends the terrible struggle.

From *Carlow Sentinel*, December 1917:

Roll of Honour.
The death in action, announced in the Roll of honour on Friday, 23rd ult, of "Bim" Nolan, and a few weeks ago of "Tom" O'Donnell— which we recorded with regret in our columns—has inspired the following feeling lines from a personal friend of both, and an esteemed correspondent; --
In Memoriam of Two Carlow Heroes.

You fought the fight for Ireland, boy,
Your mother bows her head
And weeps with pride she bore a son
Whose in the list of dead.
Her brave and gallant lad is gone,
A hero in the fight,
And he is with the chosen Race
And mingles with the right.

You fought the fight for Ireland,
boy
And died in Glory's ray
With men who heard the bugle call
And marched the shell-pocked way.
Your name's enshrined in Honour
Roll,
Incarnadined in red.
You'll tramp again to trumpet
sound
Triumphant Risen Dead!

Information from his informal will dated 20 February 1917. Effects and property received: (Mother) Mrs Lizzie O'Donnell, Staplestown Road, Carlow. I have not been able to establish who "Bim" Nolan was, or even if he died. No soldier named Nolan, B., died in 1917.

Grave or memorial reference: IV. F. 13. Cemetery: Niederzwehren Cemetery in Germany. Also listed under Carlow/ Graigue on the Great War Memorial, Milford Street, Leighlinbridge, County Carlow.

O'FARRELL, PATRICK: Rank: Private. Regiment or service: Irish Guards. Unit: 2nd Battalion. Date of death: 16 January 1918. Service No.: 7716. Born in Carlow. Enlisted in Dublin. Died. From *Nationalist* and *Leinster Times*, March 1918:

With deep regret we announce the sad news of the death in action of Private Patrick O'Farrell ooon 16th January last. He was eldest son of mr John O'Farrell, ex-R. I. C, Carlow, late of Carlow Graigue. The deceased joined the Army pay

Corps in the outbreak of war and later volunteered for active service with the 2nd Irish Guards in France, where he was in several engagements and was twice wounded. To all who knew him he endeared himself by his kindly and unassuming disposition.

From *Nationalist* and *Leinster Times*. February, 1918:

O'Farrell—Private Patrick (Pat) O'Farrell, 2nd Irish Guards. Killed in France, January 16 last. Deeply regretted by his sorrowing family and friends. —R. I. P.

Grave or memorial reference: VII. A. 28. Cemetery: Faubourg D'Amiens Cemetery, Arras in France. Also listed under Carlow/Graigue on the Great War Memorial, Milford Street, Leighlinbridge, County Carlow.

O'GRADY, STANDISH DE COURCY: Rank: Lieutenant Colonel. Regiment or service: Royal Army Medical Corps. Awarded; CMG, DSO. Date of death: 23 December 1920. Age at death: 48.

Supplementary information: Son of Captain Standish de C. O'Grady; husband of Esther Alice O'Grady, (daughter of Colonel Philip Doyne Vigor, Ester died in 1970) of Holloden, Bagenalstown, Ireland. Born at Limerick. M. B. Educated at Tonbridge School, Tonbridge, Kent and Trinity College, Dublin. Graduated with a B. A in Surgery and Obstretics (BAO). Commissioned in 1898. Fought in the

East African campaign and was mentioned in despatches. During the Great War he was mentioned in despatches three times and was decorated with the award of Companion, Distinguished Service Order in 1917 and invested as a Companion, Order of St Michael and St George in 1918. He had three children. Gerald Vigors de Courcey O'Grady, Faith O'Grady, and Philip Henry Vigors de Courcy O'Grady. From the *British Medical Journal*, 22 January 1921, page 144:

Deaths in the Services.
Lieutenant Colonel Standish de Courcy O'Grady, C. M. G., D. S. O., R. A. M. C., died at the Military Hospital, Malta, on December 23rd, aged 47. He was born at Dresden on July 27th, 1872, and educated at trinity College, where he graduated M. B., B. Ch., and B. A. O., in 1866. Entering the army as surgeon lieutenant on July 27th, 1898, he became captain in 1901 and Lieutenant Colonel on March 1st, 1915, and was appointed temporary colonel on October 30th, 1916. he had also qualified as a specialist in State medicine at the R. A. M. C. College. He served in East Africa in the Somailand campaign of 1904, was mentioned in despatches in the *London Gazette* of September 2nd, 1904, and received the medal with a clasp. In the recent war he was thrice mentioned in despatches; in the Gazette of February 17th, 1915, may 29th, 1917, and December 30th, 1918; received the 1914 star, with the war medal and the Victory medal, the D. S. O. on June 3rd, 1917, and the C. M. G. on January 1st, 1919.

Grave or memorial reference: B. XIX. Cemetery: Pieta Military Cemetery, Malta.

O'KEEFE (S D G W I M R) **O'KEEFFE** (CWGC) **KEEFE** (Great War Memorial, Milford Street, Leighlinbridge, County Carlow), **RICHARD:** Rank: Rifleman. Regiment or service: London Regiment. Unit: 8th (City of London) Battalion (Post Office Rifles). Date of death: 20 September 1917. Service No.: 371325. Born in Carlow. Enlisted in Carlow while living in Tullow. Killed in action. Brother of Thomas O'Keeffe below. Grave or memorial reference: XLI. E. 10. Cemetery: Poelcapelle British Cemetery in Belgium.

O'KEEFE/O'KEEFFE, THOMAS: Rank: Lance Corporal. Regiment or service: Royal Dublin Fusiliers. Unit: 1st Battalion. Date of death: 5 July 1915. Service No.: 11022. Born in Ballykealy, County Carlow. Enlisted in Naas while living in Ballykealy. Killed in action in Gallipoli. After his death his effects and property received by Mrs Eileen O'Keeffe, Dublin Road, Carlow. From De Ruvigny's Roll of Honour:

...29th Division, Mediterranean Expeditionary Force. Eldest son of the late Richard O'Keeffe, by his wife, Ellen (Dublin Road, Carlow), daughter of Andrew O'Neill. Born in Ballykealy Ballon, County Carlow, 10-December-1892. Educated at the Christian Brothers Academy, Carlow. Enlisted

10-Jaunary-1911. Was appointed Lance Corproal in 1912, and promoted Corporal in 1913. Served in India from November-1913 to November-1914. Left England with his regiment for the Dardanelles on 16-March-1915. Took part in the landing there 25-26-April, and was killed in action at Gallipoli 10(sic)-July-1915. A comrade wrote of him; "On one occasion we were advancing and the enemy's trenches were about three or four hundred yards in front. At this time we were halted in a ravine preparing to advance, and the enemy's fire was very heavy; at any rate, the Sergeant shouted at his men that there was a wounded man in front; would some of them go out and take him in? But the fellows all passed it down the line that there was a wounded man out in front; would someone go and bring him in? At any rate Tom heard it, and asked immediately where the wounded man was. The Sergeant showed him, and Tom shouted round at me, 'Will you come, terry?' Then without waiting for an answer he was out over the top, and between us we got the chap in. He told us he had been lying out there two days—in reality he had been there since about 11 a. m. that morning, it was then abut 6 p. m. he was wounded in the shoulder, side, arm and thigh, and had lost an awful lot of blood. He was in that much pain that he thought he had been there two days. The Dublins and Munsters were that weak then that they combined the two regiments and called us the Dubsters. Well, after bringing in that chap we advanced and succeeded in routing the Turks and dug ourselves in in a new position, from which the New Zealanders relieved us next day. Well, that is just one of the many little moves I was in with old Tom. Now I wasn't present when Tom was killed. I was in the trenches, and Tom was in charge of a ration party going back along a nullah to draw the company's rations, when he was killed by a sniper. It appears this sniper had command of the nullah, and blankets and sandbags barricades were put to knock off the sniper, but all to no purpose, he must have been concealed on a hill. It was him that killed poor Tom. The bullet pierced is brain, and he only lived for a couple of minutes afterwards during which time he was unconscious, so never spoke after being hit. The medical officer was present on the spot, but could not do anything. Tom is buried in a very nice cemetery in a separate grave." His younger brother, Richard O'Keeffe, is now (1916) on active service with the London Regment. (See Richard O'Keeffe above).

Grave or memorial reference: VII. C. 21. Cemetery: Twelve Tree Copse Cemetery in Turkey. Also listed under Ballon/Rathoe/Aghade on the Great War Memorial, Milford Street, Leighlinbridge, County Carlow.

O'LEARY, EDWARD: Rank: Private. Regiment or service: Royal Dublin Fusiliers. Unit: 8/9th Battalion. Date of death: 29 November 1917. Age at death,

41. Service No.: 14728. Born in Carlow. Enlisted in Dublin. Died of wounds.

Supplementary information: Husband of Catherine O'Leary, of 41 Usher's Quay, Dublin.

Grave or memorial reference: H. 5. Cemetery: St Leger British Cemetery in France. Also listed under Carlow/ Graigue on the Great War Memorial, Milford Street, Leighlinbridge, County Carlow.

O'MARA (CWGC and also in his records), **O'MEARA** (Great War Memorial, Milford Street, Leighlinbridge, County Carlow), **MATTHEW:** Rank: Private. Regiment or service: Australian Infantry, AIF. Unit: 15th Battalion. Date of death: 15 October 1917. Age at death: 41. Service No.: 6542.

Supplementary information: Son of Daniel and Jane O'Mara. Parents were both dead at the time of enlistment. Native of Carlow Ireland. Born, Lockland, Carlow. Occupation on enlistment: Labourer and stock keeper. Age on enlistment: 39 years 5 months. Next of kin details: (Brother)Patrick O'Mara, Mount Macquarie Station, Blackhall, Queensland. Parents deceased, medals were to be sent to his brother. Place and date of enlistment: Emerald, Queensland, 12 July 1916. Embarked at Brisbane aboard the *Boonah* and disembarked in Plymouth. Went to Etaples, France March 1917 from Folkestone. Weight, 9st 10lbs. Height, 5 feet, 7 inches. Complexion, fair. Eyes, gray. Hair, brown. Enlisted while living in Northampton Downs, Blackhall, Barcoo, O"Land (sic). Location of death; 'Traffic Control', 4th Australian Division,

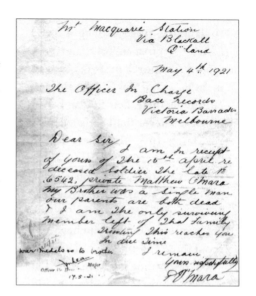

Pte O'Mara, brother's letter.

Ypres Menin Road. Age on entering Australia, 8 years 4 months.

Grave or memorial reference: I. E. 4. Cemetery: Birr Cross Roads Cemetery in Belgium. Also listed under Carlow/ Graigue on the Great War Memorial, Milford Street, Leighlinbridge, County Carlow.

O'MEARA: See **O'MARA, MATTHEW.**

O'NEILL, PATRICK LAWRENCE: Rank: Private. Regiment or service: Canadian Motor Machine Gun Brigade. Unit: 1st. Date of death: 22 April 1917. Age at death, 47. Service No.: 47640.

Supplementary information: Husband of Mary. A. M. O'Neill, of 122 Hudson Road, Plumstead. London, England. Born in Meerut, Bengal. Enlisted in Valcartier, 23 September 1914. Occupation on enlistment: Soldier.

Date of Birth: 14 January 1873. Previous Military Experience: RNW. MP, Cape Mtd, 10 years, RCD. Height, 5 feet, 10½ inches. Complexion, fair. Eyes, hazel. Hair, grey. I include this man as he is listed in *Carlow Sentinel*, May 1917:

Roll of Honour.
O'Neill—killed in action, Patrick L. O'Neill, Canadian Expeditionary Force, only surviving so of Edward O'Neill, Gotham, Carlow. R. I. P. Canadian papers please copy.

Grave or memorial reference: III. D. 14. Cemetery: Bois-Carre British Cemetery, Thelus, Pas-de-Calais, France.

O'NEILL, PETER: Rank: Driver. Regiment or service: Army Service Corps. Unit: 208th Company. Date of death: 6 January 1918. Age at death: 38. Service No.: T4/057358. Born in Ballymurn, County Wexford. Enlisted in Carlow while living in Carlow. Died in the Balkans.

Supplementary information: Son of Owen and Mary O'Neill of Ballyboy, Enniscorthy, County Wexford; husband of Kate O'Neill of Newtownforbes, County Longford.

Grave or memorial reference: 1338. Cemetery: Salonika (Lembet Road) Military Cemetery in Greece. Also listed under Carlow/Graigue on the Great War Memorial, Milford Street, Leighlinbridge, County Carlow.

O'NEILL, THOMAS: Rank: Private. Regiment or service: Leinster Regiment. Unit: 2nd Battalion. Date of death: 18 October 1914. Service No.: 7081. Born in Borris-in-Ossory, Queen's County. Enlisted in Birr, King's County. Killed in action. Grave or memorial reference: I. B. 14. Cemetery: Houplines Communal Cemetery Extension in France.

O'NEILL, THOMAS: Rank: Private. Regiment or service: Royal Dublin Fusiliers. Unit: 1st Battalion. Date of death: between 28 February 1917 and 1 March 1917. Service No.: 11429. Born in Tullow, County Carlow. Enlisted in Naas while living in Tullow, County Carlow. Killed in action. After his death his effects and property were received by: Miss Julia O'Neill, Ounagh, Tullow, County Carlow. Grave or memorial reference: Pier and Face 16 C. Memorial: Thiepval Memorial in France. Also listed under Tullow on the Great War Memorial, Milford Street, Leighlinbridge, County Carlow.

O'REILLY, MICHAEL J.: Rank: Lance Bombardier. Regiment or service: Royal Garrison Artillery. Unit: Sussex RGA (TF). Date of death: 15 August 1918. Age at death, 41. Service No.: 374474. Born in Carlow. Enlisted in Brighton. Died.

Supplementary information: Husband of E. W. O'Reilly, of 17, Ditchling Road, Brighton.

Grave or memorial reference: III. B. 14. Rosiers Communal Cemetery Extension in France. Also listed under Carlow/Graigue on the Great War Memorial, Milford Street, Leighlinbridge, County Carlow.

O'ROURKE, JIMMY: Rank: Private. Regiment or service: Connaught Rangers. Date of death: 30 September 1914. Age at death: 18. The information above comes from his inscription under Leighlinbridge/Old Leighlin on the Great War Memorial, Milford Street, Leighlinbridge, County Carlow. SDGW shows only one O'Rourke that died serving with the Connaught Rangers and he died in 1918. According to the CWGC the only James O'Rourke killed in 1914 was: O'ROURKE, JAMES. Rank: Private. Regiment or service: Irish Guards. Unit: 1st Battalion. Date of death: 6 November 1914. Service No.: 2820. Born in Kilkenny, County Kilkenny. Enlisted in Kilkenny. Killed in action. Grave or memorial reference: He has no known grave but is listed on Panel 11 on the Ypres (Menin Gate) Memorial in Belgium.

O'ROURKE, WILLIAM: Rank: Private. Regiment or service: Royal Dublin Fusiliers. Unit: 1st Battalion. Date of death: 1 March 1917. Service No.: 5354. Born in Carlow Graigue, Carlow. Enlisted in Carlow. Killed in action. Grave or memorial reference: Pier and Face 16 C. Memorial: Thiepval Memorial in France. Also listed under Carlow/Graigue on the Great War Memorial, Milford Street, Leighlinbridge, County Carlow.

O'SHEA, DAVID: See **SHEA, DAVID.**

O'SHEA, LAURENCE: Rank: Private. Regiment or service: Royal Dublin Fusiliers. Unit: 3rd Battalion. Age at death: 18. Date of death: 9 June 1915. Service No.: 5622. Born in Carlow. Enlisted in Dublin while living in Athy. Died of wounds.

Supplementary information: Son of Laurence and Elizabeth O'Shea, of Pollerton Road, Carlow, Ireland. Date of will: 9 May 1915. Effects and property received by: (Mother) Mrs Lizzie O'Shea, Kilkenny Road, Carlow.

Grave or memorial reference: Plot 1. Row L. Grave 8. Cemetery: Ferme-Olivier Cemetery in Belgium.

O'SULLIVAN, FRANCIS: Rank: Private. Regiment or service: Cheshire Regiment. Unit: C Company. 8th Battalion. Date of death: 16 April 1916. Age at death: 34. Service No.: 11260. Born in Bovis, Crannagh, Leinster, Ireland. Enlisted in Altrincham, Cheshire while living in Dublin. Died of wounds in Mesopotamia.

Supplementary information: Son of Daniel O'Sullivan, of Borris, County Carlow; husband of Elizabeth O'sullivan, of 15, Upper Buckingham Street, Dublin.

Grave or memorial reference: Panel 14 and 62. Memorial: Basra Memorial in Iraq.

P

PACK-BERESFORD, CHARLES GEORGE: Rank: Major. Regiment or service: Queen's Own (Royal West Kent Regiment). Unit: 1st Battalion. Date of death: 24 August 1914(CWGC) 10 September 1914 (ODGW, Great War Memorial, Milford Street, Leighlinbridge, County Carlow). Age at death: 45.

Supplementary information: Son of Denis William Pack-Beresford, DL, of Fenagh, County Carlow, and Annette Caroline Pack-Beresford (*née* Browne). Killed in action. Served on the North-West Frontier (India), 1897-8, and in the Boer War (Mentioned in Despatches). From 'Bond of Sacrifice':

> ...was born on the 21st of November, 1869, and was the son of denis W. Pack-Beresford, Esq., J. P., D. L., M. P., County Carlow, of Fenagh House, Bagenalstown, Ireland, and grandson of Major-General Sir Denis Pack, K. C. B.
>
> He was educated at Wellington College and the R. M. C., Sandhurst, joining the Royal West Kent Regiment as Second Lieutenant in November, 1889, becoming Lieutenant in February, 1893/. From December, 1896, to March, 1900, he was Adjutant of his Battalion, having become Captain in December, 1899, and major in March, 1908. Major Pack-Beresford was employed on the North-West Frontier of India, 1897-98, having been in Malakand and the action at Landaki; at opera-
> tions in Bajaur and in the Mamund country; at Buner in the attack and capture of the Tanga Pass. For these services he received the medal with clasp.
>
> He also served in the South African War from 1900-02, and was engaged in operations in the Orange River Colony, in 1900; in the Transvaal and Cape Colony in 1900 and 1901. he was mentioned in Despatches ("*London Gazette*" September 1901), and received the Queen's medal with four clasps. From 1903-09, Major Pack-Beresford was Officer of a Company of Gentlemen Cadets at the R. M. C., Sandhurst. He commanded the Depot of his regiment at Maidstone from 1910 to 1911. Killed in action at Wasimes, near Mons, 24-August-1914.

From *Carlow Sentinel*, August 1914:

> Major C. G. Pack-Beresford.
> Killed in action.
> The announcement of the death in action of major C. G. Pack Beresford, Kent Regiment, which appeared on the sad "honor list" issued on Wednesday, has caused intense grief to the members of his family and a large circle of friends in this his native county. Until the sorrowful news was received on Tuesday by his brother, Mr D. R. Pack-Beresford, D. L., Fenagh House, Carlow, his family were not aware that he had

reached the fighting zone. He fell with many other gallant defenders of King, Fatherland, and the Empire—hero's to a man. On both sides Major Pack-Beresford was descended from families famous in British military honours. He was second son of the late Captain Denis Pack-Beresford, who was elected Parliamentary representative of County Carlow with the late Mr Bruen, in 1865. He was grandson of the late Major-general Sir Denis Pack, K. C. B; who five times received the thanks of Parliament for his military services. Major Pack-Beresford's mother was Lady Elizabeth Louisa Beresford, youngest child of George, first Marquis of Waterford. In compliance with the will of the late Right Hon. William Carr Viscount Beresford, K. C. B., he assumed by Royal licence, in 1854, the additional name of Beresford on succeeding to that nobleman's estate in the County of Carlow, and married in 1863 Anette Caroline, only daughter of the late Robert Clayton Browne, Esq., D. L., of Browne's Hill, Carlow. It is a remarkable co-incidence that the late Major Pack-Beresford died on the battle ground not far distant from the field of Waterloo, where his distinguished ancestor, Captain Pack, won his greatest military achievements. At Thursdays meeting of the Carlow Board of Guardians, a resolution of sympathy with the family of the late Major Pack-Beresford, was adopted.

From De Rivigny's Roll of Honour:

Pack Beresford, Charles George, Major. 1st Battalion, Queen's Own Royal West Kent Regiment. 3rd son of Denis William Pack-Beresford, J. P., D. L., of Fenagh House, Bagnalstown, County Carlow, by his wife, Annette Caroline, only daughter of Robert Clayton Browne, of browne's Hill, County Carlow. Born in London on 21-November-1869. Educated at Wellington College and Sandhurst. Gazetted 2nd lieutenant in the Queen's Own, 20-November-1889. Became Lieutenant, 01-February-1893, Captain, 18-December-1899, and Major, 21-March-1908, being Adjutant 1897-1900, an instructor at the R. M. C., sandhurst, 1903-6, and Major in command of 3rd Battalion, regimental Depot, Maidstone, 1911-1914. Served with the Malakand and Buner field force on the North West Frontier of India, 1897-8, including action at Landakal, the operations in the Mamund country and Buner, also during the attack and capture of the Tanga Pass (medal with clasps); in the South African War, 1899-1901, including the operations in the Orange Free State, September, 1900-July, 1901, and in cape Colony in August, 1901, September to December 1901 (Despatches (*London Gazette*, 10-September-1910); Queen's medal with four clasps); and with the Expeditionary Force in France. Killed in action at Wasimes, near Mons, 24-August-1914.

From *Carlow Sentinel* August 1914:

How Major Pack-Beresford fell.

A Lance Corporal of the Queens Own (Royal west Kent) regiment, who was also wounded at Mons where the West Kents lost four officers killed, including Major Pack-Beresford, describes (in the "Times") what he saw of the fight;
--

We reached Mons on Saturday afternoon, August 22, the day before the battle. We at once commenced to entrench, and were still engaged on this work when the Germans fired their first shell, which wrecked a house about 20 yards away. Then, we got ready for the fight. We made loopholes in a wall near the house and remained there foe 15 hours under heavy fire of shrapnel. . The Germans came across the valley in front of us in thousands, but their rifle fire as they advanced was absolutely rotten, and much damage as they did was done by the big guns which covered their advance. Numerically the Germans were far superior to us, and as soon as one lot was shot down another took its place.

We retired from Mons about 4 o'clock on Monday morning to a little village on the borders of France. We kept up a rear-guard action all the way, and it was in that I was wounded. A shell dropped close to me, and some fragments penetrated my left leg. I was thrown to the ground, and for a time lay unconscious. When I recovered I found my rifle and ammunition were missing, having, I suppose been taken by the Germans who evidently thought I was dead. I last saw Major Pack-Beresford, who was in charge of "B" Company, about an hour before he fell. He was leading his men to the top of a hill, and I heard him shout, as he rushed forward, "Come on, boys; they are all ours," referring to some advancing Germans.

Grave or memorial reference: He has no known grave but is listed on La Ferte-Sous-Jouarre Memorial in France. Also listed under Bagenalstown/Fenagh on the Great War Memorial, Milford Street, Leighlinbridge, County Carlow.

PARR, DENIS: Rank: Sergeant. Regiment or service: Royal Dublin Fusiliers. Unit: G Company, 10th Battalion. Date of death: 29 May 1917. Age at death: 23. Service No.: 11208. Born in Carlow. Enlisted in Carlow. Died of wounds.

Supplementary information: Son of Frank and Lily Parr; husband of A. Parr, of 10, Centenary Row, Old Youxhall Road, Cork.

Grave or memorial reference: IV. M. 28. Cemetery: Duisans British Cemetery, Etrun in France. Also listed under Carlow/Graigue on the Great War Memorial, Milford Street, Leighlinbridge, County Carlow.

PARR, FRANCIS: Rank: Private. Regiment or service: Irish Guards. Unit: 1st Battalion. Date of death: 6 November 1914. Service No.: 4229. Born in Carlow.

Enlisted in Carlow. Died of wounds. Grave or memorial reference: III. B. 38. Cemetery: Boulogne Eastern Cemetery in France. Also listed under Carlow/Graigue on the Great War Memorial, Milford Street, Leighlinbridge, County Carlow.

PARR, PATRICK: Rank: Private. Regiment or service: Royal Dublin Fusiliers. Unit: D Company. 9th Battalion. Date of death: 9 September 1916. Age at death: 32. Service No.: 21892. Formerly he was with the Royal Garrison Artillery where his number was 44246. Born in Carlow. Enlisted in Carlow. Killed in action.

Supplementary information: Son of Francis and Elizabeth Parr; husband of Annie Parr, of Charlotte Street, Carlow. Date of will: 2 August 1915. Effects and property received by: (Wife) Annie Parr, Charlotte Street, Carlow. From the *Nationalist* and *Leinster Times*:

Roll of Honour.

Parr—Killed in action in France, on 9th September, 1916, Private Patrick Parr, dearly beloved husband of Annie Parr, Charlotte Street, Carlow. On whose soul, Sweet Jesus, have mercy. Immaculate Heart of Mary, pray for him.
A light from our household gone,
A voice we loved is stilled.
A place is vacant in our bosom.
That never can be filled.

Inserted by his sorrowing wife and children.

Grave or memorial reference: Pier and Face 16 C. Memorial: Thiepval Memorial in France. Also listed under Carlow/Graigue on the Great War Memorial, Milford Street, Leighlinbridge, County Carlow.

PENDER, ANDREW J.: Rank: Private. Regiment or service: Irish Guards. Unit: 2nd Battalion. Date of death: 31 July 1917. Age at death: 35. Service No.: 2267. Born in Ballyadams, Queen's County. Enlisted in Wigan, Lancashire while living in Oldleigh, Queen's County. Killed in action.

Supplementary information: Son of Michael and Alice Pender, of Oldleigh, Ballickmoyler, Carlow.

Grave or memorial reference: I. B. 2. Artillery Wood Cemetery in Belgium. Also listed under Carlow/Graigue on the Great War Memorial, Milford Street, Leighlinbridge, County Carlow.

PENDER, MICHAEL: Rank: Driver. Regiment or service: Royal Engineers. Unit: 129th Field Company. Date of death: 12 February 1916. Age at death: 21. Service No.: 90757. Born in Rathtoe, County Carlow. Enlisted in Carlow while living in Kellestown, County Carlow. Killed in action.

Supplementary information: Son of Bridget Pender, of Kellistown, Tullow, County Carlow. Grave or memorial reference: I. G. 19. Cemetery: Menin Road South Military Cemetery in Belgium. Also listed under Ballon/Rathoe/Aghade on the Great War Memorial, Milford Street, Leighlinbridge, County Carlow.

PHELAN, EDWARD: Rank: Rifleman. Regiment or service: Rifle Brigade. Unit: 2nd Battalion. Date of death: 28 March 1915. Age at death: 25. Service No.: 5301. Born in Cork. Enlisted in Carlow, Queen's County while living in Carlow, Queen's County. Died of wounds.

Supplementary information: Son of James and Elizabeth Phelan, of Charlotte Street, Carlow. Brother of James Phelan below. Date of will: 28 March 1915. Effects and property received by: Mrs E. Phelan, Charlotte Street, Carlow From the *Nationalist* and *Leinster Times*, May 1916:

PHELAN—First Anniversary—In loving memory of James Phelan, late of Charlotte Street Carlow, killed in action in the Dardanelles in R. D. F. Sacred Heart of Jesus, have mercy on him. Immaculate Heart of Mary, pray for him.
One year is gone and yet we miss him,
Words would fail our loss to tell,
But the God that sent him to us,
Took him to his heavenly care.

Inserted by his sorrowing mother, sisters and brothers.

From the *Nationalist* and *Leinster Times*, March 1918:

Phelan—Third Anniversary—In loving memory of my dear son, Eddie Phelan, late of Charlotte Street, Carlow, who died on the 28th March, 1915, from wounds received on the 12th, in the battle of Neuve Chapelle.

Sacred Heart of Jesus have mercy on him. Immaculate Heart of Mary pray for him.
Three years have gone and yet we miss him
Words would fail our loss to tell
But the God that sent him to us
Took him to his heavenly home.

From the *Nationalist* and *Leinster Times*, March 1920:

PHELAN—4th Anniversary—In memory of Eddie Phelan, late of Charlotte Street, died 28th March, 1915, in Boulogne Hospital from wounds received in Neuve Chapelle. Sacred Heart of Jesus have mercy on him.
His King and country called him,
The call was not in vain,
And British Roll of Honour
Will find this hero's name.

Inserted by his sorrowing mother. -R. I. P.

Grave or memorial reference: III. D. 64. Cemetery: Boulogne Eastern Cemetery in France. Also listed under Carlow/Graigue on the Great War Memorial, Milford Street, Leighlinbridge, County Carlow.

PHELAN, JAMES: Rank: Private. Regiment or service: Royal Dublin Fusiliers. Unit: 1st Battalion. Date of death: 30 April 1915 (SDGW, IMR) 11 May 1915 (CWGC, Great War Memorial, Milford Street, Leighlinbridge, County Carlow). Age at death: 21. Service No.: 11209. Born in

Tipperary. Enlisted in Carlow. Died of wounds. Killed in action in Gallipoli.

Supplementary information: Son of Elizabeth Phelan, of Charlotte St, Carlow, and the late James Phelan. Brother of Edward Phelan above. From the *Nationalist* and *Leinster Times,* May 1915:

Phelan—Killed in action in the Dardanelles, on May 11th, Private J. Phelan, 1st R. D. F., aged 19 years, and late of Charlotte Street, Carlow. Sacred Heart of Jesus, have mercy on him, Immaculate Heart of Mary, pray for him—R. I. P.

He lies today, in a soldier's grave
In a far-off distant land
Where, he fought and died, for his
country's pride.
And the dear ones left behind.
Yet again, we hope to meet him.
When the days of life are fled;
And in heaven, with joy to greet
him
Where no farewell tears are shed.

Inserted by his sorrowing mother, sisters and brothers. (Second son killed in action.)

The *Nationalist* and *Leinster Times,* May 1916:

Roll of Honour.
PHELAN—First Anniversary—In loving memory of James Phelan, late of Charlotte Street, Carlow, killed in action in the Dardanelles, on the 11th May, 1915, Private in R. D. F. Sacred Heart of Jesus, have mercy on him. Immaculate Heart of Mary, pray for him.

One year gone and yet we miss him,
Words would fail our loss to tell,
But the God that sent him to us,
Took him to his heavenly care.

Inserted by his sorrowing mother, sisters and brothers.

Grave or memorial reference: He has no known grave but is listed on the Special Memorial, B, 80. V Beach Cemetery in Turkey.

PHELAN, PATRICK: Rank: Private. Regiment or service: Leinster Regiment. Unit: B Company. 2nd Battalion. Date of death: 27 March 1918. Age at death: 22. Service No.: 5879. Born in Bagnalstown County Carlow. Enlisted in Carlow. Killed in action. Formerly he was with the Royal Army Service Corps, Motor Transport, where his number was 299616.

Supplementary information: Son of John and Sarah Phelan, of Strawhell, Carlow.

Grave or memorial reference: Panel 78. Memorial: Pozieres Memorial in France. Also listed under Bagenalstown/ Fenagh on the Great War Memorial, Milford Street, Leighlinbridge, County Carlow.

PHILLPOTTS, LOUIS MURR/ MURRAY: Rank: Brigadier General. Regiment or service: Royal Artillery. Unit: 24th Divisional HQ, also listed as Staff 56th Division. Date of death: 8 September 1916. Age at death: 46. Awards: CMG, DSO. Killed in action.

Supplementary information: Son of the Reverend H. J. and Mrs Phillpotts, of Shadwell, Speldhurst, Kent; husband of Mrs Phillpotts, of Russelstown Park, Carlow. From the *Nationalist* and *Leinster Times*, 1916:

Roll of Honour
Brigadier-General L. M. Phillpotts, D. S. O., C. M. G., whose death in action is announced was attached to the Royal Field Artillery. General Phillpotts, who was the second son of the Rev. R. J. and Mrs Phillpotts, of Shadwell, Speldhurst, Kent, and the husband of Mrs A. Phillpotts, of Russelstown Park, Carlow, served in the South African War, where he took part in the advance on Kimberley, including the actions at Modder River. He was also present in the Orange River Colony operations between February and May, 1900, and afterwards served in the Transvaal. He was mentioned in despatches, and received the Queen's Medal with three clasps. He attained the rank of Brigadier-General in 1915. Even before his marriage he was very well-known in County Carlow, where he was very popular, and was a good rider to bounds(hounds?).

From the *Nationalist* and *Leinster Times*, September 1916:

Late Brigadier General Philpotts.
The following has been sent to Mrs Philpotts by a brother officer of her husband's; --
24th Divn.,
9th Sept, 1916.

Dear Mrs Philpotts—It was with the greatest grief that we heard yesterday of the death of your gallant husband.

Since he has been associated with me in this Division, he has always shown himself a first class gunner officer.

His energy and resource have been pf the greatest service to his country; he has brought the artillery of the Division to a very high state of excellence, and his loss to us will be irreparable.

Personally I have lost in him a very valued friend and counsellor, on whose loyal service and good judgement I could always implicitly rely.

The whole Division deplores with me his untimely death, met with in the service of his King ans country, and fared with the unflinching courage which was his.

No task was too heavy and no danger too great to be undertaken and faced by him at the call of duty. He has done it nobly, and you will be glad to know that he was loved and honoured by his comrades of all ranks; there are none who do not mourn him. Proud you must be to have been privileged to be a wife of so gallant a soldier.

But all our pride can hardly aid to console our private sorrow, sorrow which falls so much the more greatly on you. We feel for you and in the name of the Division I command and also personally, I subscribe myself with the deepest sympathy, yours sincerely,
J. E. Capper.

We take the following from the "Morning Post" of September 13th, 1916; --

Brigadier-General Louis Murray Phillpotts, D. S. O. C., M. C, R. F. A., (killed in action on September 8th) was second son of the rev H. J. and Mrs Phillpotts, of Shadwell, Spelhurst, Kent. He was born in June, 1870, and passed out of Woolwich into the Royal Artillery in February, 1890, and in July, 1907, received his majority. During his captaincy he was divisional adjutant, and afterwards adjutant to the Royal Artillery. General Phillpotts, who held the first-class certificate in gunnery, was gazetted Lieutenant Colonel in October, 1914, and in the following year was promoted to the staff with rank of Brigadier General. He had served with great distinction in the present war, and his services were mentioned in despatches, while he was made a Companion of the Order of St Michael and St George. He won the D. S. O. in the South African War, in the early part of which he was acting Staff Officer to the Officer commanding the lines of communications, North. Afterwards he was in the advance on Kimberley, and fought in the action at Modder River. He took part in the operations at Paardeburg, and was also in the action near Johannesburg. Other services in various theatres of the campaign were rendered by him, and he was mentioned in despatches. In addition to being made a Companion of the Distinguished Service Order he was decorated with the Queen's Medal with three clasps.

From *Carlow Sentinel*, September 1916:

Roll of Honour.

PHILLPOTTS—September 8, 1916, killed in action, Brigadier General Murray Phillpotts, D. S. O., C. M. G., R. F. A., the beloved husband of Amy Phillpotts of Russelstown Park, Carlow and second son of Rev, H. J., and Mrs Phillpotts, Shadwell, Speldhurst, Kent.

Brigadier General L. M. Phillpotts.

.... served in the South African War, where he took part in the advance on Kimberly, including the actions at Modder River. He was also present in the Orange River Colony operations between February and May, 1900, and afterwards served in the Transvaal. He was mentioned in despatches, and received the Queen's Medal with three clasps. He attained the rank of Brigadier General in 1915. While stationed in Carlow the late gallant soldier made many personal friends, and enjoyed the esteem and respect of the entire community, who sympathise deeply with his afflicted widow and young son in their bereavement.

Grave or memorial reference: II. A. 1. Cemetery: Citadel New Military Cemetery, Fricourt in France.

PIGOTT, MARK: Rank: Private. Regiment or service: Army Service Corps. Date of death: 30 March 1918. Age at death: 36. Service No.: S/19785.

Supplementary information: Husband of Catherine Pigott, of Henry Street,

Graigue-Cullen, Carlow. This man is not in any other database.

Grave or memorial reference: 4. 10. 1. Cemetery: Carlow (St Mary's) Cemetery, County Carlow.

PIKE, ROBERT MAXWELL: Rank: Captain. Regiment or service: Royal Flying Corps. Unit: 5th Squadron. Age at death: 29. Date of death: 9 August 1915. Awards: Mentioned in Despatches. Killed in action.

Supplementary information: Son of Robert Lecky Pike, DL and Mrs Lechy Pike, of Kilwork, Tullow, County Carlow. From *Our Heroes*:

> …who was reported missing on August 9th last, is now reported dead. Captain Pike, who was a son of Mr R. L. Pike, Kilnock, County Carlow, entered the Navy when a young man, but owing to an injury to his knee had to leave the service. On the outbreak of the war he joined the Royal Flying Corps. He was a most daring and skilful aviator, and his place in the corps will be difficult to fill.

Nationalist and *Leinster Times*, December 1914:

> Roll of Honour.
> We also regret to learn that Captain Lecky-Pike, Grenadier Guards, son of Mr R Lecky-Pike, D. L., Kilnock, County Carlow, has been wounded in action/ His many friends will, however, be pleased to learn, that the injuries are not very serious, and that he hopes soon to rejoin his gallant Regiment at the front.

The *Nationalist* and *Leinster Times*, August 1915:

> Kilnock, County Carlow.
> Captain Robert Maxwell Pike, Flight Commander, Royal Flying Corps, was killed in action near Hooge, In flanders, on the 9th of August. Captain R. Maxwell Pike was the second son of Mr Robert Lecky Pike, D. L., of Kilnock, County Carlow, and was in his 20th year. Born on the 30 August, 1887, and educated at Harrow, he entered the Navy in 1902. Three years later he was invalided out of the Navy on account of ill health, which necessitated having his knee joint taken away, and left him with a rigid leg for life. In September, 1914, soon after war broke out, Captain Pike joined the Royal Flying Corps, and at once showed great promise. He took his pilot's certificate after a month's training, and quickly became an expert flying officer. He remained in this country until the end of January, when he went to the front. Early in April he was promoted to be a Flight Commander and temporary Captain. At 8 a. m on the 9th of August he ascended in a new, very fast, single-seater aeroplane for scouting purposes. He was seen flying at ten thousand feet, and later fighting a large German aeroplane. About 9 a. m. he was seen to have apparently driven off the enemy aeroplane and his own machine began to descend in spirals, and eventually landed in the German lines near Hooge. It has since been ascertained that captain Maxwell Pike was badly

wounded during his combat in the air, in which he single-handed fought the enemy aeroplane, and he succumbed to his wounds shortly after landing. He was buried with full military honours by the Germans in a churchyard close by. Captain Maxwell Pike was amongst the bravest of the brave; he did not know what fear was.

From the *Nationalist* and *Leinster Times*, September 1915:

Late Flight-Commander Pike.
On Friday, 10th inst., St Lappan's Church, Little Island, was the scene of a very suitable, but most impressive, memorial service to the late Flight Commander, Robert Maxwell-Pike, Royal Flying Corps.

The picturesquely situated little church, in which the deceased officer frequently worshipped was filled with the personal friends and admirers, who desired to pay their last tribute of respect to the memory of one who gave his life freely for his country's cause. Soon after the outbreak of war, Mr Pike, as he then was, with everything to look forward to in this life, set to his fellow-countrymen an example which was followed by many by equalled by none. A physical defect preventing him from joining the ordinary branches of the army, he at once qualified as a pilot, and his own merit alone obtained for him a commission in the Royal Flying Corps. Soon he was with this intrepid and heroic body of men in France, and it was not long before his great ability and

bravery as an airman were rcognised, and, in the words of his Chief-of-Staff—"His services were always perfectly invaluable." It was while so performing his duty that he laid down his life for his country, he met, in fact, a hero's end. Like many of that same corps his name will long be remembered as one who gave his all for the Empire which he loved.

For the deceased officers, parents, and, indeed, the whole of the Pike family, the greatest sympathy is felt by all classes, and Monday's service recalled to the minds of many that this was the second memorial service held in memory of members of the Pike family who have fallen on the plains of Flanders.

Twelve months ago have not elapsed since a similar service was held in Glanmire Church to the memory of Captain Gordon –Pike, son-in-law to Mr Joseph Pike, D. L., who was killed while gallantly leading his men to the attack in the third month of the war.

The service was conducted by Rev L. Swanzy, and associated with him was the Lord Bishop of Cork.

The following members of the Pike family were present—Mr Robert Lecky Pike (father). Mrs Lecky Pike (mother). Miss Lecky Pike (sister), Mr Joseph Pike, D. L. (uncle). Mrs Pike and the Misses Pike, Bessborough. (a more detailed account of his Memorial Service held at St Lappans can be read in the Carlow Sentinel.)

From *Carlow Sentinel*, August 1916:

PIKE—In loving memory of Captain Robert Maxwell Pike, Royal Flying Corps, killed in action in Flanders on August 9th, 1916, second and youngest son of Mr and Mrs Robert Lecky Pike, Kilnock, County Carlow.

[This officer was also known as Captain Robert Maxwell Lecky-Pike. Author.]

Born in Kilnock, second son of Robert Lecky Pike.

Memorial: Arras Flying Services Memorial in Faubourg D'Amiens Cemetery, Arras in France.

PONSONBY, THE HONOURABLE CYRIL MYLES BRABAZON:

Rank: Major. Regiment or service: Grenadier Guards Unit: 3rd Battalion attached to the 2nd Battalion. Date of death: 27 September 1915. Killed in action.

Supplementary information: Second son of 8th Earl of Bessborough and the Countess of Bessborough; husband of Rita Narcissa Ponsonby (now Mrs Cyril Flower, of Codicote Mill, Welwyn, Herts). From *Munster Express*, October 1915:

Major Ponsonby Killed in action.
The Hon. Cyril Myles Brabazon Ponsonby, M.V.O., the second son of the Earl of Bessborough, has been killed in action. He was born on November 16th-1881, and was gazetted second Lieutenant in the 2nd battalion of the Grenadier Guards on August 11th-1900. He served in South Africa in 1900-1, and acted

for a time as A. D. C. to the Duke of Connaught. In july 1904, he obtained his lieutenancy, and four years later was gazetted captain. In July, 1911, he married Rita, the eldest daughter of Lieutenant-Colonel M. J. C. Longfield, Castle Mary, County Cork. On May 20th in the present year he was promoted to the rank of major in the 4th battalion.

From the *Carlow Sentinel*, October 1915.

Capt. Hon. C. M. B. Ponsonby. 2nd Grenadier Guards, who has been killed in France, was the second son of Earl and Countess of Bessborough, of Garryhill, Bagenalstown. He had been at the front for some time, and was reported wounded in November last.

From De Ruvigny's Roll of Honour:

...2nd son of Edward, 8th Earl of Bessborough, K. P., C. V. O., C. B., by his wife, Blanche Vere, youngest daughter if the late Sir John Guest, 1st Bart., M. P. Born in London 16-November-1881. Educated at harrow and the Royal Military College, Sandhurst. Gazetted 2nd Lieutenant Grenadier Guards, 11 August 1900, and promoted Lieutenant 12 April 1904, Captain 03 June 1908, and Major, May1915. Was A. D. C. to Governor and Commander—in-Chief, Ceylon, 27 November 1903 to 30 September 1905; to Inspector-General of the Forces, etc, 1 July 1906, to 20 December 1907, and to the F. M.

Commanding-in-Chief (H. R. H. the Duke of Connaught) 31 December 1907, to 31 July 1909; served (1) in the South African War 1902, taking part in the operations in Cape Colony February to 31 May 1902; and (2) with the Expeditionary Force in France and Flanders from September 1914, and was killed in action 28 September 1915, while leading the 4th Battalion of his Regiment to retake Hill 70. he was at the time temporarily in command, owing to the Commanding Officer having been gassed. He received the Victorian Order (Fourth Class) 1909, and was a Knight of the Order of the Sword of Sweden, and of the Order of Isabellea the Catholic of Spain. Me married at St George's, Hanover Square, W., 20 July 1911, Rita Narcissa (44, Gloucester Square, W.), eldest daughter of Lieutenant Colonel Mountifort John Courtenay Longfield, co. Cork, J. P., D. L., and had a son, Arthur Montifort Longfield (for whom H. R. H, the Duke of Connaught was sponsor).

From the *Munster Express*, October 1915.

The Late Major Ponsonby.
A Memorial Service was held last week in London, ar St James's Church, Picadilly, for the late Major Cyril Myles Brabazon Ponsonby, M. V. O., Grenadier Guards, second son of the Earl and Countess of Bessborough, who was kille in action in France on the 28th September.

Queen Alexandra was represented by Earl Howe; Col. H. Streatfield was present on behalf of Field-Marshal the Duke of Connaught, Honoray Colonel of the regiment, and Princess Henry of Battenburg was represented by Mr Victor Corkra. The Countess of Bessborough, the Hon. Mrs Myles Ponsonby, and several other ladies did not join the general congregation, and occupied seats in the Vestry.

Among the immediate relatives present were the Earl of Bessbroough, Colonel and Mrs Longfield and the Misses Longfield, Viscoutess Duncannon, Lord and Lady Oranmore and Browne and the Hon Dominick Browne, Lady Irene Congrave, the Hon. Cyril and Mrs Ponsonby, the Hon. Walter Ponsonby., Lord and Lady Raglan and the Misses Somerset, the Hon. Mrs Somerset, Major and Lady Kathleen Skinner, and the Hon. Mrs Charles Eliot and Miss Eliot.

Amongst the congregation there were also—The Earl and Countess of Desart, the Hon. Lady Musgrave, Mr Geo. Ponsonby., Mrs A. Congreve, and nearly every office of the 5th Battalion Grenadier Guards.

After the Benediction the congregation sung the National Anthem, and the buglers and drummers of the 5th Battalion Grenadier Guards, lined up facing the west door, after a preparatory rolling of muffled drums, sounded the "Last Post."

As the congregation dispersed the organ pealed forth the Dead March from "Saul."

At a special meeting of the Iverk Farming Society, a vote of sympathy was passed on the proposition of Mr George Morris, J. P., with Lord and Lady Bessboro, and members of their family in the great loss they had sustained by the death in action of Major the Hon. C. M. B. Ponsonby.

Grave or memorial reference: Panel 5 to 7. He has no known grave but is listed on the Loos Memorial Pas-de-Calais, France. He is also commemorated on the Great War Memorial in St Canice's Cathedral, Kilkenny... 'To the Glory of God and in loving memory of the following members of the Diocese of Ossory who gave their lives for their country in the Great War 1914-1918'. Listed on the memorial under Major The Hon. Myles. B. Ponsonby.

POWELL, THOMAS CHARLES: Rank: Bombardier. Regiment or service: Royal Garrison Artillery. Unit: 191st Siege Battery. Date of death: 14 September 1918. Age at death: 32. Service No.: 74712. Born in Parkstone, Dorset. Enlisted in Colchester, Essex while living in East Mersey, Essex. Died of wounds.

Supplementary information: Son of John and Rose Powell, of New Milton, Hants; husband of Mary Powell, of Barrack Street, Tallow, County Carlow.

Grave or memorial reference: VI. H. 3. Cemetery: Duisans British Cemetery, Etrun in France.

POWER, JOSEPH: Rank: Rifleman. Regiment or service: London Regiment. Unit: 8th (City of London)

Battalion, (Post Office Rifles). Date of death: 21 May 1916. Service No.: 3928. Enlisted in London while living in Bagenalstown, County Carlow. Killed in action. Grave or memorial reference: Bay 10 on the Arras Memorial in France. Also listed under Bagenalstown/Fenagh on the Great War Memorial, Milford Street, Leighlinbridge, County Carlow.

PURCELL, STEPHEN: Rank: Private. Regiment or service: Irish Guards. Unit: 2nd Battalion. Date of death: 29 March 1918. Age at death: 22. Service No.: 7526. Born in Leighlinbridge, County Carlow. Enlisted in Naas while living in Bagenalstown County Carlow. Died of wounds.

Supplementary information: Son of Stephen and Kate Donohue Purcell, of Barrett Street, Bagenalstown, County Carlow. After his death his effects and property were received by: (Mother) Mrs Kate Purcell, Pump Street, Bagenalstown. Later address Hotel Street, Bagenalstown. His Nuncupative (or missing) will was witnessed by, Mary B Purcell, Barrett Street, Bagenalstown and William Flangann, Clergyman.

Grave or memorial reference: XXXIII. A. 22. Cemetery: Etaples Military Cemetery in France. Also listed under Leighlinbridge/Old Leighlin on the Great War Memorial, Milford Street, Leighlinbridge, County Carlow.

PURCELL, WILLIAM: Rank: Private. Regiment or service: Leinster Regiment. Unit: 3rd Battalion. Date of death: 19 July 1915. Service No.: 10135. Born in Tullow, County Carlow. Enlisted in Maryborough, Queen's County. Carlow. Died at home. Grave or memorial reference: He is commemorated on the Grangegorman (Cork) Memorial Headstones Spec. Memorial. Alternative Commemoration – He is buried in Cork Military Cemetery. Also listed under Tullow on the Great War Memorial, Milford Street, Leighlinbridge, County Carlow.

Q

QUIGLEY, TIMOTHY: Rank: Able Seaman. Regiment or service: Royal Navy. Unit: HMS *Raglan*. Date of death: 20 January 1918. Age at death: 23. Service No.: J/36080. *Raglan* was attacked by 6 German and Turkish vessels and sand with the loss of 127 men.

Supplementary information: Born in Carlow. Son of Mary Quigley, of Bridewell Street, Carlow.

Grave or memorial reference: 28. Memorial: Chatham Naval Memorial, UK.

QUINN, MICHAEL CONWAY: Rank: Rifleman. Regiment or service: New Zealand Rifle Brigade. Unit: 4th Battalion. Age at death: 29. Date of death: 12 October 1917. Service No.: 41109.

Supplementary information: Son of James and Mary Conway Quinn, of Mill Street, Tullow, County Carlow, Ireland. Occupation on enlistment, Labourer. Embarked at Wellington abord the *Navua* with Reinforcements 'J' Company on 16 Febraury 1917 bound for Devonport, England. Killed in action. Next of kin details: J. Begg (friend), Pukeawa, Otago, New Zealand.

Grave or memorial reference: N. Z. Apse, Panel 7. Memorial: Tyne Cot Memorial in Belgium.

QUINN, PATRICK: Rank: Private. Regiment or service: Royal Inniskilling Fusiliers. Unit: 8th Battalion. Date of death: 6 September 1916. Service No.: 43103. Formerly he was with the Connaught Rangers where his number was 6245. Born in Tullow, County Carlow. Enlisted in Carlow. Killed in action. Grave or memorial reference: Pier and Face 4 D and 5 B. Memorial: Thiepval Memorial in France. Also listed under Tullow on the Great War Memorial, Milford Street, Leighlinbridge, County Carlow.

R

RALPH, MICHAEL: Rank: Private. Regiment or service: Irish Guards. Unit: 1st Battalion. Date of death: 25 October 1914. Age at death: 21. Service No.: 3777. Born in Killeshin, Kings County. Enlisted in Carlow, County Carlow. Killed in action.

Supplementary information: Son of John and Annie Ralph, of Chapel Street, Carlow Graigue, Carlow. Date of will: 6 August 1914. Effects and property received by: (Mother) Anie Ralph, Chapel Street, Graigue, Carlow. Witnesses: William Mutagh(Murtagh?) and Patrick O'Donnell, 1st Battalion, Irish Guards, Wellington Barracks. From the *Nationalist* and *Leinster Times*, October 1915:

> RALPH—(First Anniversary)—In sad but loving memory of Private Michael Ralph, 4th Irish Guards, late of Chapel Street, Carlow-Graigue, who was killed in action at Wood Polygon de Yourreleke, on 26th October, 1914. —R. I. P.
>
> Jesus, our God, in silent love,
> Still at Thy feet he lay;
> Oh, take his heart, and keep it hard,
> For all eternity.
> May he dwell in peace for ever,
> In Thy blissful home above,
> In thy Sacred Heart, dear Jesus,
> In thine own eternal love.
>
> Inserted by his loving parents, brothers and sisters.

Grave or memorial reference: He has no known grave but is listed on Panel 11 on the Ypres (Menin Gate) Memorial in Belgium. Also listed under Carlow/ Graigue on the Great War Memorial, Milford Street, Leighlinbridge, County Carlow.

REDDY, PATRICK: Rank: Gunner. Regiment or service: Royal Garrison Artillery. Unit: 66th Siege Battery Date of death: 27 July 1916. Age at death: 33. Service No.: 46499. Born in Agnade Tullow, County Carlow. Enlisted in Consett, Durham while living in Leadgate, Durham. Died of wounds.

Supplementary information: Son of James and Winifred Reddy, of Carrick, Slaney Tullow, County Carlow.

> Letter from the Front.
> Our Windgap correspondent sends us a letter which he has received from a friend of his at the front, in the course of which he says;--"We are in a hot spot at present (May 20th), Ypres and Hill 60. We got a terrible dose of the gas from the Germans. It is a d----l of a war. It is impossible to escape at all. I am with the Medical Corps now, carrying the wounded off the field to the dressing station—that is a mile behind the line. Our own doctor was killed yesterday morning, he was a very nice man. I am a stretcher-bearer and wearing a Red Cross on my sleeve. We have to dress the wounded and

carry them to a doctor, and we carry a bag of bandages on our back, as well as a small bottle of medicine to put on the wound. It is awful—you would see such terrible sights. I have no rifle or ammunition. You have to go through shot and shell as quick as you can; but it has to be done. It was I carried Paddy Reddy in when he was wounded; he is gone home now, so you see how friends meet. Wash from Kilmoganny was also wounded. This is the 20th; Italy is to start today, I think. If you saw this country—it is terrible; it is knocked to the ground. This is Belgium. I was in Mons on the 23rd of last month, where we got our baptism of fire from the German shells. It was like hell opening. The ground was trembling under our feet. It is the worst war since the creation of man; but it will have to finish sometime. I shot 13 Germans—that is a good lot—so I think I have done my share. Goodbye. Remember me to all. Write soon."(ME, 07-1915. Paddy Reddy was a Carlow soldier and died of wounds in July-1916. No soldier named Walsh from Kilmoganny died in the Great War).

Grave or memorial reference: I. D. 74. Cemetery: La Neuville British Cemetery, Corbie in France. Also listed under Tullow and Ballon/Rathoe/Aghade on the Great War Memorial, Milford Street, Leighlinbridge, County Carlow.

REDMOND, JAMES: Rank: Private. Regiment or service: Canadian Infantry (Central Ontario Regiment). Unit: 58th Battalion. Date of death: 1 October 1918. Age at death: 32. Service No.: 3107077.

Supplementary information: Son of Michael and Bridget Redmond of Garryhaslin, County Wexford, Ireland. Information from his enlistment documents: Eyes, grey. Hair, dark. Complexion, dark. Height, 5 feet 10½ inches. Address on enlistment, 1845 North Broadway Street, St Louis, MO. Date of birth: 26 June 1889. Age on enlistment: 28 years 7 months. Place of birth: Newtown Barry, County Wexford. Marital status: single. Name and address of next of kin: Miss Mary Redmond, 142 Trobridge Street, Buffalo, NY, USA. Date of attestation, 4 February 1918. Location of attestation: Toronto. Occupation on enlistment: Labourer.

Grave or memorial reference: II. C. 14. Cemetery: Canada Cemetery, Tilloy-Les-Cambrai in France. Also listed under Clonegal/Kildavin on the Great War Memorial, Milford Street, Leighlinbridge, County Carlow.

REILLY, MICHAEL: Rank: Rifleman. Regiment or service: Royal Irish Rifles. Unit: 2nd Battalion. Date of death: 20 October 1916. Age at death: 27. Service No.: 2599. Enlisted in Dublin while living in Hackettstown, County Carlow. Killed in action.

Supplementary information: Son of Ellen Reilly, of Moffats Street, Hacketstown, County Carlow, and the late Thomas Reilly.

Grave or memorial reference: Pier and Face 15 A and 15 B. Memorial: Thiepval Memorial in France. Also listed under Hacketstown on the Great War Memorial, Milford Street, Leighlinbridge, County Carlow.

REILLY, MICHAEL: Rank: Shoeing Smith. Regiment or service: South Irish Horse. Date of death: 29 June 1916. Age at death: 34. Service No.: 1849. Born in Bagwalston(sic). Enlisted in Carlow while living in Carlow. Died at home.

Supplementary information: Husband of Agnes Reilly, of 32 Regent Street, Bagnalstown.

Grave or memorial reference: Close to East wall. Tullow (The Abbey) Cemetery, County Carlow. Also listed under Bagenalstown/Fenagh on the Great War Memorial, Milford Street, Leighlinbridge, County Carlow.

REILLY, PATRICK: Rank: Private. Regiment or service: Royal Dublin Fusiliers. Unit: 2nd Battalion. Age at death: 26. Date of death: 21 March 1918. Service No.: 23163. Born in Tinryland, County Carlow. Enlisted in Athy. Killed in action.

Supplementary information: Son of Ellen Doyle (formerly Reilly), of 79 Leinster Street, Athy, County Kildare, and the late Thomas Reilly. Miuchael Greene died in the same unit on the same day.

Grave or memorial reference: I. E. 2. Cemetery: Unicorn Cemetery, Vend'huile in France.

ROACHE/ROCHE, JOSEPH: Rank: Private. Regiment or service: Connaught Rangers. Unit: 1st Battalion. Date of death: 27 September 1915. Age

at death: 24. Service No.: 9667. Born in Tullow, County Carlow. Enlisted in Carlow while living in Liscoleman. Died of wounds.

Supplementary information: Son of John Roache, of Liscolman, Tullow, County Carlow. Native of Tankardstown, Tullow. Enlisted 1909. Also served in India. Date of will: 20 September 1914. Effects and property received by: Mr John Roche, Liscoleman, County Carlow, Ireland.

Grave or memorial reference: IV. F. 6. Cemetery: Merville Communal Cemetery in France. Also listed under Tullow on the Great War Memorial, Milford Street, Leighlinbridge, County Carlow.

ROBERTS, HEDLEY VICARS: Rank: Lance Corporal. Regiment or service: Norfolk Regiment. Unit: 7th Battalion. Date of death: 24 January 1918 (IMR, CWGC) 24 October 1918 (SDGW, Milford Street). Age at death: 45. Service No.: 12234. Born in County Carlow and enlisted in St Paul's Churchyard in Middlesex. Died.

Supplementary information: Son of David and Ellie Roberts (*née* Magill) of Roscrea, County Tipperary; husband of Ethel A. Roberts, of 2 Damer Terrace, West Chelsea, London.

Grave or memorial reference: II. C. 12A. Cemetery: Les Baraques Military Cemetery, Sangatte in France. Also listed under Carlow/Graigue on the Great War Memorial, Milford Street, Leighlinbridge, County Carlow.

ROBERTS, JOHN: Rank: Private. Regiment or service: Royal Dublin

Fusiliers. Unit: 9th Battalion. Date of death: 14 September 1916. Age at death: 24. Service No.: 4/19181(CWGC), 19181(SDGW). Born in Carlow. Enlisted in Carlow. Died of wounds.

Supplementary information: Son of Thomas and Ellen Roberts, of Green Street, Carlow.

Grave or memorial reference: IV. B. 21. Cemetery: Abbeville Communal Cemetery in France. Also listed under Carlow/Graigue on the Great War Memorial, Milford Street, Leighlinbridge, County Carlow.

ROONEY, PATRICK: Rank: Private. Regiment or service: Royal Dublin Fusiliers. Unit: C Company. 8th Battalion. Date of death: 8 June 1917. Age at death: 24. Killed in action. Service No.: 28723. Born in Tullow, Carlow. Enlisted in Dublin while living in Carlow.

Supplementary information: Son of William and Kate Rooney, of Donishall, Carnew, County Wicklow.

Grave or memorial reference: He has no known grave but is listed on Panel 44 and 46 on the Ypres (Menin Gate) Memorial in Belgium. Also listed under Tullow on the Great War Memorial, Milford Street, Leighlinbridge, County Carlow.

ROURKE, JAMES: Rank: Private. Regiment or service: Royal Irish Regiment. Unit: 2nd Battalion. Date of death: 21 March 1918. Service No.: 10002. Born in Leighlinbridge, County Carlow. Enlisted in Carlow while living in Bennekerry, County Carlow. Killed

in action. Grave or memorial reference: Panel 30 and 31. Memorial: Pozieres Memorial in France. Also listed under Leighlinbridge/Old Leighlin on the Great War Memorial, Milford Street, Leighlinbridge, County Carlow.

RUSSELL, CHARLES ROBERT: Rank: Sergeant. Regiment or service: Royal Field Artillery. Date of death: 23 November 1918. Age at death: 29. Service No.: 45808. This man is not in any other database.

Supplementary information: Husband of Mary E. Russell, of St Mary's Park, Carlow. From the *Nationalist* and *Leinster Times*:

An interesting ceremony took place at the meeting of the Deptford Brough Council on Tuesday when the Mayor on behalf of the Lord Kitchener Memorial Fund, presented a 'cycle chair' to Sergeant Charles Russell, Royal Artillery, who lives with his wife and three children at 19, Pender Street, Deptford. When wrar broke out Sergeant Russell who was residing in Carlow and employed by Messrs. Thomas Thompson & Son was sent to the front with the British Expeditionary Force and went through many important engagements. He was invalided home with rheumatic fever, but when he was well enough he again applied for active service and went to the front for a second time. While in action on March 16th, 1916, a shell burst at his feet, both were blown off. He has now been provided with artificial limbs and in order that he might be able to get about the Lord Kitchener Fund was approached with the result that the 'cycle chair' was provided. Sergeant Russell who had been a soldier for 10 and a half years, was escorted to the Council chamber by Mace-Bearer Mr Allen G. Mathews. Sergeant Russell left the chamber after the presentation amid the hearty cheers of the members in Carlow he was esteemed by all and took great interest in the training of the Carlow branch of the Irish national Volunteers. He is also son-in-law of Mr Denis Corcoran of Charlotte Street, Carlow, who has three of his own sons serving the colours at this time.

Grave or memorial reference: 4. 11. 4. Cemetery: Carlow (St Mary's) Cemetery, County Carlow. Also listed under Carlow/Graigue on the

Pte Ryan, letter from his records.

Great War Memorial, Milford Street, Leighlinbridge, County Carlow.

RYAN, JOHN: Rank: Private. Regiment or service: Northumberland Fusiliers. Unit: 9th (Northumberland Hussars) Battalion. Date of death: 14 April 1918. Age at death: 26. Service No.: 55931. Formerly he was with the Royal Army Service Corps where his number was 3214. Born in Carlow. Enlisted in Dublin. Died.

Supplementary information: Son of John and Mary Ryan, of Osberstown, Sallins, County Kildare.

Grave or memorial reference: Panel 2. Memorial: Ploegsteert Memorial in Belgium. Also listed under Carlow/ Graigue on the Great War Memorial, Milford Street, Leighlinbridge, County Carlow.

RYAN, JOHN PATRICK: Rank: Private. Regiment or service: Labour Corps. Date of death: 9 May 1918. Service No.: 336134 and listed in the Commonwealth War Graves Commission as G/309 and listed as transferred to the Eastern Command Labour Section under the number 336134. Formerly he was with the Royal Dublin Fusiliers where his number was 4619. Born in Tullow, County Carlow. Enlisted in Carlow while living in Crinkle, King's County. Died of wounds.

Supplementary information: Husband of Katherine Ryan, of School Street, Crinkle, Birr, King's County Born at Limerick. Grave or memorial reference: Screen Wall O1. 359. Cemetery:

Leicester (Welford Road) Cemetery, UK. Also listed under Tullow on the Great War Memorial, Milford Street, Leighlinbridge, County Carlow.

RYAN, JOSEPH: Rank: Private. Regiment or service: Irish Guards. Unit: 1st Battalion. Date of death: 16 April 1915. Age at death: 25. Service No.: 5543. Born in Urlingford, County Kilkenny. Enlisted in Dublin, County Dublin while living in Carlow, County Carlow. Died of wounds.

Supplementary information: Husband of Kate Ryan, of 7 Charlotte Street, Carlow.

Grave or memorial reference: VIII. A. 1. Cemetery: Boulogne Eastern Cemetery in France. Also listed under Carlow/Graigue on the Great War Memorial, Milford Street, Leighlinbridge, County Carlow.

RYAN, MICHAEL: Rank: Private. Regiment or service: Australian Infantry, AIF. Unit: 58th Battalion. Date of death: 27 March 1918. Age at death: 24. Service No.: 1983. Killed in action.

Supplementary information: Son of Michael and Eliza Ryan, of St Mullens, County Carlow, Ireland. Born, Glynn, Carlow. Listed on later papers St Mullins, Newross, Carlow. Occupation on enlistment, Salesman and Labourer. Age on enlistment: 19. Re-attested due to loss of original attestation papers. Next of kin details: (Mother) Mrs Elizabeth Ryam Upper Drana. Glynn, Carlow. Later changed to (father) Michael Ryan of the same address. Place and date of enlistment: 25 January 1915

at Braodmeadows, Victoria. Weight, 11 stone (10 Stone 1 lbs on later documents).. Complexion, ruddy(changed to fair in later papers). Eyes, brown. Hair, brown.

Grave or memorial reference: Sp. Mem. 3. Cemetery: St Pol British Cemetery, St Pol-Sur-Ternoise, France. Also listed under St Mullins on the Great War Memorial, Milford Street, Leighlinbridge, County Carlow.

RYAN, PATRICK: Rank: Private. Regiment or service: Royal Dublin Fusiliers. Unit: 1st Battalion. Date of death: 4 June 1915 (CWGC, IMR, SDGW) 4 June 1916 (Great War Memorial, Milford Street). Service No.: 18145. Born in Tullow, County Carlow. Enlisted in Carlow while living in Tullow, County Carlow. Killed in action in Gallipoli. Grave or memorial reference: Panel 190 to 196. Memorial: Helles Memorial in Turkey. Also listed under Tullow on the Great War Memorial, Milford Street, Leighlinbridge, County Carlow.

RYAN, PATRICK J.: Rank: Scullion. Regiment or service: Mercantile Marine. Unit: SS *Southland* (Liverpool) Date of death: 2 September 1915. Age at death: 21.

Supplementary information: Son of James, and the late Kate Ryan, of Drummond, St Mullens, County Carlow. The Belgian made tramp-steamer SS *Southland* was converted to a troop-ship to ferry Canadian soldiers from Halifax to Liverpool during the war. On 2 November 1915 the ship was torpedoed but did not sink. There may be a discrepancy in the month of death given by the CWGC. When *Southland* was struck by the torpedo she was carrying Australian troops to Gallipoli. The steamship was again torpedoed and sunk in the Atlantic 140 miles N. W1/2W from Tory Island by German submarine U70 in 1917.

Grave or memorial reference: Tower Hill Memorial, UK.

RYAN, PETER JOSEPH: Rank: Private. Regiment or service: Australian Infantry, A. I. F. Unit: 57th Battalion. Date of death: 1 October 1918. Age at death: 32. Service No.: 3775.

Supplementary information: Born at Oilgate, County Wexford, Ireland. Son of John and Cathrine McCarthy Ryan of Killoughtemane Corries, Bagenalstown, County Carlow. Date of Birth: 2 January 1893. Age on enlistment: 25. Height, 5 feet 8½ inches. Eyes, blue. Hair, dark brown. Complexion, dark. Weight 138lbs. Occupation on enlistment: Labourer. Next of kin: Mrs McCarthy (re-married), Corries, Bagelnalstown, County Carlow. Went to school in Carlow Town. Personal effects were to be sent to his brother, J. Ryan, 32 Hobson Street, Victoria. Peter

was gassed on 29 September 1918 after only being on the battlefields 4 weeks and died of gas poisoning on 1 October 1918 in the 50th Casualty Clearing Station based in Tincourt, Boucly in France.

Grave or memorial reference: V. F. 34. Cemetery: Tincourt New British Cemetery in France. Also listed under Bagenalstown/Fenagh on the Great War Memorial, Milford Street, Leighlinbridge, County Carlow.

RYAN, WILLIAM: Rank: Lance Corporal. Regiment or service: Household Cavalry and Cavalry of the line including the Yeomanry and Imperial Camel Corps. Unit: 20th Hussars, C Squadron. Date of death: 29 August 1914. Age at death: 21. Service No.: 5248. Born in St Mary's, Waterford. Enlisted in Cork while living in Cork. Died of wounds.

Supplementary information: Son of Patrick and Esther Ryan, of 14 Portland Place, Carlisle. Born at Carlow, Ireland. Listed in De Ruvigny's Roll of Honour with no new information.

Grave or memorial reference: In the south west corner. Cemetery: Moy-De-L'Aisne Communal Cemetery, Aisne in France.

S

SALLINGER, JOSEPH: Rank: Private. Regiment or service: Royal Dublin Fusiliers. Unit: 2nd Battalion. Date of death: 24 May 1915. Age at death: 35. Service No.: 6913. Born in Tullow, County Carlow. Enlisted in Carlow. Killed in action.

Supplementary information: Son of John and Elizabeth Sallinger.

Grave or memorial reference: Panel 44 and 46. Memorial: Ypres (Menin Gate) Memorial in Belgium. Also listed under Tullow on the Great War Memorial, Milford Street, Leighlinbridge, County Carlow.

SALTER, FRANCIS: Rank: Corporal. Regiment or service: Royal Irish Regiment. Unit: 2nd Battalion. Date of death: 10 November 1916. Service No.: 11676. Born in Carlow. Enlisted in Carlow. Died of wounds. Date of will: 30 March 1916. Effects and property received by: Mrs Salter, Bridewell Street, Carlow, Ireland. He is buried in the same row as Private John Hughes, another Carlow soldier with the Royal Dublin Fusiliers who died two weeks before him.

Carlow Soldier's Death.
Mrs Salter, Carlow, has received the following; --
2nd R. I. Regt, B. E. F.
France, 15/11/16.
  Dear Mrs Salter—It is with exceeding regret I have to tell you that your son, Corporal 11670, F. Salter, was seriously wounded on the evening of the 9th November, and died of his wound at an hospital in France on the evening of the 11th. I sympathise with you to the fullest in the loss of a magnificent son and soldier. I had not taken over command of this Company very long, only since the 27th of October when the Company Commander was killed, but quite long enough to recognise that your son was one of my best non-commissioned officers. Corporal Salter was most popular in the Company and was always regarded by officers and men as a brave and splendid soldier, and so he died. Who could have wished for a better character, or to have died a more glorious death. Futhermore, Mrs Slater, it will be the greatest consolation for you to know that our priest saw and administered to your son the last Sacraments before he died. He was then quite conscious and passed away as happy as a little child. R. I. P.
  Allow me to offer you out deepest sympathy at the loss of a gallant N. C. O. to the Regiment, and the best son a mother could wish to have.
—I am, Mrs Salter, yours very truly.
H. J. O'Reilly, Lieutenant,
O. C., "B" Company.
"2nd R. I. Regt.

Grave or memorial reference: III. A. 229. Cemetery: Bailleul Communal Cemetery Extension (Nord) in France. Also listed under Carlow/Graigue on

the Great War Memorial, Milford Street, Leighlinbridge, County Carlow.

SALTER, PETER: Rank: Private. Regiment or service: Irish Guards. Unit: 1st Battalion. Date of death: 1 November 1914. Age at death: 23. Service No.: 3882. Born in Kildrenagh, County Carlow. Enlisted in Dublin, County Dublin. Killed in action.

Supplementary information: Son of the late Thomas and Maria Salter, of Kildrena, County Carlow. Date of will: 6 August 1914. Effects and property received by: (Father) Mr Thomas Salter, Kildrenagh, Bagenalstown, County Carlow. Witnesses: Timothy O'Donoghue, family of James Anker Manch (sic), 67 Light, Newcastle-on-Tyne.

Grave or memorial reference: Panel 11. Memorial: Ypres (Menin Gate) Memorial in Belgium. Also listed under Bagenalstown/Fenagh on the Great War Memorial, Milford Street, Leighlinbridge, County Carlow.

SCANLON, FRED: Rank: Lance Corporal. Regiment or service: Royal Irish Fusiliers. Unit: 9th (North Irish Horse) Battalion. Date of death: 23 November 1917. Age at death: 28. Service No.: 41482. Born in Bagnalstown County Carlow. Enlisted in Antrim while living in Bagenalstown. Killed in action.

Supplementary information: Son of James and Sophia Scanlon, of Bohermore, Bagenalstown, County Carlow. Enlisted 1915.

From *Carlow Sentinel*, December 1917:

Death

Scanlon—23rd November, 1917, killed in action. Lance Corporal T Frederick Scanlon, North Irish Horse (attached Royal Irish Fusiliers) eldest and dearly beloved son of James and Sophia Scanlon, Bohermore, Bagnelastown.
Acknowledgement.

Mr and Mrs James Scalnon and family return sincere thanks to the many kind friends who sympathised with them in their great sorrow, and trust they will kindly accept this acknowledgement, as they find it impossible to reply to each individually.

(In our reference in "Roll of Honour" last week to this young Carlow soldier, the name should have been Fred. Scanlon, and his rank as lance Corporal, North Irish Horse (attached to Royal Fusiliers)—Ed, C, S.

From *Carlow Sentinel*, December 1917:

Roll of honour.

We regret to learn of the death of a young Carlow soldier, Corporal James Scanlon. North Irish Horse (attached to Royal Irish Fusilirs). He was in a business establishment in Carlow when he joined the colours and was killed in a recent engagement. His father, Mr James Scanlon, Bohermore, Bagenalstown, has received the following letter from the Military Chaplain of the forces; --

"Dear Mr Scanlon—I have to sympathise with you on the death

of your very gallant son who was killed in action here on 23rd inst. He was exceedingly popular with both officers and men, and his loss is greatly deplored. He died like a hero in a charge against an enemy position and suffered none. You have every right to be proud of your boy."

Grave or memorial reference: Panel 10. Memorial: Cambrai Memorial in Louveral in France. Also listed under Bagenalstown/Fenagh on the Great War Memorial, Milford Street, Leighlinbridge, County Carlow.

SCULLY, LAWRENCE: Rank: Acting Bombardier. Regiment or service: Royal Horse Artillery and Royal Field Artillery. Unit: C Battery, 283rd Brigade. Date of death: 50791. Service No.: 10 October 1916. Born in Tullow, County Carlow. Enlisted in Kilkenny, Ireland. Date of will: 30 May 1916. Effects and property received by: (Sister) Mrs M. Sullivan, Ballon Hill, County Carlow. Killed in action. From the *Nationalist* and *Leinster Times*, November 1916:

Roll of Honour.
Scully—10th October, Bombardier L, Scully, Royal Field Artillery, son of the late James Scully, Ardristan, Tullow, killed in action in France—R. I. P.

Grave or memorial reference: X. P. 2. Cemetery: Guards Cemetery, Lesboeufs in France. Also listed under Tullow on the Great War Memorial, Milford Street, Leighlinbridge, County Carlow.

SCULLY, THOMAS: Rank: Gunner. Regiment or service: Royal Field Artillery. Unit: 40th Trench Mortar Battery. Date of death: 16 August 1918. Age at death: 30. Service No.: 265297. Enlisted in Gosport, Hants while living in Carlow, Ireland. Died of wounds. Formerly he was with the Royal Garrison Artillery where his number was 57461.
Supplementary information: Son of Thomas and Bridget Scully, of Dublin Road, Carlow; husband of Mary Catherine Scully, of Dublin Road, Carlow.
Grave or memorial reference: IV. C. 18. Cemetery: Bagneux British Cemetery, Gezaincourt in France. Also listed under Carlow/Graigue on the Great War Memorial, Milford Street, Leighlinbridge, County Carlow.

SEERY (SDGW & IMR, Great War Memorial, Milford Street, Leighlinbridge, County Carlow), **SECRY** (CWGC), **MARTIN:** Rank: Private. Regiment or service: Royal Irish Regiment. Unit: 2nd Battalion. Date of death: 15 September 1914. Age at death: 21. Service No.: 10299. Born in Carlow. Enlisted in Carlow. Killed in action.
Supplementary information: Son of Patrick Secry.
Grave or memorial reference: He has no known grave but is listed on the La Ferte-Sous-Jouarre Memorial in France. Also listed under Carlow/Graigue on the Great War Memorial, Milford Street, Leighlinbridge, County Carlow.

SHANNON, EDWARD: Rank: Private. Regiment or service: Royal Dublin Fusiliers. Unit: 1st Battalion). Date of death: between 21 March 1918 and 29 March 1918. Age at death: 27. Service No.: 20157. Formerly he was with the Royal Garrison Artillery Secondary where his number was 52047. Born in Hackettstown, County Carlow. Enlisted in Naas while living in Hackettstown, County Carlow. Killed in action.

Supplementary information: Son of Thomas and Sarah Sharmon, of Hacketstown, County Carlow. After his death his effects and property were received by: (Mother) Mrs Sarah Shannon, main Street, Hacketstown, County Carlow, Ireland.

Grave or memorial reference: Panel 79 and 80. Memorial: Pozieres Memorial in France. Also listed under Hacketstown on the Great War Memorial, Milford Street, Leighlinbridge, County Carlow.

SHANNON, MARTIN: Rank: Private. Regiment or service: Royal Dublin Fusiliers. Unit: 2nd Battalion. Date of death: 18 June 1915. Service No.: 5603. Born in Leighlinbridge, County Carlow. Enlisted in Carlow while living in Mageney, County Carlow. Died of wounds. Grave or memorial reference: I. E. 97. Cemetery: Bailleul Communal Cemetery Extension (Nord) in France. Also listed under Leighlinbridge/Old Leighlin on the Great War Memorial, Milford Street, Leighlinbridge, County Carlow.

SHARP, HERBERT: Rank: Private. Regiment or service: Middlesex Regiment. Unit: 1/7th Battalion. Date of death: 21 March 1917. Age at death: 31. Service No.: T. F. 203483 (SDGW) 203483(CWGC). Died. Born in North Fambridge, Essex. Enlisted in Luton, Bedfordshire while living in Paglesham.

Supplementary information: Husband of Margaret Mary Sharp, of The Causeway, Church End, Paglesham, Rochford, Essex. From *Nationalist* and *Leinster Times*, April 1917:

SHARP-March 24th, 1917, at General Hospital, France, from acute bronchitis and poison, Private Herbert Sharp, 7th Middlesex Regiment, son-in-law of Bernard and Mrs Meade, Ballyhide, Carlow. (The 1911 census, lists the Meade's in Ballyhide, Queen's County.)

Grave or memorial reference: XXII. B. 1A. Cemetery: Etaples Military Cemetery, Pas-de-Calais, France.

SHAW, JOHN: Rank: Private. Regiment or service: Leinster Regiment. Unit: 1st Battalion. Date of death: 15 March 1915. Service No.: 3297. Born in Carlow. Enlisted in Heath Camp, Queen's County. Died of wounds. From the *Nationalist* and *Leinster Times*, 1916:

SHAW—First Anniversary—In loving memory of Private John Shaw, 4th leinster regiment, Pollerton Road, Carlow, who died of wounds received in action in France, on the 15th March, 1915.

One year, to-day, we parted,
'Twas a heavy trial to bear;
God gives each one their share.
Your gentle face and manner,
Are present with us still;
But Heaven, for you, is far better.
Blessed by God's Holy Will.

Sacred Heart of Jesus have mercy on his soul. Immaculate Heart of Mary, pray for him. Inserted by his mother and father.

From the *Nationalist* and *Leinster Times*, March 1917:

SHAW—(Second Anniversary)— In loving memory of private John Shaw, 4th Leinster Regiment, of Pollerton Road, Carlow, who died of wounds received in action in France, on the 15th of march, 1915, aged 19 years. Sacred Heart of Jesus, have mercy on his soul. Immaculate Heart of Mary, pray for him.

The midnight stars are shining,
upon his distant grave,
Where the one we loved is sleeping,
the was a soldier brave.
He bade us not a last farewell, he
said good-bye to none,
His spirit flew before we knew, that
from us he had gone.
He sleeps beside his comrades in
hallowed graves unknown,
But his name is written in letters of
love in the hearts he left at home.
Inserted by his sorrowing parents,
brothers and sisters

Nationalist and *Leinster Times*, June, 1918.:

Shaw—Third Anniversary-In loving memory of John Shaw, Pollerton Road, Carlow, 1st Leinster Regiment, died from wounds received in action in France, aged 19 years.

Gone from the world so quickly,
plucked like a flower in its bloom.
So fair, so young, so loving, yet
called away so soon.
He was a flower too fair for Earth,
just sent here for a while;
God marked him when he gave
him birth and took him with a
smile.
The midnight stars are shining
upon his silent grave;
The one we loved lies sleeping—
the one we could not save.

Inserted by his loving father, mother, brothers and sisters.

Grave or memorial reference: Panel 44. Memorial: Ypres (Menin Gate) Memorial in Belgium. Also listed under Carlow/Graigue on the Great War Memorial, Milford Street, Leighlinbridge, County Carlow.

SHAW, LAWRENCE: Rank: Private. Regiment or service: Leinster Regiment. Unit: 1st Battalion. Date of death: 12 May 1915. Service No.: 9462. Born in Carlow. Enlisted in Maryborough, Queen's County. Killed in action. From the *Nationalist* and *Leinster Times*, May 1915:

Shaw—May 12th, 1915, killed in action. Andrew L Shaw, aged 20 years, 1st Leinsters, son of Laurence

Shaw, Carlow. Deeply regretted by his sorrowing father, brothers, sisters and relatives. Sweet Jesus, have mercy on him. —R. I. P.

Grave or memorial reference: Panel 44. Memorial: Ypres (Menin Gate) Memorial in Belgium. Also listed under Carlow/Graigue on the Great War Memorial, Milford Street, Leighlinbridge, County Carlow.

SHEA, DAVID: Rank: Private. Regiment or service: Royal Dublin Fusiliers. Unit: 2nd Battalion. Date of death: 6 July 1915. Age at death: 19. Service No.: 18270. Born in Leighlinbridge, County Carlow. Enlisted in Carlow. Killed in action.

Supplementary information: Son of Patrick and Anne Shea, of Leighlin Bridge, County Carlow. (See Finn, Peter). Name and number on will; O'Shea, David, No 18270, 2nd Battalion, Royal Dublin Fusiliers. Date of will: 28 May 1915. Effects and property received by: (Mother) Annie O'Shea, Poes Hill, Leighlin Bridge, County Carlow.

Grave or memorial reference: Coll. grave I. D. 31. Cemetery: Bard Cottage Cemetery in Belgium. Also listed under Leighlinbridge/Old Leighlin on the Great War Memorial, Milford Street, Leighlinbridge, County Carlow.

SHEA, MICHAEL: Rank: Sergeant. Regiment or service: Royal Scots (Lothian Regiment). Unit: 11th Battalion. He was part of the 27th Brigade 9th Scottish Division. Date of death: 21 March 1917. Age at death: 27.

Service No.: 16906. Born in Crettyard, Queen's County. Enlisted in Glasgow while living in Glasgow. Killed in action.

Supplementary information: Son of James and Mary Shea, of Clonbrock, Crettyard, Carlow.

Grave or memorial reference: Bay 1 and 2. He has no known grave but is listed on the Arras Memorial in France. Also listed under Carlow/Graigue on the Great War Memorial, Milford Street, Leighlinbridge, County Carlow.

SHIEL (CWGC, SDGW, IMR) **SHIELL,** (Great War Memorial, Milford Street, Leighlinbridge, County Carlow), **MICHAEL:** Rank: Private. Regiment or service: Royal Dublin Fusiliers. Unit: 2nd Battalion. Date of death: 3 July 1918. Age at death, 29. Service No.: 21067. Formerly he was with the South Irish Horse where his number was 2790. Born in Castledermott, County Kildare. Enlisted in Ayr while living in Mageney, County Carlow. Died of wounds.

Supplementary information: Son of John Shiel, of Castleroe, Maganey, County Kildare.

Grave or memorial reference: VII. A. 12. Cemetery: Cambrai East Military Cemetery, Nord, France.

SLATER, THOMAS: Rank: Sergeant. Regiment or service: Royal Horse Artillery and Royal Field Artillery. Unit: D Battery, 285th Brigade. Date of death: 9 April 1918. Service No.: 45819. Born in Carlow. Enlisted in Dublin. Killed in action. Grave or memorial reference: Panel 1. Memorial:

Ploegsteert Memorial in Belgium. Also listed under Carlow/Graigue on the Great War Memorial, Milford Street, Leighlinbridge, County Carlow.

SMITH, JOHN: Rank: Private. Regiment or service: Royal Dublin Fusiliers. Unit: 1st Battalion. Date of death: 16 May 1915. Service No.: 4573. Born in Leighlinbridge, County Carlow. Enlisted in Carlow. Died of wounds. From the *Nationalist* and *Leinster Times*, August 1914:

Irish Guardsman's Battle Stories.
The Fighting around Mons.
The following is taken from "The Scotsman" in its issue of 22nd November. Private Smith belongs to Seskinrea, Leighlinbridge; --

Private John Smith, 1st Battalion, Irish Guards, who is at present recovering from a shrapnel wound received in the recent fighting at Ypres, tells an interesting story. Private Smith arrived at Deaconess Hospital, Edinburgh, on Saturday. He has been at the front since the beginning of the war.

He took part in the trying times at Mons, the retreat, the recovery, the fierce battles of the Marne. He was at the "siege" of the Aisne, and latterly he was in the fighting at Ypres, and Ypres, according to Private Smith and several other soldiers who took part in the operations at that place, was the worst of the lot. For 15 days Private Smith was in the trenches. He described a particularly fierce German attack, the issue, which for some time hung in the balance, being decided, as frequently happens, by "cold steel."

"On the 8th November," said Private Smith, "the Germans started shelling our trenches about eight o'clock in the morning. They kept hard at it for hours, and then the infantry came forward to the attack in great masses. It was terrific. The French were in the trenches next our regiment, and the Germans broke through their lines at several points. This made it necessary for us to retire to a new position, and in doing so we lost a lot of our men. We formed up, however, and went at them with the bayonet. But it was no use; there were far too many of them. We fell back again, and just then the 2nd Life Guards came on the scene. That decided it. They put in their bayonets and made a tremendous charge, driving the Germans back, and taking 200 prisoners. Our losses were heavy, but for every one we lost it is certain the Germans lost twenty."
The Prussian Guards.

On two occasions Private Smith came up against the German "crack" corps, the Prussian Guard. There is no doubt, he says, that the Prussian Guard is a superior soldier to any other corp in the German Army. They are picked men, many of them, if not the majority, six feet high, and strongly built. "A finer body of men," said Private Smith, "it would be hard to see. They are very plucky, and they seem to be a better class of men altogether, intellectually and physically. When they come to the attack they give tremendous shouts, and they come forward in oped order, and not in masses, as is generally the case."

One case of treachery came under Private Smith's notice. While his regiment was at Soupier, the bread was supplied to the troops by a local baker. This man came under suspicion, and he was subsequently arrested. Nothing could be proved against him, however, and he was liberated. When the British left, the place was occupied by French troops, who were warned to keep the baker under observation. On the first day that the French arrived the baker was discovered endeavouring to send information to the enemy by mans of pigeons. He was shot.
An Exciting Encounter.

It was at Soupier that Private Smith and a "chum" had a narrow escape. "We were fighting at the edge of a wood," said Private Smith. "The Germans were some distance in front. Presently some Germans showed themselves carrying a white flag. But we had been so often "had" with that dodge that the officer told us to keep on firing, which we did. Shortly afterwards we got the order to advance, and crossing a field we came upon a crowd of Germans, Some of us fixed bayonets and charged, and a number of the Germans put up their hands. We disarmed them, and sent them into a wood. We then crossed over a small hollow, and climbed a slope, and at the other side we ran into another crowd of Germans. My chum and I were somewhat detached, and three Germans came straight at us.

One was an officer with a revolver, and the other two had fixed their bayonets. One of the soldiers made a lunge at me, but I caught his bayonet and put him out with a knock on the head. When I was engaged with this fellow the second German came at me with his bayonet, but before he got close my chum ran his bayonet through him. The officer fired on us with his revolver; missed us, but one of the bullets hit one of several Grenadier Guards who were coming to our aid. We captured the officer. Some time after this we had to lie five hours in a turnip field. We got between the enemy and our own men, and there was a hot rifle fire from both sides. We lay there till dusk, when the Grenadiers advanced. One of our men was shot while we were lying in the field."
Cattle Roasted to Death.

One of the most affecting sights which Private Smith saw was at a farm near Soupier. There was a big herd of cattle on the farm, and it was as pretty a sight as one could see. During the night the Germans shelled the farmhouse and buildings, which caught fire. In the morning the soldiers went to the smouldering ruins, and in the cattle sheds they were horrified to discover that all the cattle—numbering in all 140— had been burned to death. At some of the stalls it was clear that the animals had made desperate attempts to get their liberty.

… Private Smith said that the health of the men in the trenches was very good notwithstanding their privations. This was entirely owing to the precautions that were taken. There was practically no fever, which we believed was very prevalent in the German trenches.

Grave or memorial reference: D. 109. Cemetery: Lincoln (Newport) Cemetery, Lincolnshire, UK. Also listed as **SMYTH, JOHN** under Leighlinbridge/Old Leighlin on the Great War Memorial, Milford Street, Leighlinbridge, County Carlow.

SMULLEN, JOHN: Rank: Private. Regiment or service: Royal Dublin Fusiliers. Unit: B Company 2nd Battalion. Date of death: 24 May 1915. Age at death: 17. Service No.: 5606. Born in Leighlinbridge, County Carlow. Enlisted in Carlow. Killed in action.
Supplementary information: Son of Charles and Maggie Smullen, of Church Street, Leighlinbridge, County Carlow.
Grave or memorial reference: Panel 44 and 46. Memorial: Ypres (Menin Gate) Memorial in Belgium. Also listed under Leighlinbridge/Old Leighlin on the Great War Memorial, Milford Street, Leighlinbridge, County Carlow.

SMYTH, JOHN: See **SMITH, JOHN.**

SMYTHE, ALBERT EDWARD: Rank: Private. Regiment or service: Irish Guards. Unit: 1st Battalion. Date of death: 1 November 1914. Age at death: 18. Service No.: 4480. Born in Old Leighlin, County Carlow. Enlisted in Carlow while living in Rathdrum, County Wicklow. Killed in action.
Supplementary information: Son of Edward Henry and Esther Hamilton Smythe, of Knockbawn, Enniskerry, County Wicklow. One of five sons who served in the Great War. From the *Nationalist* and *Leinster Times*. April 1916:

Roll of Honour.
SMYTHE—Killed in action, near Ypres, on November 1st, 1914, Albert Edward Smythe, 1st Irish Guards, fourth son of Edward H. and Mrs Smythe, Grove Hall, Rathdrum (late of Seskinrea, Leighlinbridge) age 19 years. (Smythe is recorded in the 1901 census as being born in Carlow, as is his family.)

Grave or memorial reference: He has no known grave but is listed on Panel 11 on the Ypres (Menin Gate) Memorial in Belgium. Also listed under Leighlinbridge/Old Leighlin on the Great War Memorial, Milford Street, Leighlinbridge, County Carlow.

SPARKS, MARGARET: Rank: Unknown. Regiment or service: Unknown. Unit: SS *Leinster.* Date of death: 10 October 1918. Steamship *Leinster* was hit by a German Torpedo and sank with the loss of over 400 people. It was the greatest maritime disaster in Irish Waters.
Supplementary information: Address at Farquar Road, SW 19. Only daughter of the late the Richard Sparks of Carlow. Information above compliments of Peter Lecane.

Grave or memorial reference: Has no known grave but is commemorated on the Tower Hill Memorial, London.

STAPLETON, JAMES: Rank: Private. Regiment or service: Royal Irish Fusiliers. Unit: 1st Battalion. Date of death: 1 July 1916. Service No.: 8921. Born in Bagnalstown, County Carlow. Enlisted in Carlow while living in Bagnalstown, County Carlow. Killed in action. Grave or memorial reference: I. I. 7. Cemetery: Sucrerie Military Cemetery, Colinclamps in France. Also listed under Bagenalstown/Fenagh on the Great War Memorial, Milford Street, Leighlinbridge, County Carlow.

STEEDMAN, WILLIAM (CWGC, SDGW)**:** Rank: Sergeant. Regiment or service: Royal Field Artillery. Unit: C Battery. 40th Brigade. Date of death: 19 September 1917. Age at death: 27. Service No.: 49975. Born in Tennessee, USA. Enlisted in Edinburgh. Died of wounds.

Supplementary information: Husband of Anna Steedman, of Mill Street, Carlow, Ireland. From the *Nationalist* and *Leinster Times*, 1917:

Late Sergeant Steadman.

My dear Mrs Steadman—You will have heard from his own Captain and Battery Commander of the gallant end of your boy, Sergeant William Steadman of the 6th Battery. I Joined this division over six months ago, and since that time I had grown to know and love your husband. He was a splendid soldier, a most efficient section commander, cheerful, resourceful and calm, yet full of spirit under the most trying circumstances; but what I most like to tell you is that always and invariably he was a sterling Catholic, regular in his practice, most devoted to his religion, and offering a magnificent example to the Catholics of his battery. I heard his confession only three days before the end came, and it came as it does to so many of us out here very suddenly. A shell landed just outside the muzzle of the gun, and he got a shock, had his left shoulder torn and was killed instantaneously—almost one might say painlessly. His body was brought down from the position to the lines and there yesterday evening I took his funeral and buried him at about 6 p. m. in the military cemetery. The sergeant in charge of the party (a very fine Catholic) assisted me at the burial and the officer commanding the lines was present, as also were so many of the men, though they had been up from three that morning and---fully overworked. It was a beautiful tribute to the affection and reverence inspired by your boy's life and death. I myself must now hurry up to the guns, in order to be with my other boys, and I am sure you will forgive this brief and hurried note in consequence. To say that I loved your boy is to utter a platitude. He won the affection of all, and he died doing his duty to his King and Country, having never forgotten his duty to God. What a comfort that must be to you in your sad bereavement. Believe me I shall not forget him at Holy Mass, nor you either who need all the comfort God and his holy Mother, the consoir(?) of the afflicted, can give to you. Often I feel that there are sadder things happening in distant English homes, and in the hearts of loving mothers and wives and sweethearts than we ever see out here, where death and its horrors are so manifest. God bless you, my dear Mrs Steadman, and may the Passion of His own beloved Son be your strength and the Mother of Sorrows your comforter in your great sorrow. I shall not forget to pray for your son, Pray too, for my men and for me a poor Catholic Priest who needs al the help of God—Believe me, my dear Mrs Steadman, with the deepest sympathy, ever yours sincerely in Christ.

L. E. Bettanti, S. J., C. P.
19th September, 1917.

Dear Mrs Steadman—It is with the greatest regret that I have to inform you that your husband, Sergeant Steadman, of the Battery under my command, was killed in action at about 10 p. m. last night.

A shell entered the gun-pit killing him instantly and wounding three others. I am perfectly certain his death was painless, and I don't think he ever knew he was hit.

Sergeant Steadman was one of the best N. C. O's in my battery, and his loss to me is a great one. The loss to you is infinitely greater, and at first must seem overwhelm-

ing, but believe me, after a time you will feel proud of the death he died, and of the sacrifice you have made for our King and Country, and your sorrow will be so much the less. The Officers, N. C. O's, and men join with me in offering you our sincerest sympathy in your sad bereavement.

Sergeant Steadman's personal kit, etc, will be sent to you in due course. —Yours sincerely,

E. Munt, Captain.
Commanding 6th Battery, R. F. A.

From the *Nationalist* and *Leinster Times*, 1917:

STEADMAN—September 19th, 1917, killed in action, Sergeant William Steadman, Royal Field Artillery, deeply regretted by his sorrowing wife, R. I. P. Queen of the Holy Rosary pray for him.

Grave or memorial reference: I. F. 17. Cemetery: Brandhoek New Military Cemetery No. 3 in Belgium.

STEWART, ALASTAIR DUNCAN: Rank: Private. Regiment or service: Royal Dublin Fusiliers. Unit: 1st Battalion. Date of death: 4 October 1917. Service No.: 29762. Born in Marylebone, Middlesex. Enlisted in Dublin while living in Bagnalstown, County Carlow. Killed in action.

Supplementary information: Son of Mrs L. Stewart, of Blair-Atholl, Perthshire. Grave or memorial reference: Panel 144 to 145. Memorial: Tyne

Cot Memorial in Belgium. Also listed under Bagenalstown/Fenagh on the Great War Memorial, Milford Street, Leighlinbridge, County Carlow.

STORRAR, ANDREW WYNNE:
Rank: Second Lieutenant. Regiment or service: Royal Dublin Fusiliers. Unit: 2nd Battalion, attached to the 48th Trench Mortar Battery. Date of death: 16 August 1917. Age at death: 35. Killed in action.

Supplementary information: Son of Major David Morrison Storrar, TD, and Lily Hodgson Storrar, of Plasnewydd, Crumlin, Mon. L. D. S. Edin. and Liverpool. From the *Carlow Sentinel*, August 1917:

Lieutenant E Wynne Storrar.
News which reached Carlow on Tuesday announcing (unofficially) that Lieutenant Wynne Storrar, Dublin Fusiliers, had been killed in action in France, has caused widespread regret. A few weeks since when on active leave, previous to returning to France, Lieutenant Storrar visited friends in Carlow, where for several years he enjoyed a large practice in dental surgery, which he relinquished and joined the colours at the call of King and Country. As yet no particulars connected with his death have been received.

From the *Carlow Sentinel*, September 1917.

Roll of Honour.
Second Lieutenant A. W. Storrar.
A fortnight back we announced that friends in Carlow had received infor-mation that Second Lieutenant A. W. Storrar had been killed while serving with the colours in France. In the absence, however, of an official announcement, hopes were entertained that a mistake might possibly have occurred, but the inclusion of his name in last Monday's casualty list left no room for doubt, as he was reported killed in action on August 6th. (listed in the 1911 census living in Dublin Street, Carlow.)

Grave or memorial reference: II. E. 18. Cemetery: Potijze Chateau Grounds Cemetery in Belgium. Also listed under Carlow/Graigue on the Great War Memorial, Milford Street, Leighlinbridge, County Carlow.

SULLIVAN, JOHN:
Rank: Lance Corporal. Regiment or service: Royal Dublin Fusiliers. Unit: W Company. 1st Battalion. Date of death: 3 June 1918. Age at death: 22. Service No.: 14523. Born in Dublin Enlisted in Dublin. Died of wounds.

Supplementary information: Son of Bridget Sullivan, of Borris, County Carlow, and the late Michael Sullivan. From the *Nationalist* and *Leinster Times*, November 1918:

Carlow Soldier's Death in Palestine.
News has reached Carlow of the death in Palestine of Private Thomas Sunderland, 13 R. I. R. Deceased belonged to Castle Hill, Carlow. He was killed in action on September 21st during the advance in Palestine. At the outbreak of the war Private Sunderland was in India and served

two years in France, where he was wounded. Captain Pilworth, writing to the dead soldiers mother, says that after being hit he was attended by the Chaplain, Rev. Father O'Carroll, and also received medical aid. He was a gallant soldier, continued the captain, and always performed his duty with commendable bravery and pluck. Rev. Father O'Carroll also wrote informing the parents that he administered the last Rites of Holy Church.

Grave or memorial reference: Panel 10. Memorial: Ploegsteert Memorial in Belgium. Also listed under Borris/Ballyellin on the Great War Memorial, Milford Street, Leighlinbridge, County Carlow.

SUNDERLAND, THOMAS: Rank: Private. Regiment or service: Royal Irish Regiment. Unit: 1st Battalion. Date of death: 21 September 1918 (CWGC, IMR, SDGW) 20 September 1918 (Great War Memorial, Milford Street, Leighlinbridge, County Carlow). Age at death: 25. Service No.: 9709. Born in Carlow. Enlisted in Maryborough while living in County Carlow. Died of wounds in Palestine.

Supplementary information: Son of James and Mary Sunderland, of Castle Street, Carlow.

Grave or memorial reference: Panel 18. Memorial: Jerusalem memorial in Israel. Also listed under Carlow/Graigue on the Great War Memorial, Milford Street, Leighlinbridge, County Carlow.

SUTTON, FRANK: Rank: Private. Regiment or service: Leinster Regiment. Unit: Depot. Date of death: 16 October 1915. Age at death: 30. Service No.: 3017 and 6/3017. Born in Clydie, County Carlow. Enlisted in Dublin. Died at home.

Supplementary information: Husband of Ellen Sutton, of 14 Railway Avenue, Inchicore, Dublin.

Grave or memorial reference: Mil. Con. C. 3562. Cemetery: Plymouth (Weston Mill) Cemetery, Devon, UK. Also listed under Leighlinbridge/Old Leighlin on the Great War Memorial, Milford Street, Leighlinbridge, County Carlow.

SWAINE, LAWRENCE: Rank: Private. Regiment or service: Leinster Regiment. Unit: 1st Battalion. Date of death: 15 March 1915. Age at death: 21. Service No.: 3413. Born in Tullow, County Carlow. Enlisted in Maryborough, Queen's County. Killed in action.

Supplementary infortmation: Son of Mrs Teresa Swayne, of Main Street, Stradbally, Queen's County.

Grave or memorial reference: Panel 44. He has no known grave but is listed in the Ypres (Menin Gate) Memorial in Belgium. Also listed under Tullow on the Great War Memorial, Milford Street, Leighlinbridge, County Carlow.

T

TALLON, PATRICK: Rank: Private. Regiment or service: Royal Dublin Fusiliers. Unit: 1st Battalion. Date of death: 3 September 1915. Age at death: 43. Service No.: 21586. Formerly he was with the Royal Army Medical Corps where his number was 39486. Born in Clanmore, Hackettstown, County Carlow. Enlisted in Liverpool. Died of wounds in Gallipoli.

Supplementary information: Son of the late James and Anne Tallon. Served in the Boer War.

Grave or memorial reference: Panel 190 to 196. Memorial: Helles Memorial in Turkey.

TEEHAN, CHRISTOPHER: Rank: Private. Regiment or service: Royal Dublin Fusiliers. Unit: 9th Battalion. Date of death: 7 June 1917. Service No.: 28023. Born in Tullow, County Carlow. Enlisted in Naas while living in Tullow, County Carlow. Killed in action. Grave or memorial reference: I. B. 1. Cemetery: Lindenhoek Chalet Military Cemetery, Heuvelland in Belgium. Also listed under Tullow on the Great War Memorial, Milford Street, Leighlinbridge, County Carlow.

THOMAS, AUBREY JOCELYN NUGENT: Rank: Captain. Regiment or service: Lancashire Fusiliers. Unit: 1st Battalion. Date of death: 25 April 1915 (CWGC) 1 May 1915 (ODGW, Great War Memorial, Milford Street,

Leighlinbridge, County Carlow, he is not listed in IMR). Age at death: 29.

Supplementary information: Son of Captain J. H. W. Thomas (retired), of Belmont, Carlow, Ireland. From De Ruvigny's Roll of Honour:

>…elder son of Jocelyn H. W. Thomas, of Belmont, Carlow, Ireland, formerly captain, Scots Fusiliers Guards. Born at Belmont, County Carlow, 23-September-1888. Educated at Harrow and Sandhurst. Gazetted 2nd Lieutenant, 1st Lancashire Fusiliers, 16-August-1905, and promoted Lieutenant, 29-May-1909, and Captain, 20-January-1915. Served with the Mediterranean Expeditionary Force, and was killed in action during the landing of the Lancashire Fusiliers at Beach W, Gallipoli, 25-April-1915.

From *Carlow Sentinel*, May 1915:

>Captain A. H. N. Thomas.
>On Monday last a wire reached Carlow announcing the sad intelligence of the death of Captain Aubrey Jocelyn Nugent Thomas, Lancashire Fusiliers (killed in action at the Dardanelles on the previous Saturday.) He was the elder son of Captain Jocelyn H. W. Thomas, of Belmont, Carlow, was bron in September, 1885, and entered the service in 1905. He obtained promotion in 1909, and secured his company in January of this year.

He recently returned to England with his Regiment, which was serving in India, and during his short stay before proceeding to the Dardanelles, paid a hurried visit extending over only a few days, to his home. The sad news of his untimely death, was received with feeling of sincere regret by the residents of this his native town, where he was held in the highest esteem. The deepest sympathy is extended to his father and family in their bereavement.

At a meeting of the Carlow Refugee Committee on Wednesday a resolution, proposed by Mr Henry Bruen, D. L., and seconded by Mr Walter McM. Kavanagh, D. L., was passed expressing deep sympathy with captain Thomas and family in their bereavement.

Grave or memorial reference: I. 99. Cemetery: Lancashire Landing Cemetery in Turkey. Also listed under Carlow/Graigue on the Great War Memorial, Milford Street, Leighlinbridge, County Carlow.

THOMPSON, SIMON: Rank: Rifleman. Regiment or service: Royal Irish Rifles. Unit: 2nd Battalion. Date of death: 9 July 1916. Service No.: 8866. Born in Tullow, County Carlow. Enlisted in Waterford. Killed in action. Grave or memorial reference: Pier and Face 15 A and 15 B. Memorial: Thiepval Memorial in France. Also listed under Tullow on the Great War Memorial, Milford Street, Leighlinbridge, County Carlow.

TIERNEY, MARTIN: Rank: Private. Regiment or service: Leinster Regiment. Unit: 2nd Battalion. Date of death: 20 May 1916. Service No.: 106.

Supplementary information: Son of Mr Tierney, of 3, East Cottages, Burry Port, Carmarthenshire. Born in Carlow. Enlisted in Maryborough, Queen's County. Killed in action. Date of will: 1 April 1916. Effects and property received by; Mrs Johanna Tierney, Bridewell Street, Carlow, Ireland. From the *Nationalist* and *Leinster Times*, 1916.:

Roll of Honour.
TIERNEY—Killed in action in France, on May 20th, 1916, Private Martin Tierney, Bridewell Lane, Carlow, 2nd Battalion, Leinster Regiment.

He bade us not a last farewell,
He said good-bye to none.
His spirit flew, before we knew,
That from us he had gone.

Inserted by his loving mother, father, and sisters. —R. I. P.

Grave or memorial reference: II. B. 20. Cemetery: Ration Farm Military Cemetery, La Chapelle-Darmentieres, Nord in France. Also listed under Carlow/Graigue on the Great War Memorial, Milford Street, Leighlinbridge, County Carlow.

TIMMINS, JAMES: Rank: Private. Regiment or service: Leinster Regiment. Unit: 2nd Battalion. Date of death: 31 July 1917. Service No.: 3328.

Born in Carlow. Enlisted in Carlow. Killed in action.

Supplementary information: After his death his effects and property received by his mother. His Nuncupative (or missing) will was witnessed by Mrs E. Heaens(sic), Mill Lane, Carlow.

Grave or memorial reference: Enclosure No. 4 VIII. C. 8. Cemetery, Bedford House Cemetery in Belgium. Also listed under Carlow/Graigue on the Great War Memorial, Milford Street, Leighlinbridge, County Carlow.

TOOLE, JAMES: Rank: Private. Regiment or service: Leinster Regiment. Unit: 2nd Battalion. Date of death: 6 May 1915. Service No.: 3415. Born in Tullow, County Carlow. Enlisted in Maryborough. Killed in action.

Supplementary informaion: From his estate, after he died, £5 was given to Mrs Fanning, and the rest of the property to Mrs Fanning, Castlemore, Tullow County Carlow.

Grave or memorial reference: C. 7. Cemetery: Ferme Buterne Military Cemetery, Houplines in France. Also listed under Tullow on the Great War Memorial, Milford Street, Leighlinbridge, County Carlow.

TOWNSEND, JOHN: Rank: Gunner. Regiment or service: Royal Garrison Artillery. Unit: 242nd Siege Battery. Date of death: 14 August 1917. Service No.: 126540. Born in Leighlinbridge, County Carlow. Enlisted in Carlow while living in Bagenalstown, County Carlow. Died of wounds.

Supplementary information: Son of William and Kate Townsend (*née* Walsh), of Barret Street, Bagenalstown, County Carlow.

Grave or memorial reference: I. D. 6. Cemetery: Godewaersvelde British Cemetery in France. Also listed under Leighlinbridge/Old Leighlin on the Great War Memorial, Milford Street, Leighlinbridge, County Carlow.

TOWNSEND, MICHAEL: Rank: Private. Regiment or service: Royal Irish Regiment. Unit: 2nd Battalion. Date of death: 20 November 1917. Age at death: 22. Service No.: 7924. Born in Carlow Graigue, County Carlow. Enlisted in Carlow while living in Carlow Graigue. Killed in action.

Supplementary information: Son of Mary Townsend, of Leighton Street, Graigue, Carlow, and the late John Townsend.

Grave or memorial reference: II. D. 18. Cemetery: Croisilles British Cemetery in France. Also listed under Carlow/Graigue on the Great War Memorial, Milford Street, Leighlinbridge, County Carlow.

TUITE, PATRICK: Rank: Private. Regiment or service: Royal Dublin Fusiliers. Unit: 1st Battalion. Date of death: 15 July 1917. Service No.: 19747. Born in Bagnalstown, County Carlow. Enlisted in Carlow. Died of wounds.

Supplementary information: After his death his effects and property received by his wife, Mrs Maggie Tuite, Kilcarrig Street, Bagenalstown, County Carlow.

Grave or memorial reference: III. B. 24. Cemetery: Bard Cottage Cemetery in Belgium. Also listed under Bagenalstown/Fenagh on the Great War Memorial, Milford Street, Leighlinbridge, County Carlow.

V

VENABLES, ALFRED C.: Rank:
Private. Regiment or service: Royal
Irish Regiment. Unit: 7th (South
Irish Horse)Battalion. Date of death:
21 March 1918. Service No.: 25918,
South Irish Horse number was 1275.
Born in Carlow. Enlisted in Dublin
while living in Drumcondra, County
Dublin. Killed in action. Grave or
memorial reference: Panel 30 and
31. Memorial: Pozieres Memorial in
France. Also listed as **ALFRED C.
ENABLES** under Carlow/Graigue on
the Great War Memorial, Milford Street,
Leighlinbridge, County Carlow.

WALKER, THOMAS: Rank: Sergeant. Regiment or service: Royal Dublin Fusiliers. Unit: 1st Battalion. Date of death: 12 July 1915. Age at death: 21. Service No.: 5486. Born in Carlow Graigue, County Carlow. Enlisted in Carlow. Killed in action in Gallipoli.

Supplementary information: Son of Peter and Ellen Walker, of Green Lane, Carlow. After his death his effects and property was willed to, and received by, his mother, Mrs Walker Greene, Carlow, Ireland.

Grave or memorial reference: VII. D. 18. Cemetery: Twelve Tree Copse Cemetery in Turkey. Also listed under Carlow/Graigue on the Great War Memorial, Milford Street, Leighlinbridge, County Carlow.

WALL, EDWARD: Rank: Sergeant. Regiment or service: Royal Dublin Fusiliers. Unit: 9th Battalion. Date of death: 9 September 1916. Service No.: 15717. Born in Tullow, County Carlow. Enlisted in Dublin while living in Carlow. Killed in action. Date of will: 3 September 1916. After his death his effects and property was willed to, and received by, his brother, Mr Michael Wall, Barrack Street, Tullow, County Carlow, Ireland. From the *Nationalist and Leinster Times*, 1915:

Private Stephen Wall, late of Green Street, writing to Mrs McWey, thanks her and the ladies of Carlow for their thoughtfulness in sending gifts. In a letter to his parents, Private Wall also mentions the kindness of the Carlow Red Cross Society. He says he has no chance of getting home unless he gets wounded, which he is not anxious for. (Stephen was a brother of Edward and survived the war.)

Grave or memorial reference: He has no known grave but is listed on Pier and Face 16C on the Theipval Memorial in France. Also listed under Tullow on the Great War Memorial, Milford Street, Leighlinbridge, County Carlow.

WALSH, JAMES: Rank: Private. Regiment or service: Royal Irish Regiment. Unit: 1st Battalion. Date of death: 16 March 1915 Service No.: 4202. Born in Muckalee, County Kilkenny. Enlisted in Kilkenny while living in Coolcullen, County Kilkenny. Killed in action.

Supplementary information: Son of John and Margaret Walsh, of Seskin Rea, Old Leighlin, Bagenalstown, County Carlow.

Grave or memorial reference: Panel 33. Memorial: Ypres (Menin Gate) Memorial in Belgium. Also listed under Leighlinbridge/Old Leighlin on the Great War Memorial, Milford Street, Leighlinbridge, County Carlow.

WALSH, MICHAEL: See **WELSH, MICHAEL.**

WALSH, PATRICK MALACHY:
Rank: Private. Regiment or service: Royal Munster Fusiliers. Unit: 8th Battalion. Date of death: 16 September 1916. Service No.: 1707. Born in Mageney, County Carlow. Enlisted in Swansea while living in Swansea. Died of wounds. Grave or memorial reference: B. 19. 35. Cemetery: St Sever Cemetery, Rouen in France. Also listed under Carlow/Graigue on the Great War Memorial, Milford Street, Leighlinbridge, County Carlow.

WALSH, WILLIAM ARTHUR:
Rank: Bombardier. Regiment or service: Royal Garrison Artillery. Date of death: 28 December 1916. Age at death: 34. Service No.: 1454. Formerly he was with the Royal Garrison Artillery, 137th Deptford H. B., where his number was 1454. Died of wounds in the War Hospital in Halifax.

Supplementary information: Son of the late Henry and Jane Walsh, of Rutland, Bennekerry, Carlow. Born in Dublin. Enlisted in Dublin while living in Bennekerry, County Carlow. Personal effects: Ready Cash in change to (brother) R. Walsh, R/m Nengh, County Tipperary. (Mother or if deceased, two brothers and sister at home) 50 Dufferin Avenue, S.C. Road, Dublin, Ireland. Insurance Policies on mother to (brother) Richard Gunner Walsh, 1454 Rutland Binekerry, Carlow, Ireland. Gold ring watch and chain to (fiancee), Millie Gilbert, 6 Dame Street, Dublin, Ireland. From the *Carlow Sentinel*, January 1917.

Roll of Honour.
Tribute to a Carlow Soldier.
The many friends of Bombardier William A. Walsh, will learn with sincere regret that he succumbed last week to the wound recently received in action in France. He was a native of Rutland, County Carlow, but resident for many years in Dublin, where he held the position of buyer in the plumbing department of Messrs John C Parkes and Sons, Ltd, of whose staff he was one of the most popular members. Though never of a robust constitution, he responded to the call of duty by joining in November, 1915, the Royal Garrison Artillery, proceeding with his battery ij May last, where he saw constant active service until November, when he received the wound which subsequently proved fatal. He had proved a keen soldier and earned the regard of his officers and comrades, by whom his loss will be felt as keenly as by the large circle of friends who mourn the passing of a true and loyal comrade. He was a member of the Executive Committee of the Pickwick Club, and was also well known in other social circles in the city.

Grave or memorial reference: J. A. 92. Cemetery: Halifax (Stoney Royd) Cemetery, Yorkshire, UK. Also listed under Palatine/Urglin on the Great War Memorial, Milford Street, Leighlinbridge, County Carlow.

WALSH, WILLIAM: Rank: Private. Regiment or service: Irish Guards.

Unit: 2nd Battalion. Date of death: 15 September 1916. Service No.: 7532. Born in Carlow. Enlisted in Carlow. Killed in action. From the *Nationalist and Leinster Times*.

Killed in action.

Official news reached Bagenalstown this week intimating that Private William Walshe, Irish Guards, was killed in action in France. Previous to joining the army he was employed at Messrs. Brown and Croswaith's Flour Mills, where he was a general favourite with his fellow-workmen. In Gaelic circles he won more laurels as a footballer and hurler. His stamina on the field secured for his team easy wins over opponents.

Grave or memorial reference: Pier and Face 7D. Memorial: Thiepval Memorial in France. Also listed under Carlow/ Graigue on the Great War Memorial, Milford Street, Leighlinbridge, County Carlow.

WALSH, WILLIAM: Rank: Private. Regiment or service: Royal Irish Regiment. Unit: 2nd Battalion. Date of death: 24 May 1915. Age at death: 24. Service No.: 6487. Born in St Patrick's, Waterford. Enlisted in Waterford. Killed in action.

Supplementary information: Son of William and Johanna Walsh, of Philip St, Waterford.

Grave or memorial reference: He has no known grave but is listed on Panel 33 on the Ypres (Menin Gate) Memorial in Belgium. Also listed under Bagenalstown/Fenagh on the

Great War Memorial, Milford Street, Leighlinbridge, County Carlow.

WATCHORN, ABRAHAM: Rank: Private. Regiment or service: Royal Dublin Fusiliers. Unit: 5th Battalion. Date of death: 26 April 1916. Age at death: 21. Service No.: 25026. Born in Wicklow. Enlisted in Naas while living in Rathvilly, County Wicklow. Died at home.

Supplementary information: Son of Abraham Watchorn, of Williamstown, Rathvilly, County Carlow. From De Ruvigny's Roll of Honour:

Elder son of Abraham Watchorn, of Williamstown, Rathvilly, County Carlow, Farmer, by his wife, Jane, daughter, of George James. Born at Dundrum, County Dublin, 20 Oct, 1894. Educated at Lisnavagh and was a farmer. Enlisted 22 Nov, 1915; and was killed in action during the Dublin Rebellion, 26th April, 1916.

He is also listed on the Casualty List in the *Waterford News*, May 1916. He was named on a list of wounded in the *Waterford News*.

Grave or memorial reference: CE. 625. Cemetery, Grangegorman Military Cemetery in Dublin. Also listed under Rathvilly on the Great War Memorial, Milford Street, Leighlinbridge, County Carlow.

WATERS, JAMES: Rank: Private. Regiment or service: South Lancashire Regiment. Unit: 8th Battalion. Date of death: 31 October 1918. Age at death:

24. Service No.: 34193. Born in Carlow. Enlisted in Llanelly, Glamorganshire while living in Carlow. Died at home. Grave or memorial reference: R.C. 594. Cemetery: Grangegorman Military Cemetery in Dublin. Also listed under Carlow/Graigue on the Great War Memorial, Milford Street, Leighlinbridge, County Carlow.

WELSH (IMR, SDGW, CWGC) WALSH (Great War Memorial, Milford Street, Leighlinbridge, County Carlow), MICHAEL: Rank: Gunner. Regiment or service: Royal Garrison Artillery. Unit: 287th Siege Battery. Date of death: 22 November 1917. Age at death, 44. Service No.: 41807. Born in Arls, Carlow, Queen's County. Enlisted in Reading while living in Ballyfoyle, Queen's County. Killed in action.

Supplementary information: Son of John and Mary Ann Walsh, of Ballyfoyle, Maganey, County Kildare.

Grave or memorial reference: III. B. 3. Cemetery: Ypres Reservoir Cemetery in Belgium. Also listed under Carlow/Graigue on the Great War Memorial, Milford Street, Leighlinbridge, County Carlow.

WESTROPP-DAWSON, WALTER HENRY MOUNTIFORD: Rank: 2nd Lieutenant Regiment or service: Cheshire Regiment. Unit: 2nd Battalion. Date of death: 24 May 1915. Age at death: 22. Killed in action.

Supplementary information: Son of Frank and L. C. Westropp-Dawson, of 'Frondeg', Holyhead, Charlesfort, County Wexford and Utpon, County Carlow. His medals and death plaque were sold in an English auction house in 2004. From an article in The *Enniscorthy Guardian*:

County Wexford Officer reported killed. Second-Lieutenant W. H. M.. Westropp-Dawson, 15th Hussars, who is unofficially reported killed in France on 25th July, was the eldest son of Mr F Westropp-Dawson, Charlesfort, County Wexford.

Grave or memorial reference: He has no known grave but is listed on Panel 19-22 on the Ypres (Menin Gate) Memorial in Belgium.

WHEATLEY, ANTHONY: Rank: Gunner. Regiment or service: Australian Field Artillery. Unit: Headquarters Staff, 2nd Brigade, 5th Reinforcements. Date of death: 8 July 1915. Service No.: 4205. Died of wounds in Gallipoli.

Supplemtary Information: Son of Anthony Weatley, Hacketstown later changed to Barkle, Kittegan, Baltinglass, Count Wicklow, Ireland. Height, 5 feet 6 inches. Eyes, blue. Complexion, fair. Hair, fair. Weight, 11st 2ozs. Born in Hacketstwn, County Carlow. Enlisted 8 January 1915 at Liverpool, N. S. W. Age on enlistment: 29 years 10 months. Occupation on enlistment, labourer.

Grave or memorial reference: II. D. 10. Cemetery: Beach Cemetery, Anzac, Turkey.

WHELAN, MICHAEL: Rank: Rifleman. Regiment or service: London Regiment. Unit: 8th (City of London)

Battalion (Post Office Rifles). Date of death: 15 September 1916. Service No.: 371322. Born in Tullow, County Carlow. Enlisted in Tullow while living in Tullow, County Carlow. Killed in action. Grave or memorial reference: Pier and Face 9 C and 9 D. Memorial: Thiepval Memorial in France. Also listed under Tullow on the Great War Memorial, Milford Street, Leighlinbridge, County Carlow.

WHELAN, NICHOLAS: Rank: Private. Regiment or service: Irish Guards. Unit: 2nd Battalion. Age at death: 25. Date of death: 19 December 1916 Service No.: 7736. Born in Tullow, County Carlow. Enlisted in Carlow. Died.

Supplementary information: Son of Thomas and Mary Whelan (*née* Byrne), of The Green, Tullow, County Carlow.

Grave or memorial reference: B. 37. Cemetery: La Neuville Communal Cemetery, Corbie, Somme, France. Also listed under Tullow on the Great War Memorial, Milford Street, Leighlinbridge, County Carlow.

WHELAN, RICHARD: Rank: Private. Regiment or service: Irish Guards. Unit: 2nd Battalion. Date of death: 12 September 1917. Age at death: 20. Service No.: 9356. Born in Jamestown, County Carlow. Enlisted in Maryborough, Queen's County. Killed in action.

Supplementary information: Son of Thomas and Mary Whelan, of Coolnafearagh, Monasterevan, County Kildare.

Grave or memorial reference: Panel 10 and 11. Memorial: Tyne Cot Memorial in Belgium. Also listed under Carlow/ Graigue on the Great War Memorial, Milford Street, Leighlinbridge, County Carlow.

WHELAN, THOMAS: Rank: Lance Corporal. Regiment or service: Royal Dublin Fusiliers. Unit: 9th Battalion. Date of death: 27 April 1916. Age at death: 40. Service No.: 23969. Born in Tullow, County Carlow. Enlisted in Carlow while living in Tullow, County Carlow. Killed in action.

Supplementary information: Brother of Patrick Whelan, of Paulwille, Tullow, County Carlow.

Grave or memorial reference: Panel 127 to 129. Memorial: Loos Memorial in France. Also listed under Tullow on the Great War Memorial, Milford Street, Leighlinbridge, County Carlow.

WHELAN, THOMAS: Rank: Private. Regiment or service: Royal Inniskilling Fusiliers. Unit: 2nd Battalion. Date of death: 16 May 1915 (CWGC, IMR, SDGW), 27 August 1914 (Great War Memorial, Milford Street, Leighlinbridge). Age at death: 39. Service No.: 13226. Born in Rathrush, County Carlow. Enlisted in Liverpool while living in Carlow. Killed in action.

Supplementary information: Son of Patrick and Bridget Whelan, Rathrush, Tullow, County Carlow.

Grave or memorial reference: Panel 16 and 17. Memorial: Le Touret Memorial in France. Also listed under Ballon/Rathoe/Aghade on the

Great War Memorial, Milford Street, Leighlinbridge, County Carlow.

WHELAN, THOMAS: Rank: Private. Regiment or service: Royal Dublin Fusiliers. Unit: 2nd Battalion. Date of death: 24 October 1914. Service No.: 7556. Born in Carlow. Enlisted in Carlow. Killed in action. Grave or memorial reference: Panel 10. Memorial: Ploegsteert Memorial in Belgium. Also listed under Carlow/Graigue on the Great War Memorial, Milford Street, Leighlinbridge, County Carlow.

WHELAN, WILLIAM: Rank: Private. Regiment or service: Royal Dublin Fusiliers. Unit: 2nd Battalion. Date of death: 27 August 1914. Age at death: 24 Service No.: 10149. Born in Rathoe, County Carlow. Enlisted in Carlow while living in Castledermot, County Kildare. Killed in action.

Supplementary information: Son of the late Patrick and Mary Whelan, of Castledermot; husband of Bridget Whelan, of Carlowgate, Castledermot, County Kildare.

Memorial: La Ferte-Sous-Jouarre Memorial in France. Also listed under Ballon/Rathoe/Aghade on the Great War Memorial, Milford Street, Leighlinbridge, County Carlow.

WHELAN, WILLIAM: Rank: Private. Regiment or service: Royal Dublin Fusiliers. Unit: Depot. Date of death: 9 March 1917. Service No.: 26960. Born in Tinyreland (sic), County Carlow.

Enlisted in Carlow. Died at home. Grave or memorial reference: E. 13. 26. Cemetery: Naas (St Corban's) Catholic Cemetery, County Kildare. Also listed under Tinryland on the Great War Memorial, Milford Street, Leighlinbridge, County Carlow.

WHITTAKER, BENJAMIN: Rank: Private. Regiment or service: King's Own (Royal Lancaster Regiment). Unit: 1st Battalion. Date of death: 8 May 1915. Age at death: 37. Service No.: 8485. Born in Carlow. Enlisted in Spennymoor. Killed in action.

Supplementary information: Son of Leonard and Mary Whittaker; husband of Annie Whittaker, of Henry Street, Graigue Cullen, Carlow. Date of will: 17 September 1914. After his death his effects and property were received by: (Wife) Annie Whittaker, Henry Street, Carlow, Ireland. From the *Nationalist* and *Leinster Times*, April 1915:

County Carlow at the Front.
Dear Sir—I wish to thank the ladies of Carlow for parcel received. I am very pleased to receive such useful articles. They are just the thing for the trenches. It is very wet and cold in the trenches just now, but I am in very good health and have been spared, thank God. We came out on Christmas Eve for four days, so we spent our Christmas out of the firing line, but not out of sound of shell and fire. I cannot tell you too much about the war, only just what is happening on our own front. We are holding a position against the enemy; we are very far advanced; we

are only about 40 yards between. I am sorry some of my comrades from Carlow have fallen in the war. It is very hard, but they have given their lives, not only for their King, but for their homes. Every Irish Soldier fighting here knows what would happen if the Germans ever got on the Irish shore. Their women and children would be murdered, and their churches and homes destroyed as they have done here. I am glad the Irish Volunteers have answered to the call so well. But we want more to finish this lot for good. I shall be very glad when it is all over and going home again, please God.
Yours Truly.
Corporal B. Whittaker.

From the *Nationalist* and *Leinster Times*, June 1915:

Killed in action.
The following is a letter received by Mrs Whittaker, Carlow Graigue, notifying her of the death of her husband, Corporal B. Whittaker, at Armentieres, on May 8th last. Whittaker was a native of Carlow-Graigue, and was one of the first to be recalled for service on the commencement of the war on August last. Since then he has been in the firing line.

1st Battalion, King's Own R. L. Regiment.
7th June, 1915.
   Dear Madam—In reference to your letter of June 1st, your husband, be Whittaker, was shot through the head in action on may 8th. His pay-book and such belongings as he had on him were handed to the orderly room sergeant by my Sergeant Major, who has the care of such things. I believe among his belongings was a rosary which tyou will receive in due time.
His remains were interred about 100 yards in rear of our trench borders, together with those of Lieutenant Maculloch, and Captain Scott, and a small wooden cross with his name was placed over his grave.
He died at his post like a brave man, an example to his comrades. —I am, madam, yours faithfully.
A. B. Woodgate.
   Captain, O. C. B Company.

From the *Nationalist* and *Leinster Times*, May 1915:

WHITTAKER—Killed in action, on May 8th, 1915, at Armentieres, Corporal Ben Whittaker, 1st Royal Lancaster Regiment, and late of Carlow-Graigue. Sacred Heart of Jesus, have mercy on his soul—R. I. P. Inserted by his sorrowing wife and children.

From the *Nationalist* and *Leinster Times*,. May 1916:

Roll of Honour.
W H I T T A K E R — First Anniversary—In loving memory of Benjamin Whittaker, Carlow-Graigue, killed in action at Ypres on May 8th, 1915. On whose would, Sweet Jesus, have mercy. Immaculate Heart of Mary, pray for him. Inserted by his wife and children. —R. I. P.

Grave or memorial reference: Panel 12. Memorial: Ypres (Menin Gate) Memorial in Belgium. Also listed under Carlow/Graigue on the Great War Memorial, Milford Street, Leighlinbridge, County Carlow.

WHYTE, PATRICK: Rank: Private. Regiment or service: Royal Dublin Fusiliers. Unit: 6th Battalion. Date of death: 8 October 1918. Service No.: 19269. Born in Leighlinbridge, County Carlow. Enlisted in Carlow. Killed in action.

Supplementary information: Son of Mr Richard. F. Whyte, of The Cottage, Milford, County Carlow.

Grave or memorial reference: A. 23. Cemetery: Guizancourt Farm Cemetery, Guoy, Aisne in France. Also listed under Leighlinbridge/Old Leighlin on the Great War Memorial, Milford Street, Leighlinbridge, County Carlow.

WILLOUGHBY, CHARLES: Rank: Private. Regiment or service: South Irish Horse. Date of death: 20 June 1917. Age at death: 22. Service No.: 1497. Born in Tullow, County Carlow. Enlisted in Dublin while living in Mayo, Queen's County (sic). Killed in action.

Supplementary information: Son of Samuel and Anne Willoughby, of Mayo, Ballickmoyler, Carlow. From the *King's County Chronicle*, July 1917:

Life at the Front.
Letters from Birr Lance Corporal.
In a couple of letters from the front, Lance Corporal Willie O'Hara give an interesting account of life out there, within the past couple of weeks. "We are working in the trenches." he writes, "making them as little in front of our own, that is, in no man's land. It is not a very safe sort of work for if Fritz spots you he makes it very hot. We have had a couple of fellows killed so far. We have our billets in a wood a good distance back, and we walk it at night. We have made ourselves very comfortable. Technical training comes in very handy when you have to build your own house. The weather is splendid, but if anything too hot. In a second letter the wrtier states he was admitted to hospital, feeling a bit shaken after a rough night. "Poor Charlie Willoughby was killed the same night a few yards away. He died immediately after being hit somewhere in the stomach. We got him into an old German dug-out that happened to be near where we were working. There were no others killed in our regiment, but three fellows near me were badly wounded. One of them was blown with some earth on top of me. I was trying to give a hand with a stretcher case when got a bruise on the arm from a piece of shrapnel. It did not cut me and the mark has nearly disappeared. I am having a good time now and will probably be here for a few days, when I should be quite well again. "

Grave or memorial reference: XIX. A. 24. Cemetery: Loos British Cemetery in France. Also listed under Tullow on the Great War Memorial, Milford Street, Leighlinbridge, County Carlow.

WILLOUGHBY CHARLES: Rank: Private. Regiment or service: Royal Irish Regiment. Unit: 1st Battalion. Date of death: 18 May 1915. Service No.: 1729. Born in Coolcullen County Kilkenny. Enlisted in Carlow. Killed in action. Grave or memorial reference: He has no known grave but is listed on panel 4 on the Le Touret Memorial in France. Also listed under Leighlinbridge/Old Leighlin on the Great War Memorial, Milford Street, Leighlinbridge, County Carlow.

WILLOUGHBY, SAMUEL: Rank: Private. Regiment or service: Royal Dublin Fusiliers. Unit: A Company. 2nd Battalion. Date of death: 27 August 1914. Age at death: 27. Service No.: 8966. Born in Hackettstown, County Carlow. Enlisted in Carlow. Killed in action.

Supplementary information: Son of Samuel and Anne Willoughby, of Church Road, Hacketstown; husband of Annie Willoughby, of Mill Street, Hacketstown, County Carlow.

Memorial: La Ferte-Sous-Jouarre Memorial in France. Also listed under Hacketstown on the Great War Memorial, Milford Street, Leighlinbridge, County Carlow.

WILSON, HUMPHREY WORTHINGTON: Rank: Lieutenant/ Temporary Captain. Regiment or service: Yorkshire Regiment, attached to the 2nd Battalion, East Yorkshire Regiment. Date of death: 4 October 1915. Killed in action. From the *Nationalist* and *Leinster Times*, October 1915:

WILSON—Killed in action in France, between 2nd and 4th October, 1915, Captain Humphrey Worthington Wilson, Yorkshire Regiment, dearly loved husband of Emily Wilson Scarborough and youngest son of the late Mr and Mrs James Wilson, Carlow; aged 30 years. Canadian papers please copy.

From the *Nationalist* and *Leinster Times*, also in the *Carlow Journal*, October 1915:

How Captain Wilson Died.
The "Scarborough Evening News" of October 11th publishes an account of the death of captain H, W. Wilson, who was killed gallantly leading a charge against the Germans. The account was given in a letter from the Colonel to Mrs Wislon, 13 Pavilion Square, Scarborough. Captain Wilson belonged to Carlow. The letter speaks highly of Captain Wilson; "I very much regret, " it says, "to have to report the death of your husband, who as killed whilst gallantly leading a charge against the German positions. His death was instantaneous, as his body was found some 50 or 60 yards from our front trenches. All of us mourn the death of a most gallant and conscientious officer, whose place it will be difficult to fill. We also offer you our deepest and most heartfelt sympathies in your great loss. Captain Wilson was always cheery and bright even in the most arduous circumstances. I wish there were ore like him. "

Surely a finer tribute to an officer could not be paid by his superior, and the letter will be a consolation to his widow, who has to mourn his death after being married only six months. As stated on Saturday, she is the youngest daughter of the late Mr W. Fairbank, and Mrs Fairbank, her mother, as indicated above, resides at 13 Pavilion Square.

Gained the D. C. M.

Captain Wilson, who was a native of Carlow, had had the most distinguished military career, He fought through the Boer War, receiving the King's medal, and the

Queen's medal, the latter having six clasps—Wittebergen, Diamond Hill, Johannesburg, Driorontein, Paardeburg, and the relief of Kimberley. He also, in the South African War, won the Distinguished Conduct Medal—"For distinguished conduct in the field, " as it is recorded on the medal, and this, with other medals, will be prized by Mrs Wilson. A fourth medal he possessed was; For long service and good conduct.

Captain Wilson was well known in Scarborough, where he was attached for two and a half years, as Sergeant major, to the 5th Yorks. His military career would have concluded in June last, but he continued after the war, gained his captaincy, and went out to France, attached to the 2nd East Yorkshire Regiment. In South Africa he fought with the mounted infantry, and in addition to winning the D. C. M. , in that war, as stated, he was twice mentioned in despatches.

From the *Carlow Nationalist* in September 2002:

Acting Captain Humphrey Worthington Wilson, D. C. M.

Wilson, 4157 Sergeant H W, 1st Prince of Wales Own Yorkshire Regiment (2nd Battalion Mounted Infantry)

Humphrey Worthington Wilson was born on 19 March 1876, the son of James and Elizabeth Wilson of Carlow, Ireland. He enlisted as a Private in the Yorkshire Regiment on 1 June 1893 and was posted to and joined the 1st Battalion at Jersey on 7 June. He served in Gibraltar, January 1898 to March 1899 and proceeded to service in South Africa, 22 September 1899 where he served until 6 October 1902. On the outbreak of the Boer War he joined the Yorkshire Regiment section of the 2nd Battalion Mounted Infantry on its formation as a Sergeant. He took part in the Relief of Kimberley, including the action at Klip Drift, the battles of Paardeberg and Driefontein, the Sannah's Post engagement, operations near Thabanchu, actions at Hont's Nek and Welkom Kopjes, the battle of Diamond Hill, the pusuit of De Wet, the relief of Elands River and operations in the western Transvaal, October 1900-July 1901, including the action at Nooitgedacht. For his distinguished service with the 2nd Battalion Mounted Infantry he was mentioned in despatches and awarded the DCM. Promoted to Colour Sergeant in April 1903, he was posted to the 5th Battalion and appointed Acting Sergeant-Major on 12 October 1912, having been awarded the Army LS&GC with a gratuity in April 1912. He was commissioned a 2nd Lieutenant in the Yorkshire Regiment on 8 April 1915 and promoted to Lieutenant on 10 June 1915. He reached the rank of Temporary Captain, attached to the 2nd Battalion East Yorkshire Regiment in September 1915. He was killed in action whilst gallantly leading his men in a charge against German positions on 4 October 1915. Having no known grave, his name is commemorated on the Loos Memorial.

Grave or memorial reference: Panel 127 to 129. Memorial: Loos Memorial in France. Also listed under Carlow/Graigue on the Great War Memorial, Milford Street, Leighlinbridge, County Carlow.

WILSON, PATRICK JOSEPH:
Rank: Private. Regiment or service: Manchester Regiment. Unit: D Company, 17th Battalion. Date of death: 30 July 1916. Age at death: 18. Service No.: 28875. Born in Bagesltown (sic), County Carlow. Enlisted in Manchester while living in Collyhurst, Manchester. Killed in action.
Supplementary information: Son of Mary Ann Wilson, of 46 Clare Street, Chorlton-on-Medlock, Manchester, and the late Joseph Wilson.
Grave or memorial reference: Pier and Face 13 A and 14 C. Memorial: Thiepval Memorial in France. Also listed under Bagenalstown/Fenagh on the Great War Memorial, Milford Street, Leighlinbridge, County Carlow.

WILSON, SYDNEY: Rank:
Lieutenant. Regiment or service: Scottish Infantry. Date of death: 10 November 1918. Age at death: 27. The only information I have found on this man comes from his inscription under Leighlinbridge/Old Leighlin on the Great War Memorial, Milford Street, Leighlinbridge, County Carlow.

WILSON, WILLIAM EDWARD:
Rank: Private. Regiment or service: Royal Irish Regiment. Unit: 7th (South Irish Horse) Battalion. Date of death: 30 November 1917. Service No.: 25894, South Irish Horse number 1968. Born in Carlow. Enlisted in Carlow while living in Fenagh, County Carlow. Killed in action. From the *Carlow Sentinel*, December 1917:

Wilson—killed in action William Wilson, South Irish Horse, son of Sergeant Wilson, R. I. C. , Fenagh County Carlow.

From the *Nationalist* and *Leinster Times*, December 1917:

Private W. E. Wilson.
It is with regret that we have to chronicle the death of Private W. E. Wilson, S. I. Horse, son of Sergeant and Mrs Wilson, R. I. C, Fenagh, County Carlow, who was killed in action in France on the 30th November. At the age of 18 this promising young lad enlisted in the South Irish Horse, which was then quartered in Cahir, County Tipperary, where he did his training and then went to France; saw a good

deal of fighting, and his comrades state that he always faced danger cheerfully and fearlessly. He was an expert horseman, and on several occasions won regimental horse jumping competitions while serving in France. All who came in contact with him mourn his untimely end.

From De Ruvigny's Roll of Honour:

. . son of William Wilson, Sergeant, Royal Irish Constabulary of Fennagh, Bagenalstown, County Carlow, by his wife, Marion, daughter of the late Edward Watters. Born in Carlow 4 January 1898. Educated at fennagh National School, and Skerries College, Dublin. Was Clerk in an estate office. Joined the South Irish Horse 25 January 1916; subsequently transferred to the Royal Irish Regiment. Served with the Expeditionary Force in France and Flanders from 25-July following and was killed in action near Crosielles 30 November 1917. Buried in Croiselles British Cemetery. Major Roche Kelly wrote; "Your poor lad was one of the smartest boys in my company, and a very great favourite with all his companions, " and the Chaplain; "He was a fine man and a splendid soldier. "

Grave or memorial reference: I. B. 14. Cemetery: Croiselles British Cemetery in France. Also listed under Bagenalstown/Fenagh on the Great War Memorial, Milford Street, Leighlinbridge, County Carlow.

WORLEY, JAMES: Rank: Private. Regiment or service: Royal Dublin Fusiliers. Unit: 10th Battalion. Date of death: 29 May 1917. Age at death: 28. Service No.: 10216. Born in Walworth, Surrey. Enlisted in Carlow while living in Tullow, County Carlow. Died of wounds.

Supplementary information: Son of Alfred and Katherine Worley (*née* Aughney).

Grave or memorial reference: Bay 9. Memorial: Arras Memorial in France. Also listed under Tullow on the Great War Memorial, Milford Street, Leighlinbridge, County Carlow.

WYNNE, CHARLES WYNDHAM: Rank: Captain. Regiment or service: Royal Garrison Artillery. Unit: ; 182nd Siege Battery. Date of death: 24 June 1917. Age at death: 22. Died of wounds.

Supplementary information: From De Ruvigny's Roll of Honour:

Youngest son of Albert Augustus Wynne of Tigroney, Avoca and Glendalough Cottage, County Wicklow, Civil Engineer, by his wife Alice K. , daughter of the Revd John Wynne of Corrie, Bagenalstown. Born: 29 May 1895. Educated: Lancing College (Methematical Exhibition), and Balliol College, Oxford, where he was a member of the O. T. C. Gazetted 2nd Lt RGA. 28 February 1918. He was promoted to Lieut. and Captain, September 1916, served for a time in Ireland. Subsequently volunteered for foreign service, and served with the

Expeditionaly Force in France and Flanders from September, 1916. Second in Command of the Battery, took part in the battle of Arras, 9 April 1917, and of Messines, 7 June and died at the General Hospital, St Omer, 24 June 1917 of wounds received in action at Armentieres 10 June. Buried in St Omer. A brother officer wrote; 'He was one of the best. Beloved by his men, and excellent officer, with a tremendous interest and whole-heartedness in our work' and a Private; 'You will understand what a high opinion we all had of him, and now that he is no longer with us, we realise of what irreplaceable value he was, and would give all we know to have him with us again.'

Grave or memorial reference: IV. C. 38. Cemetery: Longuenesse (St Omer) Souvenir Cemetery in France. He is also listed on the Balliol College WW1 Memorial.

WYNNE-STORRAR, ANDREW: See **STORRAR, ANDREW WYNNE.**